MIRACLE RUN

MIRACLE RUN

Watching My Autistic Sons Grow Up—
and Take Their First Steps into Adulthood

CORRINE MORGAN-THOMAS
with GARY BROZEK

BERKLEY BOOKS, NEW YORK

THE BERKLEY PUBLISHING GROUP
Published by the Penguin Group
Penguin Group (USA) Inc.
375 Hudson Street, New York, New York 10014, USA
Penguin Group (Canada), 90 Eglinton Avenue East, Suite 700, Toronto, Ontario M4P 2Y3, Canada
(a division of Pearson Penguin Canada Inc.)
Penguin Books Ltd., 80 Strand, London WC2R 0RL, England
Penguin Group Ireland, 25 St. Stephen's Green, Dublin 2, Ireland
(a division of Penguin Books Ltd.)
Penguin Group (Australia), 250 Camberwell Road, Camberwell, Victoria 3124, Australia
(a division of Pearson Australia Group Pty. Ltd.)
Penguin Books India Pvt. Ltd., 11 Community Centre, Panchsheel Park, New Delhi—110 017, India
Penguin Group (NZ), 67 Apollo Drive, Rosedale, North Shore 0632, New Zealand
(a division of Pearson New Zealand Ltd.)
Penguin Books (South Africa) (Pty.) Ltd., 24 Sturdee Avenue, Rosebank, Johannesburg 2196,
South Africa
Penguin Books Ltd., Registered Offices: 80 Strand, London WC2R 0RL, England

This book is an original publication of the Berkley Publishing Group.

While the author has made every effort to provide accurate telephone numbers and Internet addresses
at the time of publication, neither the publisher nor the author assumes any responsibility for errors
or for changes that occur after publication. Further, the publisher does not have any control over and
does not assume any responsibility for author or third-party websites or their content.

Copyright © 2009 by Corrine Morgan-Thomas
Cover art by Alamy
Cover design by Pyrographx

First edition: March 2009

Library of Congress Cataloging-in-Publication Data

Morgan-Thomas, Corrine.
    Miracle run : watching my autistic sons grow up—and take their first steps into adulthood / Corrine
Morgan-Thomas with Gary Brozek.— 1st ed.
        p. cm.
    ISBN 978-0-425-22582-0
    1. Morgan, Phillip—Mental health.   2. Morgan, Stephen—Mental health.   3. Morgan-Thomas,
Corrine.   4. Autistic children—United States—Biography.   5. Parents of autistic children—United
States—Biography.   I. Brozek, Gary.   II. Title.
    RJ506.A9M675 2009
    618.92'85882—dc22   2008052317

PRINTED IN THE UNITED STATES OF AMERICA

10   9   8   7   6   5   4   3   2   1

PUBLISHER'S NOTE: This book describes the real experiences of real people. The author has dis-
guised the identities of some, and in some instances created composite characters, but none of these
changes has affected the truthfulness and accuracy of her story.
Most Berkley books are available at special quantity discounts for bulk purchases for sales promo-
tions, premiums, fund-raising, or educational use. Special books, or book excerpts, can also be created to fit specific needs. For details, write: Special Markets, Penguin Group (USA) Inc., 375 Hudson
Street, New York, New York 10014.

Dedicated to my father and mother, Ralph and Lupe Mount,
who taught that one's potential is not limited by an infirmity

ACKNOWLEDGMENTS

To run a great cross-country race, you have to assemble a great team. My thanks to my agent at Artisans and Artists, Adam Chromy, who started us down the right path. Without the insight and hard work of Denise Silvestro at Berkley, who worked on the book up until days before giving birth, we might have wandered off course. She put us in the capable hands of Andie Avila, who helped get us to the finish line. Thanks also to everyone in the Berkley publicity department, who helped spread this important message.

To run a race, you have to be prepared. Our family will never forget Gary Brozek, who immersed his mind in the psychological, physiological, and spiritual aspects of autism and brought the dynamics of our family to life on the page. Gary dove into medical consults, school homework, team scores, medications, IEPs, and much more to make our story complete.

I also want to thank everyone at Agoura High School, and especially Coach Bill Duley, who transformed many lives by not questioning the ability of a quiet autistic young man. I will never forget that you let Stephen borrow running shoes for his first big win. From such small gestures great things spring.

To everyone at Patriarch productions and Lifetime television—especially the wonderful and caring cast, Mary Louise Parker, Aidan Quinn, Zac Efron, and Thomas Lewis—thank you for helping to bring such an important message to the world.

A big treat to my therapy dogs, Carebear, Baby, Ms. Likki, Snowflake, Song, Princess, and their offspring, who have given comfort and support. Many thanks to Serena, Lindsay, and Gaby Diller, who helped train them.

To run a race, you need nourishing food. I would like to thank the Rolettis for providing food and donations for our Miracle Run and sometimes for our family, who at times faced hardship. Thanks also to all those who provided much-needed spiritual and emotional nourishment: Laura Nielsin; Kiwanis; Peggy Doherty; Irma Haldane; the Thomas family; Autism Speaks; Big Steve Morgan and his wife, Maria; and of course Doug and Ali. Special thanks to my oldest son, Richard, who spent most of the last year in the Persian Gulf, defending our country on the USS *Abraham Lincoln*.

And, finally, to win a race, you need a purpose. Thanks to Stephen and Phillip, who give me direction and strength to make it to the finish line.

INTRODUCTION

SOMETIMES the things we have forced on us, the things we'd rather not do above all else, turn out to be the best things we can possibly do for ourselves. I don't know; maybe there's somebody up there looking out for us. Just when you think you have everything figured out, that your life has settled into a pattern, it calls on you to rethink every assumption you've ever made. It requires you to reexamine your most entrenched beliefs and to understand that what you thought were conclusions were really just jumping-off points to learn even more about yourself and others. The universe is a funny place. Not funny, ha-ha funny, but funny strange, funny outrageous, funny extraordinary.

Back in the early evening of September 23, 1998, you wouldn't have been able to convince me that much of anything was funny. Not humorous, not exceptional, not quirky, not anything special. I was tired that evening. Not the usual "I worked hard all day and the traffic was bad on the way home, how did so many dishes get stacked up in the sink, I can't think of a single thing to make for dinner tonight, and I don't want to get up and do *this* all over again" kind of tired that most working mothers feel. No, I would have gladly traded *my* tired for *that* tired. My tiredness was the kind that put to the test the idea that God never gives anyone more than they can handle. I was feeling all of the above, and then some. I'd begun to believe that maybe God was using me as a test subject, seeing just how far he could go before one of his creations snapped. I sometimes felt as if I were a prototype product in a factory being subjected to all kinds of abuse. Some technician was hoping I'd fail so he could see what flaws were inherent in the design and determine what could be improved in the next model to keep the same thing from happening again.

In other words, I was living the tumultuous life that most parents of autistic children do. Only in my case I had a double dose, since both of my twin sons shared the same diagnosis.

So when my autistic sixteen-year-old son Stephen came to me that evening in September and said, "Coach says the parents have to go to the games," I bit my lip and didn't say to him, "You can tell Coach where he can go, and remind him to bring plenty of sunscreen, too." I'd learned that jokes don't go over so well with Stephen or with his identical twin brother, Phillip. Their minds function more or less logically, sometimes in a way that I can't at first comprehend. But when I try to think as literally as I'm capable of, I can usually figure out what they are thinking and what they mean.

Even though Stephen made his statement in his usual very subdued, deadpan, matter-of-fact way, his intent was very serious, and it took some mental gymnastics to figure that out. I'd eventually come to learn that the Agoura High School Chargers cross-country team's coach was a man whose requests were not to be taken lightly. At that point I knew him only as a local legend and a stern but fair taskmaster. I also knew that if Stephen knew that Coach Duley had made that demand, then I'd better not shirk my duty, and I'd better go to the meet the next day. Stephen is my no-nonsense son, the true literalist, the dutiful soldier, all of the things you might associate with someone who has chosen to be part of a cross-country team. I knew that Stephen liked to run. Starting in junior high, he'd begun taking off and roaming the neighborhood and the surrounding areas on foot. I simply figured it was the natural expression of a boy's desire to roam. I also knew that he and Phillip both loved the *Rocky* movies and watched them over and over again. Stephen had started his own physical fitness regimen; I could hear him mornings just after the sun rose. More precisely, what I heard was the clanking of the metal weights he'd load onto his barbells, the sound of his sneakers and his hands clapping together when he did jumping jacks on the stone patio, a thumping kind of exhalation when his back bounced off the stones during his sit-ups.

Stephen didn't talk much, and I'd come to learn about his states of mind based on the sounds produced during his activities. If the refrigerator clicked and whirred, that meant Stephen was hungry. If the flat of his hand thumped the kitchen table and the swiping sound of eraser dust being cleared came from the kitchen table, that meant Stephen was frustrated. He hated making mistakes in his schoolwork. He expected a lot of himself, and he expected me to be at his race.

I had a whole set of excuses lined up like dominoes. Chief among them was that I didn't have the energy to drag myself over to the high school to watch a cross-country race, let alone do whatever "volunteer" task Coach Duley had in mind for all the parents. I was so drained because I'd been worrying so much about Phillip. Phillip's condition had worsened as he got older. On top of his autism, he'd developed a variety of symptoms from Tourette's syndrome. Though it isn't uncommon for the autistic to develop Tourette's syndrome, there's little comfort to be found in its not being a rarity. I also knew my time wouldn't be spent watching my son compete in the race. I am all for being supportive of my kids and cheering them on; however, I couldn't imagine how humiliating it would be for Stephen to have his mother watch him perform his duties as a water boy.

Talk about water torture; I didn't know how I was going to feel standing there amid all the other parents of track stars. I imagined wanting to go into tic mode right in those bleachers—curling up into a protective ball. As I did far too frequently back then, I let my imagination and insecurities get the best of me. As the parent of autistic children, I felt as if all the stares, all the isolation, all the taunts—and even worse, the whispered or unstated unkind remarks—that Phillip and Stephen had endured had also been directed at me. On top of that, I imagined that all the other parents would be gathered there in a gaggle of designer labels, blinding one another with their Rolex watches, their capped teeth nearly outdueling the shine on their Mercedes and BMWs that sat glittering like gemstones in the parking lot. Where I'd gone to school, there would have been shards of broken glass littering the parking lot. Besides, I didn't want to endure the stares or, worse, the bank shot of their eyes meeting mine and then angling off to some other, safer direction.

I'm not proud of how I dealt with my feelings of inadequacy and unfairness before the Miracle Run, or how for a long time I allowed my bitterness to infect me. I admit that that evening when Stephen told me I had to go to his cross-country meet, I hosted a pity party for myself. Here was another thing being asked of me when I'd already felt for years as though I'd been giving daily as much as I possibly could.

Having so many demands placed on you is all part of the package you receive along with the diagnosis. On and off, I would think of autism as a gift—sometimes a cruel gag of a gift and other times a genuine bounty that helped me better understand myself and the world.

Today I recall those impressions and marvel at just how much of a miracle the boys have been, how their example could have transformed that small but very real and very resentful part of me into who I am today. I needed to vent my frustrations somehow, and if that expression took the form of those bitter thoughts, I can at least be proud that I never allowed them to poison what I said to or did with my children. I also understand now that it was important for me to give myself the freedom to feel bad some of the time, to understand that while it sometimes took superhuman effort to parent autistic twins, I was still a fallible human being. So if I misdirected some of my anger at the world, I was committing—or so I thought back then—a victimless crime.

An hour after Stephen's first announcement, he slunk back into the living room. I was seated on the couch, trying to lose myself in some television show. He sidled up to me and said again, "Coach says the parents have to go to the games."

I nodded.

"I'll be there tomorrow, Stephen. Don't you worry."

And I meant both parts of my statement. I'd be doing enough worrying for all of us. I hadn't mentioned to Stephen that many of the reasons why I didn't want to go had to do with how exhausted I was from dealing with Phillip's Tourette's syndrome. I felt so bad for Phillip, felt that life was so unfair to him. How much is too much for a kid to handle? I wasn't about to complicate Stephen's life by letting this get in the way of supporting him and thereby letting him down. I too often felt that I had done this before.

I looked Stephen in the eye and gave him my best "We're all in this together" smile. He immediately pushed his glasses up on his nose and scanned the ceiling before retreating to his room. I'd see if my oldest son, Richard, and youngest child, Ali, would want to come out to support their brother. Richard and Ali had been spared the diagnosis but not the collateral damage that autism imposes on families. My first marriage hadn't been able to survive it, and the father of all three of my sons was now more of a vestigial presence in our lives. The same was true of Ali's father, a man I never married but whose hasty and untimely retreat from our lives was as much responsible for my resentment toward my more affluent neighbors outside Malibu Lake as any direct confrontation or conflict with them. Guilt by association and all that. I also felt guilty that my disastrous choice in boy-friends had destroyed the precarious balance of the household.

The next morning I woke up to the sounds of the kids getting themselves ready for school. I mostly heard Phillip, the family chatterbox, going on and on to himself about some vocabulary test he was going to have to take that day. I could hear the note of anxiety in his voice, the near-whine that too often characterizes so much of what he says. If I focused on the sound of his voice, I could block out the image of his tics and spasms, his head rocking back and forth like the spring-mounted horses at the playground.

Phillip didn't sound out of breath, and I counted that as a good thing. Maybe his anxiety level wouldn't spike and go off the charts. A woman can hope, can't she? A few moments later the door swung shut, the voices drifted off, and I closed my eyes again. I heard my husband's truck start up and crackle across our stone driveway.

I lay in bed for a while, mentally preparing for another long day, certain that the weather was gray and dreary to match my mood. Of course, this being Southern California, when I finally got up and looked out the kitchen window, another gloriously clear day in Malibu Lake smacked me in the face. I know the kinds of images that the mention of Malibu must conjure up. Well, there's Malibu and then there's Malibu Lake. Malibu is coastal, exclusive, and up-market. Malibu Lake is hillside, bohemian, and down-market. We're an hour from downtown L.A. and Hollywood geographically, but eras away philosophically. A little bit of the sixties sensibility drifted off like smoke and settled into the valleys and hills that surround us. All the winds of change do is drive that smoke deeper into the nooks and crannies of the place.

We love it here. It's a great place to raise my four kids. Our house is in the Malibu hills, far from the big city and far from the sprawling affluence of more typically suburban Agoura and the surrounding communities. Truth be told, the place is a little retreat for me. After the twins were diagnosed with autism at five years old, I literally and figuratively headed for the hills. The little enclave that we carved out of the hillside suited me just fine. The less I had to interact with people, the better. I'd come to believe that autism and Tourette's syndrome were taboo, that other people marked us as lepers, that we were better off among our own kind.

By noon I'd taken a break, and with my glass of water I went out to sit on a bit of the hillside to the west of our house that we'd leveled off. I'd had visions of a gazebo sitting on that spot, but a plastic deck chair and worn patch of dirt would have to suffice until the proverbial "someday" came along. As I sat there admiring the patchwork of vegetation that quilted the near and distant hills, I was able to admit that if we were in exile—and admittedly partially in self-imposed exile—we'd been forced into and not out of our version of paradise.

I took some comfort in knowing that my work situation was better than it had been in years. I worked from home as a bookkeeper and accountant for a small service. I had several permanent clients, and the pay was decent. Best of all, I could, for the most part, set my own schedule, giving me the flexibility to constantly monitor Stephen's and Phillip's progress at school, attend meetings, and explore other treatment options. It hadn't always been like that, though; I'd done my share of begging bosses for time off, tested the patience and goodwill of too many coworkers. I was glad to have most of that behind me.

Sitting there in the sun, my thoughts drifted to Stephen and Phillip. I wondered how their day was progressing and how Phillip had done on his vocabulary test. I tried not to think too much about the cross-country meet that was coming up. All along, I believed that Stephen had joined the team by accident. The twins were sophomores, and they'd both come home from Agoura High the first week with a sheet of paper that listed all the activities they could join. I was sure that one of the aides in the special education department had told Stephen to check some other box. He'd inadvertently filled in the one next to cross-country.

He asked me to sign the approval form and told me he needed a check for $100. I had put off signing the sheet and check, and tried to once again figure out how to move decimal places in our bank account farther to the left without resorting to fraud or extortion. Any parent can tell you how hard it is to deny their kids the things they want, but when it comes to denying what they need, that's another kind of anguish entirely. I knew that Stephen needed to feel like he *belonged* somewhere besides the special education department. It took a couple of weeks, but with a background in accounting, I was able to cook the books in such a way that Stephen could have his money and I could avoid bouncing a check. I hoped the effort would pay off.

Just as Stephen had wanted to, and did, join the debate team his freshman year, I suspected that he didn't have the skills it took to succeed at cross-country. At least as the water boy he'd enjoy some sense of belonging, contribute in some way unlike in debate. Participation was something the boys craved, and understanding their need was one of the first lessons I had to learn. As much as I tried to isolate myself, I was determined that they not be shut out of anything. Even if Phillip was having his most difficult of Tourette's days, he was going to come with me to the meet, just as he went with me everywhere the rest of the family went. I wasn't sure he'd enjoy being at a cross-country meet, but it was better than sitting at home.

At three o'clock I found myself at the intersection of Cornell and Kanan Roads. If I turned left, I'd head toward the beach. Twelve twisty miles later, and I could dip my toes in the waters of the Pacific. Calm. Peaceful.

The choice was easy.

I drove straight through the intersection and continued on my way to Agoura High School. I'd told myself earlier that afternoon that it was time to take a stand, to let go of the worrying I'd been doing about appearances. To that end, I'd decided that not only would Phillip and I go to the race but I wouldn't give a damn about what anyone else thought, either. I would pick up Ali, and then continue on to the high school. Strength in numbers and all that.

Consciously or unconsciously, to this day I'm not completely certain which, I had put on a pair of sweatpants and a tattered pair of boots. Fog had rolled into the valley shortly after noon, the temperature had dropped, and the blotted sun and overcast shrouded everything in a dull gray swath. As I wound my way through the canyon road, I kept telling myself, "I can do this. I can do this." With each repetition, I felt a little of the tension ease out of my jaw. I took one hand from the wheel and rubbed the back of my neck, feeling the resistance there.

Crossing the bridge over the 405 freeway, the landscape was transformed from dry scrub and country roads to suburban sprinkler-fed lushness. Even in the dank fog, the greens—moneyed greens, I always thought—couldn't be conquered. Instead of the eclectic mix of architectural styles that marked my neighborhood, I entered into the planned homogeneity of Agoura Hills. Something about the Spanish-style strip malls and their Taco Bell tackiness had always struck me as odd. When I recognized that I was walking down a well-worn thought path, I chastised myself.

Give it a rest, Corrine. It wasn't all *their* fault. *They* (everyone else) weren't responsible for the boys being autistic. *They* hadn't made some of the poor choices I'd made, so cut them some slack.

Maybe by working as a part-time real estate broker before getting remarried I'd come to know a little too much about the financial lives of the people with whom I shared a ZIP. Just because they made more money than I did, and could afford homes that cost more than I might expect to make in a lifetime, didn't make them bad people. I was letting my bad mood get the better of me. I needed to be more charitable. Little did I know that in less than an hour I was going to learn some valuable lessons about faith, hope, and charity and a few other virtues that I possessed but didn't always put into practice.

Picking up Ali from school improved my spirits. Having two older brothers who by necessity took up a lot of her mother's time and attention didn't seem to faze her at all. She greeted me with her usual smile, equal parts gratitude at not having to ride the school bus and appreciation for having a few minutes alone with me. She loves her brothers, has never expressed any resentment about the inequity she inherited as her lot in life, but I sometimes wondered if she and Richard ever felt the same exhaustion of spirit that I did. Richard had had his own issues to deal with—his excess weight and the resulting self-image problems—

and had experienced a lot of teasing, just as Stephen and Phillip had. I assumed that made him naturally more empathetic.

Climbing a rise, I pulled into the high school's parking lot. A small crowd was already gathered near the football field and the track that encircled it. I always thought it odd that the athletic facilities stood at the entrance to the school and wondered what signal this was sending. Even in the dingy light the electric blue bleachers and the gold-trimmed Charger Stadium seemed to shout a peppy chant. I looked for a spot as close to the main entrance as I could. Phillip was sitting on a bench, his face skewered in concentration, and I could see his lips and cheeks twitching. I got out of the car, and as I walked over to him, he looked up from whatever was holding his attention. He pushed his glasses higher up on his nose and told me that his stomach was a bit upset. It could have been the Haldol or the Thorazine that had him feeling out of sorts. Considering that the preliminary dosages the doctors prescribed to combat his Tourette's syndrome had rendered him zombielike for a week, a little bellyache wasn't such a bad thing.

Phillip, Ali, and I walked along the sidewalk back toward the football field and track. Even in the brief time it had taken me to park and retrieve Phillip, the crowd had grown from about a dozen to nearly fifty or more. I felt an adrenaline buzz in my stomach, the kind of bladder-burning sensation that I experienced when I had to give an oral presentation as a student. I'm not fond of crowds even on the best of days, and this was certainly not shaping up to even rank in the top one thousand.

The three of us stood off to the side of the main group of parents and students waiting for the start of the race. We were on the far side of the track, opposite the parking lot. The area bordered the bleachers and an open rolling field, where a group of girls were already running. I kept looking at the track, where clusters of students from each of the six schools sat. The Chargers were easy to identify by their bold colors, and I saw a group of laughing and smiling young men trotting around the track clad in black and yellow with an Oak Park eagle emblazoned on their T-shirts. They looked so relaxed and carefree, and their easy, welcoming chatter drifted over to me like the smoke and banter from a nearby campsite. I felt a palpable longing in my chest and gut. I wished that instead of standing with the coaches and the other adults, Stephen could be wrapped in the similar embrace of a team's camaraderie.

I leaned down and asked Ali if she saw Stephen. She shrugged her shoulders and said, "I can't see him." I craned my neck and stood on tiptoes to try to spot him but couldn't. I thought of asking the woman next to me if she knew who Stephen was and where he might be, but my shyness clutched my throat. Better perhaps not to draw any attention to myself. I knew that Stephen would be disappointed if he didn't see us, so I asked a young woman who looked to be about Stephen's age if she knew him.

She smiled a mouthful of metal and said, "Sure, I know him. He's right over there." She pointed to the starting line. A man with a megaphone was announcing the start of the boys' frosh-soph race. He was calling all the runners to the starting gate. I could see Stephen running his hand over his close-cropped hair. I was surprised to see him without his glasses. He looked so different, so much younger, so much more vulnerable. Then the truth of what I was seeing registered. Stephen was wearing a pair of running shorts and a sleeveless T-shirt—what I later learned was called a singlet. He wasn't carrying water bottles, didn't have a towel hung over his shoulder. He wasn't a mascot or a charity case; he was actually one of the runners.

At first I was worried for him, then I was angry. What were they doing letting my son, an autistic young man, run this race against his peers? This was ludicrous. Didn't they know? I now realize my initial reaction was irrational, but at the time, I thought he was going to get trampled. I had visions of the fox being run down by the hounds and horsemen. And worse, the fox was nearsighted and without his glasses. What kind of a sick joke was this? I grabbed Ali and Phillip by their elbows, and the three of us lurched toward the start of the race. We got only a few paces ahead of where we started when I heard the gun go off.

Stephen bolted from the pack and took the lead. They ran down the track toward where we were standing, and I could see that the smile that had been on his face was replaced with a look of steely determination. Stephen's jaw was set, and without his glasses, I could clearly see the focus and determination in his eyes. I was also stunned by the physical transformation I saw in him. I remembered how when he was a toddler and even after, I thought of him as being so spindly. When I bathed him and Phillip, I thought of how insubstantial their bones were, how easily someone could have just come along and squeezed the nest of their rib cages and crushed them, squeezed the life out of them. As he sprinted past me, I could see the layer of muscle that now covered his legs and arms and chest. Sinew and vein stood out against his flesh like mountains on a relief map.

I found myself shouting something unintelligible, something equal parts surprise, anxiety, pride, and fear. They exited the track and headed out across the field with Stephen still in the lead. I could hear other people shouting encouragement to their kids, to their school's runners. I could barely stand. My knees felt weak; my pulse throbbed at my temples. You would have thought I was the one out there running and not Stephen. I looked at Ali and her eyes shone. Phillip stood transfixed. For a moment his motor tics idled. Ali clung to my hip, bouncing up and down. For a moment my vision blurred and then cleared.

We followed a group of spectators as they edged away from the main pack to keep the runners in better view. The lead group disappeared over a rise and down a slope, but Stephen was still in the lead.

I held my breath.

When Stephen crested the next hill still in the lead, I let out a yelp of delight. I looked around but no one was staring at me; instead, they were all focusing on the runners. As the lead pack barreled toward us, Stephen was still out in front. I was amazed to see his arms pumping like pistons. Maybe the fox could out-run the hounds?

As they came toward us and the home stretch, I saw Stephen's head turn from side to side. I thought he was checking to see where his competition was, but a moment later he veered off course, and a group of six to ten runners passed him. Stephen came to a stop. He looked bewildered for a moment, his head swiveling from side to side, but then he took off again. I realized that without his glasses, he wasn't able to see the direction he was supposed to be taking. My heart sank momentarily. He'd gone the wrong way.

With only about a half mile left in the three-mile race, there wasn't enough time for Stephen to catch up completely. He passed a number of runners, and as they made their way back onto the track for the finish, I could see that he wasn't going to win the race. That didn't seem to matter to him. He kept chugging furiously.

I realized that I'd forgotten about Phillip and Ali. Ali was still right nearby, but Phillip was gone. A moment after I recognized that fact, I could hear Phillip's shouting. I thought his vocal tics had kicked in again, but I quickly realized that wasn't the case. I saw Phillip trotting along outside the fence from the racers. He had his arms raised over his head, fists clenched Rocky-style, and he was shouting, "Freedom! Freedom!"

Stephen breezed across the finish line in fourth place overall and as the first finisher for Agoura High. I literally fell to my knees and covered my face in my hands. I could swear that I'd witnessed some act of divine intervention. That couldn't have been my son, and yet it was. I was reexperiencing the kind of joy I'd had as a young parent, the moments when a first step, a first word, a smile, filled your heart to bursting with love. I'd come to the meet expecting the worst, and instead I'd been greeted with the best surprise. After years of training myself not to expect anything good to happen, to be handed this gift was an act of incomparable kindness, divinely wrapped and presented to me. It was as if I were being told, "See, you didn't believe me, but you never get more than you can handle."

I'd like to say that the clouds lifted, the fog burned away, and Stephen stood bathed in a pool of angelic light as he received his medal for being one of the top finishers. Hollywood would have it end that way, but life with autistic kids is seldom like how Hollywood depicts families. I'd love to be able to tell you that Stephen went on to win a string of races, that he became an all-American athlete, competed in the Olympics, and won gold medals. That might be how some people define winning, but when you live with autism in your life, you are beyond grateful for a fourth-place finish—you are amazed. You truly have witnessed a miracle. And if the smile on your son's face isn't a thousand-watt screen gem, it's still capable of burning off your personal fog and transforming your life, and your family's life, in ways you can't even begin to imagine.

I have a Buddhist friend who uses the expression, "After the ecstasy, the laundry." I had never been sure what she meant by that, but she then explained that we often have experiences in life that transcend our normal expectations, but we still have to live our lives after those experiences. Although I didn't have to do the laundry right after the race, I would have to go on with the less exciting tasks of motherhood. But before I'd return to the regular and mundane, I would enjoy that moment for as long as I could. We waited for Stephen to exit the locker room after the final races were run, and when I saw him, I rushed up to him and gave him a big hug. I felt Stephen tense up and immediately released him. My eyes still brimming with tears, I told him how proud of him I was, how amazed I was at his effort.

"I ran 18:26. My first mile was 5:49. The second was 6:29. The last was 6:08. I averaged 6:08." Though Stephen does not have mathematical abilities that would qualify him as a savant, he does love numbers. One particularity of his condition is that he can remember dates quite well. He seemed pleased with those numbers, but he didn't display the same kind of genuine expression of satisfaction when the medal was looped around his neck. I would have loved to see that same smile on his face again. I would eventually learn in follow-up conversations with Stephen's coaches that he'd been a full member of the squad for the entire season. In fact, Coach Duley was as surprised to find out that Stephen was an autistic as I was to find out that he was one of the team's top runners.

All of this called for a celebration—I'd make us a nice meal at home. Inspired by my son's courage and ambition, I decided that I would pick up a few things at Von's supermarket, just a few blocks from the school. It's one of the major chain stores in our area, but I hadn't shopped there in nearly a decade, preferring to do my shopping at Ralph's Market. From their names, you can pretty much guess that the former is slightly more upscale and trendy. That's one of the reasons I didn't go there. The other reason was a little more complex, but given what I'd seen Stephen do, I decided it was time to conquer that demon.

Several years before, the twins, who were as yet undiagnosed, and I were in the cereal aisle at Von's. Ali wasn't born yet, and I had left Richard at home with his father. Like a lot of young kids, Phillip and Stephen were entranced by the siren song of Sugar Smacks and were willing to dash themselves against the Scylla and Charybdis of Smurf Berry Crunch and Count Chocula. They were too big and too active to sit in the cart, so they walked beside me, grabbing their sugary favorites from the shelves and tossing the boxes into the cart. Naturally I took selections out of the cart and replaced them with sensible cereals like Cheerios and Raisin Bran. They'd scream and cry, grabbing more boxes of what they wanted. We went back and forth, throwing in and removing cereal boxes from the cart, with me trying to reason with them. Eventually, I had to pull them both by their arms and lead them not into temptation, while muttering an Our Father in the hopes that we'd stop making such a spectacle of ourselves.

We got to the end of the cereal aisle, and I felt a bit of relief wash over me. The only thing staring at us at that point was the benevolent face of the Quaker Oats man. I turned my back on the boys for a moment, and when I turned around, they had taken the nonsugary cereals out of the cart and set them on the floor. They proceeded to unzip themselves and urinate on the boxes. I was mortified. I felt as if I were on the verge of passing out. My vision narrowed, and though I could hear the whispered "Oh my Gods" and muffled shrieks and a few stifled laughs, I couldn't see anyone. My imagined expressions of shock and horror on the other shoppers' faces could have been grossly exaggerated, but none of that mattered. I wanted out of there.

I made my way to the checkout line. Stephen and Phillip must have known that what they'd done was wrong. I didn't have to yell at them, cajole them, or say anything at all. They stood side by side, ambling along beside the cart and crying. My heart and mind were racing. I looked at the clerk. She appeared to be about my age, likely a mother just like me, so I pointed to the cereal boxes that I'd segregated from the rest of my purchases by placing them in the seat of the cart.

"I don't want these, but I want to pay for them. Have to pay for them. Can they be thrown out?"

The woman paused from her mechanical scanning of the

other items to look at me, a question poised on her lips. When she saw that I was crying and was clearly distraught, she raised one eyebrow and shook her head in disgust. "Whatever."

I don't know if I was angry or delusional, but I felt the need to explain. "My sons peed on them. I don't want anyone else to touch them."

"That's disgusting." Her horrified look added an exclamation point to her statement.

"Please, I just want to pay and get home."

She shook her head and swiped the last remaining items across the scanner. She turned her back to me and began whispering to the bagger. I saw the total on the register and left my money on the conveyor belt. Not bothering to wait for any change, I took the few bags of groceries and a couple of empty ones with me. Using the bags as gloves, I put the cereal boxes in a garbage can outside the door. I hustled the boys to the car and drove home, my hands trembling. By that point, the boys seemed to have forgotten what they'd done. They stared out the window, their faces blank, all evidence of their rage seemingly erased from their memory.

Even the high I'd experienced in watching Stephen in the race couldn't erase my memory of that embarrassing day years ago. As I stepped on the rubber mat at the Von's entrance, the door shuddered and hesitated before swinging open, as though it were expressing the same trepidation I felt now, nearly a decade after the cereal fiasco.

Though no one had officially requested that I never come back to Von's, I knew that my family and I were less than welcome. I suppose one function of autism is that it makes everyone in the family more self-conscious than they need to be. Now that they were sixteen years old, I imagined that most people wouldn't recognize the severity of the boys' condition. They might recognize Phillip's Tourette's when it was up at full flame with physical and verbal tics, but when they were under control, both boys might appear just a bit nerdy. I'm certain it was just my imagination, but as the four of us paraded down the aisle at Von's, I felt as if all eyes were on me, that everyone in the store recognized me from the peeing incident so many years before.

Nine or ten years is a long time to endure self-imposed exile from anything, yet in the time I was away, my sense of Von's as a place I wasn't going to feel comfortable in persisted, no matter what the current condition of my sons. A new olive bar sat in the produce section, each of the different varieties spotlit like runway models. A refrigerated case of exotic cheeses exhaled its funky breath, and for a moment I thought of really splurging but decided better safe than sorry.

I had just picked up the few things we needed for dinner—some pasta, a stick of butter, and a canister of grated Parmesan cheese—when I started to cry. I wasn't feeling sorry for myself, wasn't bemoaning the meager celebratory dinner I was going to prepare; I think I was just releasing so many years of bottled-up stuff. I didn't care that I was now the one who was the object of the other shoppers' attention, the bedraggled-looking mother in sweats leading her motley brood of less-than-perfect kids. I guess I was crying also because I'd let what other people thought dictate so much of how I'd conducted my life. If I let strangers' opinions of me dictate where I shopped, what else and how else had I been altered? What else had I hidden from the world?

All those thoughts were swirling through my mind as we made our way to the checkout line. Stephen was wearing his school-issued warm-up suit and staring at the floor. Phillip was cradling a package of Chips Ahoy! cookies in his arms and rocking side to side like a mother soothing an infant. Ali was glancing at the magazine rack. I inhaled and tried to compose myself. When we got to the head of the line and the clerk began ringing us up, I was overcome by an urge to share our news. This time it wasn't to fill someone in about my sons' condition and how it contributed to their doing something awful. Instead I said, "My son, Stephen, he's right here behind me. He's autistic. And he ran this race today. He did great. Better than great. Awesome. I'm crying because I'm so happy for him. I wish you could have seen him." I blathered on for what felt like minutes to me, letting her know every detail.

The woman had stopped scanning the bar codes midway through my story. She looked at me. I could tell that what she saw was me, a very proud mother. She wasn't seeing the bad outfit and hair badly in need of styling or a dye job. Before I was finished, she reached across the conveyor and put her hand on my forearm. Her skin felt warm and soft. She looked me in the eye and then at each of the kids. "That's so great. I think I might cry. You're giving me goose bumps just talking about it."

I thanked her and paid. I didn't know her, but I'd shared just that little bit of my life with her and made a connection. I can't tell you the number of times I've told my story since—in one-on-one conversations with parents of autistic kids, to large groups, to anyone willing to listen. So many times they've told me the same thing that clerk at Von's did. It's never been easy for me to open up. I was always the shy kid, the one reluctant to step into the spotlight. Drawing attention to oneself just wasn't something you did in my family.

Suffer in silence.

Be seen and not heard.

Everyone's got a tough row to hoe.

You'll get your reward in heaven.

I grew up hearing and believing all those kinds of things.

What follows is the story of how Stephen's "Miracle Run" transformed our lives. It does involve a little bit of Hollywood and a whole lot of hope. Even without the first, the second one would have been there in ample supply. As it turned out, in a lot of ways it was me—and not my sons—who was the slow learner, the so-called able-minded one who needed to see the light, to have her attitude readjusted. In the pages that follow, I hope that you'll come to understand as I did that miracles are as much made as they are granted, that they are equal parts grace and guts, magic and mundane.

I understand all the risks inherent in calling this book *Miracle Run*. I know that using a cross-country race as a metaphor for living your life doesn't just border on cliché but resides right in the middle on the corner of Cliché Avenue and Sappy Street. In our case the metaphor, as trite as it may seem, really does fit. We'd all been running a race for a long time, and the sight of Stephen crossing the finish line brought that into sharper focus than it had ever been in before. His victory—technically he hadn't won that Oak Park Invitational race, but in my mind he had—energized me in a way that nothing else had in the eight years since the twins were diagnosed. I was energized, and I was crying great big heaving sobs.

I was crying because my son had shown me that you never quit. You take a wrong turn, you figure out your mistake, and you get after it again. I was also crying because I had underestimated my son. I'm not proud of that, and it's no easy admission to make, but the truth of it was staring me in the face. My son wasn't the water boy, wasn't an oddity, a curiosity, a charity case trotted out there so everyone could nod their head and feel tears welling up in their eyes and a lump forming in their throat.

No, Stephen was an honest-to-God competitor on one of the most literally uneven playing fields in high school sports. He neither asked for nor did he receive any special treatment. In fact, his coach assumed that Stephen was just one of those shy, quiet kids who meander the halls of high schools across America—the kids who tread so cautiously they don't even take the shine off the janitor's freshly polished floors. Stephen succeeded on his own terms, independently of me. I was so pleased and so proud, but at the same time I was so ashamed of myself for assuming that he was so much less than he really was. My pride and my shame were like two feuding neighbors; it would take a long time before they each came to understand the other's point of view and settle matters peaceably.

I'd like to say that Stephen's showing at the Oak Park Invitational altered all of our lives immediately and irrevocably. Telling you that would be a lie. While he crossed the finish line of that race, we all had, and continue to have, other seasons of competition to face. What I learned, and what I will share with you in the pages that follow, is that even though when the twins were first diagnosed as autistic I believed that I had been given a lifetime prison sentence, in fact, as Phillip had reminded me with his shout, I'd been granted a privileged kind of freedom.

As I sit here writing this nearly a decade after Stephen's Miracle Run, I'm only just beginning to put all the pieces together that enable me to understand how we were all able to overturn that original life sentence. Ironically enough, as I sit here, Janis Joplin's "Me and Bobby McGee" is drifting down the hillside from Phillip's "pad." He spends most of his time in an outbuilding my husband, Doug, built for him. Phillip is what some people call an old soul. Like Doug and me, he loves the music of the sixties, and this morning he's doing his best imitation of Janice's wail.

I'm sure that he understands the significance of the line "Freedom's just another word for nothing left to lose." We had to lose a lot to better understand autism's gift to us. Some of our losses were literal, some figurative, but they've all contributed to our learning to enjoy and appreciate all the colors in life's rich palette. For a long time I saw things in black and white, then I evolved a bit and some tones of gray edged their way in. I still see Stephen's Miracle Run in vivid Technicolor brilliance.

What I had to lose in order to gain our freedom and truly embrace autism's gift is what I want to share with you. I had to give up blaming and judging myself and others, had to tear down the walls of self-imposed exile I'd constructed for reasons real and imagined. I could still be fierce in advocating for them without giving up being fair to them, to myself, and to others.

I had to release the twins from my protective cocoon in order for them to enjoy the freedom of participation that meant so much to them and to me. When I was finally released from the push and pull of the twin impulses to protect them and yet to demand that their rights to a full life be honored, I felt a freedom I never thought possible.

I had to let go of one set of expectations for what the twins' lives would be like in order for their own set of desires to grow. I had to come to understand that my own desire that they be "normal" and achieve things on a timetable imposed by others resulted in me placing another obstacle in their path.

I also had to let go of my own fears and reticence, my long-standing desire to blend in. If I hadn't, I'd never have been able to become the advocate I had to become for my own children and now in a larger sense for autistics generally.

Along the way I learned that just because you are broke doesn't mean you're broken, that we could allow ourselves to be vulnerable without becoming victims, that we could all arrive at a compromise without compromising ourselves and our most deeply held values and beliefs.

I learned that even though I was, and remain, introverted, I needed to find someone who could listen to me. I didn't always want or need advice; I simply needed my voice to be heard. In time, I discovered that it was often easier to speak to a stranger, to simply say to someone who was looking either askance or with kindness at us, "My twins are autistic. It's hard." Even that simple admission acted as a relief valve. I selectively spilled my guts, scattering the various pieces along a wide swath of friends, coworkers, casual acquaintances, and people I didn't know at all so as not to be too large a burden on any one of them. That approach worked for me but may not for you.

There are more lessons than that, as you will eventually see, but I think you get the picture. I also want to let you know up-front that I am not someone who is prone to cheerleading and pumping people up with false enthusiasm. What follows is no Hallmark greeting card. You can get those sentiments from other people, very sincere and well-intentioned people. I speak the plain and simple truth as I experienced it. I believe the reason that I get hundreds of phone calls a month from parents struggling with issues related to autism is that I am a good listener and offer a grounded been-in-the-trenches perspective. The view from there isn't always pretty, nor is it always bleak. Please know this: Just as there is no cure for autism, there is no cure for being the parent of an autistic child. No one is going to come along and magically relieve you of the responsibility and worry that come with living this reality—the good, the bad, and the indifference of it. The foundation I eventually started doesn't focus on finding a cure but on helping parents deal with the day-to-day realities of autism and its effect on families, and that's what I hope you will take away from reading this book. Put another way, the focus is on treatment and not on cures. My main goal is that you will focus also on treating yourself. You've got a heavy cross to bear, and it does get easier, but the work is long and you have to take the best care of yourself so that you can provide the best care for others. That's the reality; that's the message.

My Buddhist friend explained to me the concept of the "beginner's mind," which means in a sense that you look at the world from a child's perspective. I know that when I was a kid, days seemed to last forever. At my age, they can seem to rush by in an instant. Why the difference? Well, when we're kids, what we experience is still new to us. We haven't gone through the experience so many times that we end up blocking out so many of its sensations. When we're kids, we're bombarded with new and fresh stimuli.

I used to think that it was unfortunate that autistics lacked the filtering mechanisms the rest of us have. Those filters enable us to tune in and tune out the flow of sensations that are out there. I know that for Stephen and Phillip, the world was often painful for them because so much intense stimulation was constantly bombarding them.

I hope this book will enable you to use a beginner's mind when looking at your life with an autistic. I know that when the diagnosis was handed down, I immediately based my perceptions on what I'd heard and read about autism. This book is my chance to review some of the major episodes in our lives, for me to exercise my beginner's mind and to show you the errors of my way and have you benefit from the hard-earned lessons that resulted from a young man saying to himself and others, "I want. I can. I will. I have."

Victories come in many shapes and sizes, and I've come to treasure each and every one of them. All of our victories required us to take that first baby step, to crawl before we walked or ran. Leaps of faith can span inches or miles, and sometimes it's just a matter of turning the page and moving on.

Chapter One

Signs and Wonders

I glanced in the rearview mirror. My five-year-old twins, Stephen and Phillip, sat stock-still in the backseat, their expressionless faces obscured momentarily by the shadows cast from the trees. I focused ahead again and, out of habit, reached up and touched the rosary that hung from the mirror's stalk. I rolled down the window, and the refreshing ocean coolness of a November morning in Southern California smoothed the hair from my forehead. I needed that caress, and it felt as much like a benediction as some meteorological phenomena. Signs and wonders. That was what I was looking for—along with the University of Southern California at Los Angeles medical campus.

On the recommendation of a kindergarten teacher, I was taking the boys to UCLA for an evaluation. They weren't nearly as verbal as they ought to have been at that age, she told me, as if I didn't know that, and they cried all the time. Didn't a plus cancel out a minus? So what if Stephen hadn't said a single word in school and had maybe uttered a single word less than a handful of times at home? He could scan a diagram and assemble a model car at the same age. Didn't the label on the model's box say it was intended for ages nine and above? Surely that had to mean something.

Mrs. Andrews whispered the word "autism," but it barely registered with me. In 1988, the word wouldn't have meant much to anyone outside a few medical and psychological specialists. Like a lot of people, I associated the "A word" with retardation. My kids weren't retarded, and I told myself they suffered from some kind of speech acquisition delay. I'd done some reading about childhood development, enough to convince myself that all their problems were speech related. I'll admit I was in denial—I could speculate and worry and analyze, but if anyone else said anything negative about my kids, I recoiled. My protective motherly instincts were in hyperdrive; I was acutely sensitive to any vibrations I felt that signaled even the faintest kind of judgment about my kids. After all, anything negative said about them was an indictment of me.

I couldn't continue on my path of denial, and so I finally made an appointment for Stephen and Phillip with Dr. Ritvo. Despite the diagnosis we all faced, I was feeling hopeful that morning. Among the signs and wonders I'd experienced, the legendarily nasty Southern California traffic had cooperated. Instead of accidents and gaper's blocks, slow and go and stop and simmer, we had had a relatively smooth ride; the only excitement had been a lane-splitting motorcyclist who clipped my passenger mirror, wobbled momentarily, and sped on. The thump of handlebar-to-car contact had startled us all; stirring the boys from their reverie. I viewed them from the rearview mirror, wondering what they were thinking. I constantly wished I knew what they were thinking. That morning I asked them how they were doing, what they thought of as they were looking out the window, but I could only guess. Phillip rambled on about something I couldn't really make out over the road noise, and I couldn't get him to speak louder. I could see Stephen in the mirror turn toward Phillip. Stephen's mouth was moving, and again I wished I could understand the shared babble the twins had developed to communicate with each other. Phillip shook his head, and then let loose with a string of no's, each one with a different inflection, ranging from crisply matter-of-fact to drawn-out teasing.

I knew that twins often developed their own language—sometimes verbal and sometimes preverbal. In Stephen and Phillip's case, their language was the latter. They made sounds—grunts, wheezes, whimpers, and an assortment of other noises. What made it seem like a language was how they used those sounds in sequences, with pauses and intonations that mimicked the way the pitch of our voices rises at the end of a question, or the way we emphasize a particular word by increasing our volume.

When they had settled into silence again, I imagined that in their minds they were naming and manipulating the images of the cars that we passed and that passed us. In my head, I heard Phillip, his voice low like the burbling of an idling car's exhaust, as he recited, "Chevrolet Malibu, Ford Mustang, Oldsmobile Toronado, Toyota Celica."

All kids are different, though, and I embraced that they were different. From about age one, the only guaranteed way to pacify the twins' worst tantrums was to open the hood of a car and let them stare at it. They'd be screaming, rocking, and biting themselves, and I'd take them outside and show them an engine, and immediately they'd be calm and focused, taking it all in. From their earliest days, the boys had loved to draw and color and would regularly cover their canvases (scrap paper, paper towels, discarded magazines, and newspapers) with automobiles.

At a time when most kids their age only had sufficient fine motor skills to hold on to their Hot Wheels cars or send them spinning down an adult-constructed track, Phillip and Stephen were able to assemble sophisticated model car kits unassisted. I'd sit and watch them as they'd scan the instruction sheets, use nail clippers to trim the pale white pieces from their "trees," test-fit the parts to be joined, and then, their focus riveted on the task at hand, looking more like laboratory technicians at a missile assembly plant than four-year-olds, they'd diligently squeeze out a drop of glue to cement the parts together. They'd hold the parts together between the fingers of one hand, arm held out away from their body, and with the other hand they'd scan the instruction sheet for the next step. For years, building those cars seemed to bring them the kind of peace and contentment that nothing else could. We'd run to the store, their biological father, Big Steve, and I, sometimes two or three times a week, to buy them more kits. AMT, Revell, Monogram, and Testors were brands I was investing in more so than Max Factor or Covergirl. The acrid smell of polystyrene glue can still evoke vivid memories for me, just as the familiar scent of a favorite aunt's Wind Song perfume might for someone else.

Surely this skill meant that my boys weren't retarded or disabled. They were simply different. By the time they were five, I had mostly come to terms with that intellectually. They exhibited behaviors I could take some pride in. Along with their model making, they'd taught themselves to read before they were three. They showed no interest in kids' books; instead, I'd see them sitting in the tiny chairs in their room, surrounded by shelves of stuffed animals, reading the newspaper like two contented men in a city park.

I didn't feel that their oddities were the result of some disability—just the opposite. They possessed some form of genius, and I was too limited in my own skills and abilities to relate to them on their level. Kids who could do the things they were doing at their age had to be far smarter than I was. They were okay; it was me who was struggling developmentally.

As much as I tried to tell myself that was the case, doubts lingered.

Physically, the twins were healthy. I'd had them checked out by various pediatricians time and again. Yet they terrified me. They seemed so distant, so aloof, more like celestial bodies that orbited around our family than fully engaged members of it. They communicated with each other only a little, only enough to get what they needed from one another. They were comfortable being alone together, and Stephen had only just begun to communicate with anyone besides Phillip. He'd occasionally grunt in response to something Ali or Richard said to him, but most of the time he barely acknowledged their presence. The rest of the world seemed to frighten and overwhelm them; only when they were fully involved in a task did the hand flapping, crying, and frenetic rocking cease.

And now here we were, five full years of worry and speculation later, pulling up to the parking gate at UCLA. I'd say that my heart was in my throat, but that would be an enormous understatement. I ran my tongue around the rim of my lips for perhaps the hundredth time. I forced myself to relax my jaw, but it felt as if I'd been biting down hard on the stickiest taffy for the last twenty-four hours. I had to remind myself to breathe.

Walking into the center did little to alleviate any of my anxiety. The lobby was a sterile glass and steel space that was designed to be light and airy but felt claustrophobic. The sunlight and ambient lighting played off the glass, refracting at odd angles, and was more disorienting than anything. It was as if the place were floating, tethered to the ground somehow but in danger of breaking free from its moorings. I had to consciously focus my attention on where I placed each foot or I might stagger. After signing in at reception, I kept bumping elbows with the staff member who led me down a series of corridors to the evaluation facility. A fresh-faced Asian woman who looked no more than twelve, she smiled each time our bodies came in contact. She'd tug her lab coat more tightly across her chest and tell me she was so sorry. Signs and wonders? Her apology didn't bode well.

I stood behind a glass panel honeycombed with wire, while two staff members worked with Phillip and Stephen. A honey-blond woman in a too-tight skirt sat Phillip down on a rug. The

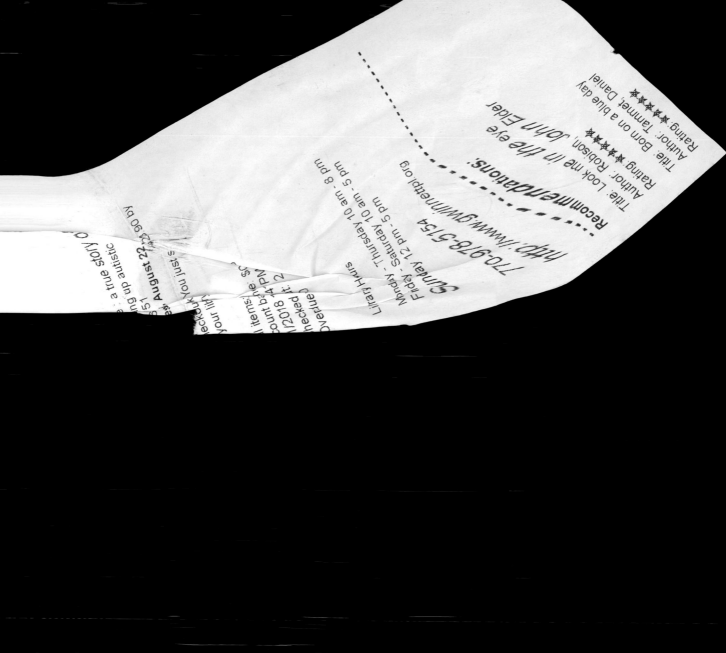

Recommendations:

Title: Look me in the eye
Author: Robison, John Elder
Rating: ★★★★★

Title: Born on a blue day
Author: Tammet, Daniel
Rating: ★★★★★

http://www.gwinnettpl.org

770-978-5154

Sunday 12 pm - 5 pm
Friday - Saturday 10 am - 5 pm
Monday - Thursday 10 am - 8 pm
Library Hours

Checked At:
.../2018 2...
count ba PM
All items: $C...
your lib...
Checkout You just...
...90 by
August 22
...ing up autistic
... a true story

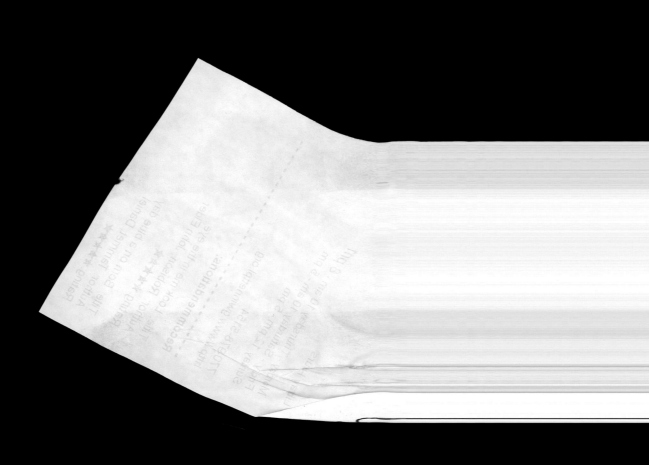

other, a young man who reminded me of Ichabod Crane, did the same with Stephen.

AT first the adults didn't interact with the boys at all. They just scattered a few toys around the floor, then took a few steps back and watched. After a few moments of this, I was furious. They were standing there in their lab coats with their clipboards and pens jotting notes, whispering and conferring with the kind of clinical detachment I would come to hate in some doctors. Stephen and Phillip weren't some specimen on a slide, which is how I felt they were being treated. They were flesh-and-blood human beings, little boys who had a different idea of play and were not a freak show because of what they did or didn't do on this rug. I couldn't get the image out of my mind from television medical shows of a group of doctors standing around a light frame viewing X-rays, coming up with a diagnosis—as though what they were observing was the sum total of a person's life and spirit. This wasn't like seeing your kids subjected to a physical exam. They were being judged as "normal" or not, having some standard of right or wrong imposed on them. I hated feeling so helpless, hated myself for putting them through this ordeal.

I told myself to calm down, that they were just doing their jobs, but my kids were far more to me than just another routine day at the office.

The evaluators—I never knew if they were doctors or what their official titles were—tried to get the boys to interact with them, but Phillip and Stephen essentially ignored them. I could see how rigidly the boys held their bodies. They were frightened and anxious, and they began flapping their hands and rocking. At one point Stephen bit his arm, a habit he'd developed fairly early on, a form of self-abuse that I much preferred to the head banging he'd done when much younger. Stephen coiled his hair around his fingers and scratched at the eczema that had recently developed on his face and arms. I so wanted him to just sit and look at the woman doing the testing, but he wouldn't. I'd spent the last few days preparing them for this evaluation. I talked with them about appropriate behavior, urged them to look adults in the eye. I knew that neither of them responded well to changes in their routine, but all of my efforts seemed to be going to waste. They were distracted and irritable. To be honest, so was I.

Eventually the specialists stopped observing the twins and led first Stephen and then Phillip into another room. I was asked to join the doctors and Stephen in one room, and after the evaluation, I would join Phillip in the other. In each space, they began by asking a series of simple questions—questions that any kid the age of the twins could have easily answered.

"Stephen, how is a cow different from a horse?"

Stephen squirmed in my lap, turned, and looked at me pleadingly.

"Stephen, what do you sleep on at night?" Hoping against hope, I pursed my lips to form the first sound of the answer. Stephen shook his head and grunted.

"Stephen, I'm going to tell you some numbers. I want you to repeat them to me. Six, seven, two, nine, eight." I bounced my head in imitation of the rhythm of the sequence. I imagined Stephen looking at me and saying, "Six, seven, two, nine, eight." In reality, Stephen kicked and thrashed.

This was going badly. I was used to Stephen ignoring me, and I'd seen him act out physically in ways far worse than this, but I knew these specialists were taking notes, checking items off a list, drawing conclusions; they weren't like me, simply accepting the boys' behavior for what it was. In time, the questions piled on one another like cereal flakes in a bowl.

"Stephen, look at this picture of a bicycle. What part of the bicycle is missing?"

"Stephen, look at these pictures. What can you find that is in all of the pictures?"

"Stephen, what is four plus three?"

"Stephen, what does the word 'angry' mean?"

"Stephen, put a line through the object on the page that doesn't belong with the others."

"Stephen, put the red and white blocks together so that they look just like the picture on this paper."

"Stephen, I'm red. I'm found on a tree. I'm a good after-school snack. What am I?"

I shut my eyes and twisted my face into a grimace, willing him to focus and answer the questions correctly, to do the tasks assigned. I knew the boy who read the newspaper knew the answers, but what was it that prevented him from just announcing, "These questions are silly. I know the answers. I just don't feel like answering."

If only the twins were deaf, I thought; I could deal with that. They could learn sign language, learn to communicate with others besides themselves, participate more fully in the world around them. But I knew there was something else at work shutting my kids out. Whether it was autism or some other mental delay—one of the hardest obstacles to face with this evaluation was the possibility that the doctors might not be able to do anything about it.

The woman asking him the questions smiled and used her voice like a musical instrument to elicit something other than the deadpan expression on his face. I imagined her as the Pied Piper emerging from Stephen's mouth, a happy trail of words tagging along behind her.

Stephen never smiled.

Stephen never spoke.

When Stephen really wanted something, he let his body do the talking for him. I'd learned to interpret a lot of his gestures, and much like parents do with preverbal children, I'd developed the bad habit of giving him what he wanted without him really asking for it. When, like Stephen, your child doesn't talk, you resort to what's most expedient and not what may be best for him in the long term.

When they were through with testing Stephen, I went into the evaluation room with Phillip. Things proceeded much as they had before. The notable exception was that Phillip was a chatterbox in comparison to Stephen. He didn't really speak, but at least he made sounds approximating language. True, it was muttering and babbling, seemingly a language of his own invention, but grunting and squeaking, to me, was better than Stephen's nearly constant silence or crying. That was typical of Phillip, and though I'd told him that he would have to keep his answers short and to concentrate, he slipped back into his usual form.

I don't remember how long the boys were in the evaluation room, but it seemed like hours. A week passed before I was called back to review the evaluation results. This time, I couldn't find anyone to take Ali, so I dragged her along with the twins to Westwood. I had to practically drag Stephen into the waiting room. He bit his arm and started to cry. Phillip sat on the floor facing a wall. One of the office assistants brought Stephen some paper and a pencil and he calmed down once he was able to draw. Before I was summoned to Dr. Freeman's office, another woman in the office sat next to me. She took Ali's hands in hers and started to play patty cake with her. Ali giggled and smiled. The woman said it would be best if Ali didn't go back into the office with me. I'd need to concentrate. A few moments later I was in Dr. Freeman's office. She stepped around her desk and offered her hand to me. An attractive woman in her early thirties, she had a wide smile that disconcerted me. She struck me at first as someone who had a lot of practice delivering bad news to people. She started in on an explanation of the work they were doing at the Neuropsychiatric Institute, how the two tests they administered—the Weschler Intelligence Scale for Children and the Vineland Adaptive Behavior Scale—worked, that it had taken a few days to compile all the results.

There was a knock on the door, and Dr. Ritvo stepped in. I had been to UCLA a few times before and consulted with him. I liked him; he had that solid, substantial fatherlike air about him. He apologized for being a few minutes late, and then he started in. "We have the assessment of current level of cognitive functioning, based on the WISC, and Phillip obtained a verbal IQ of—"

I help up my hand like a crossing guard would.

All I wanted to know was that my kids were going to be okay, that they were normal, that this was a phase, something that could be straightened out with speech therapy, with time and attention. Tears were forming in my eyes. "Please, Dr. Ritvo, what is wrong with Stephen?"

All that I had been thinking was lost in the tumult of emotions I felt when the smiling Dr. Freeman said, "Based on all our preliminary indications and analyses, Stephen and Phillip are autistic."

My mind raced. A thousand images, thoughts, bits of prayer, and curses tumbled around in my head. Autism? Autism. The kindergarten teacher had been right. Finally, the kaleidoscope stilled and formed an image—a prison. I quickly shattered that perception and mumbled, "What about medicine? An operation? There has to be something you can do for him," I begged. I could barely speak.

"There's no medicine, no surgery," she told me, and I heard her voice as you might through a fog. "We find that with most autistic youngsters, placement in an institution is best. This can be done at no cost to you."

"I can't do that to Stephen."

Dr. Ritvo started to speak and then stopped. When I looked over at him, I could see tears welling in his eyes. "Corrine, I just want to make sure you understand. Dr. Freeman is talking about both boys. They're both autistic."

Right then, the twins screamed in unison. Then the room fell silent.

THE silence lingered when I sat across from the man who had fathered the twins. I'd just recounted to my husband, Stephen Sr. (aka Big Steve), what I'd experienced at UCLA. He stared down at his hands and picked at his cuticles for a moment. He scratched his neck and then nodded. My eyes followed his as they glanced up at the clock on the soffit above the kitchen sink. We'd bought it at a little shop in Laguna Beach, a rare trip and rarer extravagance; I'd moved out but the clock had stayed. We gave it to his parents as a gift, and it hung in their house— the same house in West Hills we had been sharing with them because Big Steve couldn't hold down a job.

The clock was shaped like the sun, a smile spread across its face and its rays splayed out from the center like the tentacles of an octopus. As I sat there, it struck me for the first time that the clock's shape resembled the sunshiny figure depicted on boxes of Raisin Bran. I almost had to laugh. The man who sat across from me, the man who'd provided some of the genetic material necessary to produce my sons, had the habit of eating Raisin Bran cereal every morning. His Raisin Bran habit took on sinister importance in the light of the boys' diagnoses. What had once seemed harmless, something easily dismissed as a quirk, now loomed large in my mind. Regular as clockwork, he'd pour himself a bowl, pick out all the raisins, set them in a coffee mug, and then replace those raisins with a supply from the

Sun-Maid box he'd set alongside his bowl. With a quarter-cup measure, he'd spoon out the new raisins and sprinkle them over the bowl. He reasoned that he didn't like the hard sugar-coated raisins that came in the cereal, so on one level it made sense to remove them. Why he didn't just let me buy bran flakes without raisins didn't make sense on any level.

I knew from the time I met him that he was different. My parents had encouraged the match—he was from a family as deeply religious as ours—and it was my duty to get married and have children. He was shy and reserved, highly intelligent and skilled, but socially awkward—well, okay, socially inept. He treated me well, but sometimes he would lapse into awkward silences, or he would do things that just didn't quite match the situation. One night before we were married we went out to dinner, and afterward the waiter brought out the check. Big Steve didn't make a move to pay, so I did. I thought that his stalled reaction to the check was a little untraditional, but I had enjoyed his company and we had a nice night. I didn't say anything that might ruin the evening, but I did mention it to one of his friends a few days later. I wasn't trying to rat him out or paint him in a bad light; I was just trying to understand him better and hoped his friend could help with that.

At the end of that week, Big Steve and I were supposed to go out on another date. He came to my place to pick me up, and when I got in the car, he handed over a stack of bills. He hadn't said hello to me, hadn't even come to my door, just handed me the cash. He put the car in gear and we drove off. I sat there holding the bills in my hand, looking over at him. His brow was deeply furrowed, and I could see that the blood had drained from his hands as he held the wheel in a death grip. I didn't know if I should apologize or what. Before I could say anything, he reached into his shirt pocket and pulled something out.

"Hold out your hand. I was going to give this to you as well."

I held out my hand. He dropped an engagement ring into it.

I sat there staring at it, dumbfounded. I was wondering if maybe he thought this was some kind of clever, original way of proposing to me, but I knew he wasn't that good of an actor. He simply didn't know what to do, what was appropriate for the situation. If you were going to plan the perfect autistic proposal scenario, that would have been it. Stilted communication. Odd choice of situation. Little or no emotion.

I'm not sure what my accepting this less than "romantic, down on one knee" proposal says about me, or the level of denial I was in. As I said before, my parents approved of him. I'd even spoken to my mother directly about my concerns that Big Steve was a little off. She responded, "He's a good Catholic boy. You need to marry a good Catholic boy." So I did. I was young and shy and was flattered that any man would have considered me marriage material. And Big Steve, his quirks aside, was a remarkably good-hearted person.

As you might suspect, Big Steve wasn't the most communicative of men, and though we'd obviously been physically intimate, there was little emotional intimacy between us. And even though we were now ending our marriage, I wanted the man I had married to reach out to me, to, at the very least, extend his hand and hold mine. What I really needed was for him to get out of the chair and come over to me and hold me. Instead, he sat with his lips pursed, his eyes darting around the room in avoidance of mine.

He cleared his throat. "Excuse me."

I waited some more, thinking he'd offer me the support I so needed as I absorbed the news that our sons were autistic. Surely he was feeling what I was feeling, like a life sentence had been handed out to Phillip and Stephen; I wanted to scream and rock myself in a fury.

Finally, he gave a response. "What do you want to do?"

I started laughing. At first it was just a kind of derisive snort, but in a few seconds it was transformed into a shoulder heaving but silent laugh of resignation and despair.

What did I want to do? I wanted to go back in time, frankly. I wanted Superman to fly into space, grab the planet, and spin it back on its axis just long enough to get to the point when whatever genetic mutation, whatever fluke of cell division, whatever misstep of mitosis could be stopped in freeze frame and cleaned up in the editing room. I wanted my boys to experience a life without autism. I just wanted whatever it was that had broken them to be fixed. I could only think about how their lives would be easier if they didn't have this condition.

I wanted to be able to go back in time when Phillip and Stephen were about three years old. The two of them had just developed what doctors call "twin speak." They communicated with each other using words, sounds, and gestures that I could never correctly interpret. I felt shut out, and struggled to come to terms with what I felt was my own inadequacy, my failure to discover the Rosetta stone that would unlock their secret language and consequently their secret lives.

I wanted to go back to that time because, at least at that point, my not being able to communicate effectively with them was my fault and not a result of them being autistic. I could live with my failings but not their diagnosis.

Since I couldn't go back in time, what I wanted to do next was to understand why they were diagnosed with autism. My parents were devout Catholics, and I grew up going to church and Sunday school in addition to attending parochial schools. I knew that Adam and Eve's fall from grace in the Garden of Eden had let evil loose in the world and stained us all with original sin. I wanted and needed to know what had let this evil loose in our lives and stained Stephen and Phillip. I realize now how horrible it sounds to think that their condition was somehow a curse, but back then I still clung firmly to the belief that whenever something bad happened in your life, you could trace it back to some sin you had committed. I didn't like to think of God that way, as an avenging force who didn't care about the collateral damage to my sons for something I did. I wasn't interested so much in the metaphysical why as I was the medical why.

I wasn't immune from self-suspicion either. Through the years, and in particular in the hours since I'd heard those words at UCLA, I'd done a mental rundown of everything I might have possibly done to contribute to the boys' condition. Did I eat too much sugar while pregnant? Did the pregnancy vitamins have a bad reaction in me? Was I too stressed? Did I not exercise enough? Did the toxemia I'd experienced while pregnant mess things up? Were Stephen's low birth weight and five days in the hospital postbirth the cause of this?

The list went on and on. I did the dance that every parent of a sick, injured, or disabled child does—the tango of blame and denial.

THE twins' father and I were in the process of getting a divorce. We'd stopped living as husband and wife well before the diagnosis. The cause of the division between us was abundantly clear. He could not support a family financially. He'd struggled to keep a decent job, and after being repeatedly let go from one position after another, he finally just gave up. I was struggling to raise our three children; trying to protect Stephen and Phillip from the cruelty that I knew was going to be heaped upon them once they left the protective cocoon of our home; and attempting to work enough hours as a loan officer at our local bank to feed, clothe, house, and transport the entire family. After a while it all simply became too much for me to come home to a husband who seemed incapable of helping us. We were foundering financially, and instead of being a lifeline, he was an anchor. Had the stress in our household caused Stephen and Phillip to withdraw so completely?

I knew Steve was a bright and intelligent man, but he lacked certain social skills. I knew that contributed to his failure to hold down jobs and to do anything resembling meaningful work for a man with his level of education. Coming from me, however, an analysis of social awkwardness was pretty ironic. I was no social butterfly myself; I was more like a slug. You'd

see me come out early in the morning, especially after an overnight rain, but the rest of the time I was fairly invisible. As a
result of our shared social ineptness, I think we were drawn to
one another more out of need than desire, though our court-
ship and the early years of our marriage were happy ones. We
both doted on Richard when he was born, did all the things
and made all the mistakes that new parents do. I have to admit
that the strain of the twins' early expression of symptoms contributed to the dissolution of my marriage, but only to a small
degree.

If Phillip and Stephen were echolalic, then my husband and
I were also. We kept repeating the same steps, carried the same
grudges, had the same arguments, until finally I'd had enough
and he had, too.

When I told him about the diagnosis, he was unfazed by
the news. I wasn't surprised by that. A lack of affect, or the
appropriate expression of emotion, is one hallmark of autism.
I'd seen that in the boys, but it didn't really register with me
as a problem. I simply chalked it up to them taking after their
father. I figured that boys aren't as verbal as girls, didn't express
their emotions easily; and especially since I wasn't particularly
verbal myself or likely to easily emote, alarm bells didn't go off
for me initially.

After the diagnosis and after learning more about autism, I
suspected that Big Steve was a high-functioning autistic. Nev-
ertheless, he would go on to make a good life for himself—he's
long since been remarried, has a steady job as an over-the-road
truck driver with his new wife, and for him, the twins' autism
hasn't caused any appreciable ill effects. I don't blame him for

wanting to forget the number of times we had our power turned off, the rent was past due, or he came home unable to explain why it was that he was asked not to come back to work the next day. In some ways I envied him that lapse of memory, that persistent ability to live in denial.

The truth was, there was a disconnect between us, and there was a larger one between him and the world in general. I mean, I was shy and inhibited, but Big Steve was nearly a recluse. The other thing I noticed was that loud noises *really* bothered him. I tried my best to keep the kids quiet, but Stephen and Phillip cried persistently. Richard was becoming a teenager and music was a big part of his life. Occasionally one of us would drop something, a dog would bark nearby, and life would just, well, it would just happen—sometimes loudly and sometimes not at exactly the right time. Any loud noise would get Big Steve pacing the floors maniacally. I had enough on my mind without worrying about whether I was putting the silverware away in the drawer too loudly.

After the boys were diagnosed, something else led me to suspect that my husband might be autistic. In 1979 I'd seen the movie *Son-Rise: A Miracle of Love* on television. Back then I'd thought of it as just another of those tacky made-for-TV disease-of-the-week flicks in which the writer and director plucked at your heartstrings with all the subtlety of a hyena tearing at a carcass. Later on, when the subject matter meant more to me, I looked up the film to learn more about it. It was based on the real-life experiences of Barry Neil and Samahria Kaufman. Their son, Ruan, was diagnosed with autism in the late 1960s, when the prevailing wisdom was that autistic chil-

dren were unreachable, unteachable, and should be institutionalized. Rather than accept the grim prognosis, the Kaufmans
devised a program to teach their son how to interact with
others and the larger world, and eventually started the Option
Institute and Autism Treatment Center of America, an educational foundation dedicated to educating other parents and
professionals about working with developmentally disordered
children. James Farentino and Kathryn Harrold played the parents. The Kaufmans wrote a book in 1976 called *Son-Rise*, and
copies can still be found. In 1995 they released another book—
Son-Rise: The Miracle Continues. Ruan cowrote it, and it is still
in print.

That movie and the behavior of the young actor who portrayed Ruan aroused my suspicions about Big Steve. I realize
that my portrait of him doesn't exactly show him in the best
light. The truth is that he was a remarkably handsome, extremely
intelligent man with fascinating insights into the world. He
didn't have a college education—unlike his parents, who were
both engineers—but his work as an automotive technician paid
him well. I think the boys got their love for and fascination with
cars from him. He loved, and still loves, the boys deeply.

As I mentioned, Big Steve's parents were both engineers.
His mother, Mary, was literally a rocket scientist, who for-
mulated a fuel that NASA eventually used in its program.
She was a brilliant and delightful woman. I got to know her
really well six months after the twins were born in June 1982. I
had gotten a job transfer to Coeur D'Alene, Idaho, so we lived
very near Big Steve's parents. They had a lovely five-bedroom
home, and they couldn't have been more welcoming. While

I was working at Kay Dee Contempo, Big Steve was unem-
ployed and looking for a job. In 1982 we were still feeling the
effects of the recession, and work as a mechanic was difficult to
find, especially for someone with the spotty employment track
record Big Steve had. He stayed home and watched the kids
while I worked.

At the time, I knew something wasn't quite right with Mary,
but there was so much else that was wonderful about her that
it was easy to dismiss some of her eccentric ways. Everything
Mary did, with one or two exceptions, she did nearly to perfec-
tion. She was a great cook, an amazing seamstress and knitter,
and an accomplished engineer and businesswoman. She and her
husband, Richard, started a business called American Energy
Consultants, and it was thriving. Richard was a licensed struc-
tural engineer, and they were involved in the construction of
some of the finest homes in Malibu. They worked out of their
home, and to help them out, I did a lot of their bookkeeping in
addition to my full-time bookkeeping job.

They needed me. Though Mary was brilliant, she was one
of those classically untidy people whose orderly thinking wasn't
reflected in how she kept her desk. She also lived by a rigid routine. She ate the same lunch every day—yogurt and an apple.
She also washed her hair only once a week—every Friday at
7:00 p.m. I've since come to learn that grooming issues are significant to autistic individuals. Now, I love Mary, and she was
a dear woman who loved my sons with all her heart and soul.
It pains me to report this, but as you can well imagine, Mary
needed to wash her hair more frequently than once a week.

I think if she hadn't developed that routine of Friday washings, she would have ignored her hair altogether. I learned later that Mary's body carriage, her stooped, stiff-legged, balls-of-her-feet gait, is typical of autistic individuals. Before the twins' diagnosis, I chalked all this up to quirks. After the diagnosis, as I started to learn more about the condition via books, movies, consultations with experts, and doctors' pamphlets, I came to recognize that Mary was likely a high-functioning autistic with some characteristics of a savant. I didn't love her any less because of that; in fact, I likely loved her more because she helped me find the answers I so desperately needed to the "why" question of my sons' condition.

With my accounting and bookkeeping background, I was able to help out with my in-laws' business. One afternoon, I was sitting at my desk going over their books when I heard a distant shout. At first I dismissed it as something coming from outside the house. Then I heard a similar cry, this time a bit louder and more distinct. I pushed myself away from the desk and crept into the hallway. I was certain the sounds were coming from somewhere inside the house. I waited. I heard the clicking of one of the radiators. Then I heard it again—a high-pitched, almost musical sound coming from the end of the hallway where Mary had her office. I took a few more steps toward the source of the sound and stopped in my tracks when I heard it again. I was still standing there when Mary stepped out from behind her closed door. She had a blueprint in her hands and she scanned it as she walked down the stairs. She was staring so intently, she didn't see me standing there. When she reached the first landing and made a ninety-degree turn toward the first floor, I could see her face.

At first it was placid and expressionless, and then one cheek twitched and her head bobbled momentarily before her mouth opened and she emitted the sound I'd been hearing. She disappeared down the stairs, and I heard her rummaging in the kitchen. I went back to work and didn't think about the incident for a long time. Only when Phillip began to exhibit symptoms of Tourette's syndrome did I remember Mary's little outbursts and tics. It was another "aha" moment but not one I took a great deal of satisfaction in having.

I wasn't connecting certain behaviors between the twins and their father's family in an effort to absolve myself of guilt. I was simply trying to rationalize, to identify a cause, to understand what was happening within my family. Connecting a few dots didn't satisfy me, though, and I started to feel helpless. Why me? I wondered.

I'd like to think that I've always been beyond self-pity, but the truth of the matter is that I'm a fallible human being, and I did ask God why he chose me to suffer this way. I started questioning everything: Why my boys? Why autism—something few people knew much about? Why did I marry Steve? I was shy and a little uncertain of myself, but I had had other boyfriends along the way, a few other young men who'd shown interest in me. I think that I suspected all along that Big Steve's employment troubles and his emotional distance from me were the product of something more profound than simply his being different. At the same time, I was attracted to that difference. I valued and marveled at his unique perspective, and was attracted to his knowledge of all things mechanical. It was as if he spoke another language, came from another culture that was so different from my own conservative, traditional, blue-collar dyed-in-the-wool Catholicism. Being with him made me feel special. If I was able to see beyond the social awkwardness and the inability to hold down a steady job, then that meant that I wasn't like everyone else who cared about those mundane matters. Being able to see the goodness at the center of such a rough exterior made me one of the good gals, so different from the social climbers and the pursuers of the MRS degree I'd known in college and elsewhere.

Back then, if the measure of a woman's worth was the kind of man she could attract, then by conventional standards, I wasn't worth a whole lot in the minds of other people. But in my mind, I was wealthy beyond measure because of my ability to see beyond the immediate and the superficial. In a way, my choice to spend my life with someone whom others underestimated made me even more certain that my reasoning was sound.

Of course, all of that rationalizing and soul searching took place much later on. In the moment, I was simply struggling to deal with the reality of trying to support a family financially, raise three children in a place nowhere near my own far-flung family, and come to terms with having two sons who were rather seriously behind developmentally.

While I did ask the "Why me?" questions and wondered why God had done this to my sons, my faith did give me a lot to rely on. I continued to attend Mass regularly and found a great deal of comfort there. I had always appreciated the Psalms for their beauty, and in them I found so much that I could apply to my life and my situation. I'm not talking about the usual Psalm 23 "Yea though I walk through the valley of the shadow of death" inspiration, but others like Psalm 104, which talks about the natural world that the Lord has created and oversees. It reminded me of the beauty of the world and all its creations. That's how I felt about Stephen and Phillip. I never stopped thinking of them as children of God, as wonderful creations. In spite of all my questioning and wondering, I never for one nanosecond wished they hadn't been born. If there were times when I felt their torment, their frustration, and saw it acted out, I wasn't angry at God for having done that to them but I was pierced by a feeling of my own inadequacy, my own, and eventually others', inability to help them.

I know that all parents experience anguish when their infant children are experiencing distress and can't explain through words what is troubling them. That feeling of helplessness at their helplessness tears at your heart. I experienced that for many years. I knew, even then, that asking why was a natural part of the process I had to go through to better understand and to come to terms with their condition. I also knew that at some point after the diagnosis, I had to focus on more important questions, the questions that beat as the bass line of their frequent and improvisational crying spells. I sometimes imagined the two of them as jazz musicians, riffing on a melody that only they could hear, possessors of a language and an intonation whose origins were a mystery to us, but with an internal logic and beauty of their own devising. What next steps could I take? What could we all do to offset the prognosis that there was no pill, no treatment, no hope?

Chapter Two

Building a Fortress of Solitude

MY current husband, Doug, recently made me aware that Superman is famous for having his Fortress of Solitude. I'd heard the term before but never associated it with the man of steel, the archetypal American Superhero. I make no claim that I'm in any way heroic, let alone superheroic, and the trifocal lenses in my glasses are a testament to my myopia and not some Clark Kent–like disguise.

All I really remember of the Superman movies was the late Christopher Reeve flying around with Margot Kidder in his arms, but when Doug filled me in on Superman's story, I realized that maybe there were some similarities between us. While I wasn't bent on rescuing the world, I certainly did adopt that kind of attitude with my kids and in particular with the twins. I took it on as my sworn duty to protect them from all harm. I'll talk much more in chapters to come about the twin tensions of protecting them and letting them experience life fully.

For now, I want to focus on another set of tensions that I realize made my life more difficult than it needed to be. I already told you that I became obsessed with finding the answer to why the twins were autistic. I related that I danced the twin tango of blame and denial. One moment I was certain that something I had done during pregnancy had caused it; the next I was convinced that the boys' father and his genetic legacy were responsible. When those obsessions proved unhelpful—in the sense that I couldn't definitively say that one or the other or even a combination of the two were the guilty parties—I had to do some other mental gymnastics.

Both before and after the diagnosis, I was in denial. As a way to cope with the twins' unpredictable behavior, I'd become a master actress. If I got in line at the grocery store and Stephen stood in front of the cart staring and waving his arms and shouting, I'd pretend that I didn't see him. I'd adopt a casual "My, my, would you look at that? The *National Enquirer* has an article about a boy who is half-rat, half-human" attitude. Isn't that just the most fascinating thing? I wonder if he really likes cheese. Where do you shop for clothes when you have a rat boy? Oh, mustn't linger too long, I've got to put my groceries on the conveyor belt.

Later on, after years of pretending, if the boys' outbursts were too loud or happened too close to one of the clerks or another shopper, I'd simply look the person in the eye and say, "They're autistic," as if that could explain anything and everything. I'd seldom wait for a response; I'd just let my eyes find something else to hold my shattered attention.

Only when really pressed would I use the A word, and when I did, I wielded it like a weapon, daring anyone to respond in any way that I deemed inappropriate. All the pop psychology books tell us that denial is a defense mechanism, and I was about as defensive as they come.

Even when the first reports came back from their school that the boys weren't talking at all and I'd gotten a phone call from Mrs. Andrews, their teacher at Chaparral Elementary School, telling me that Stephen was "antisocial" and needed to be tested, I covered up. "What do you mean by 'cases' like Stephen? He's not a case; he's a twin. He doesn't need to speak so much. My doctor tells me he'll outgrow this. I don't have medical insurance to cover the testing you're talking about."

I'd only rarely lash out like that. For the most part, I retreated behind the first layer of stone going up on my fortress's walls.

Even after the diagnosis, I fixated on Stephen's apparent inability or disinclination to speak. I knew that he was smart, and I didn't need any specialized intelligence tests to verify that. I'd seen it. The kid could draw the inside of an automobile engine when he was four. The drawing would be so detailed, you'd think it came from the desk of an engineer assigned with the task of making a cutaway diagram. That's what I wanted to do, to cut away whatever it was that was impeding him and his ability to speak so that he could go on to lead a so-called normal life.

The very first day after the diagnosis, I stepped behind that wall of my fortress. I drove to the campus of Cal State University Northridge—with the exception of Pepperdine University, it was the closest college campus to our house—and posted a flyer on several bulletin boards and walls in and near the education and psychology buildings. "Help Wanted: A Graduate or Undergraduate Student in Speech Pathology or Psychology to Tutor Two Twins, Age Six." I then gave my contact information.

Today, I cringe at the tongue-twisting syntax of "to Tutor Two Twins," but at that stage in my life I wasn't saying anything three times fast, just doing everything three times faster than I ought to have been. Regardless of the construction of my plea, I had several people respond to my ad within days. One of those who called, and the young woman who eventually worked with Stephen and Phillip, turned out to be the daughter of the actor Robert Blake. This was 1989, long after his popular TV show *Baretta* had gone off the air. Delinah told me about her father reluctantly, casually passing it off as just another fact, a filler to ease the silences that lingered far too long whenever she came to work with the kids.

She would sit on the floor with them, pat it, and say the word "floor." Her cherubic face and wide-eyed encouragement had me mouthing the word, but Phillip and Stephen would just pat the floor mechanically and stare at her equally wide-eyed but without any encouragement. I was sad to tell our young tutor that things weren't working out. It was nice to have such a vibrant presence in the house, but it was clear the boys needed greater help than any she could offer.

Eventually, I got them in to see a speech pathologist, a

woman whose name I cannot recall. I sometimes wish I had the ability to go back in time and freeze-frame the countless faces the first time I met them—all the specialists, assistants, receptionists, and clerks. I would scan each of those faces, searching for some sign, any indication at all that they were either the one or the one who would lead me to the one who was going to unlock the vault that held my sons captive. Which one of them would decrypt the Rosetta stone, revealing the mystery of the Tower of Babel in which my sons were held hostage?

Even though I'd gotten the speech pathologist to work with Stephen and Phillip, I noted no real difference in the frequency or quality of their speech. Stephen remained taciturn, and Phillip's echolalia had increased to the point that it infuriated his older brother, Richard. Once, Richard was in the bathroom brushing his teeth, and Phillip came in.

"Stop watching me!" Richard said.

"Stop watching me!" Phillip parroted.

"Stop it!" Richard's voice rose in pitch and volume.

"Stop it!" Phillip's voice matched Richard's.

"You idiot." Richard's tone wavered between disgust and empathy.

"You idiot," Phillip confirmed.

I know that children often play this parroting game to rile one another, the verbal equivalent of "Why are you hitting yourself?" But this was clearly different. There was no malice in Phillip's echoing his brother's statements; it was as if he were a canyon wall reverberating mindlessly.

In some sense, what I was hoping to find was a voice that could parrot what I was thinking and feeling. I wanted to find a

book written by the mother of an autistic boy who had successfully transitioned to his teen years and beyond. I scoured the
shelves of the Agoura Hills library, not wanting to bother the
librarians, and came up empty. Finally, in desperation, I asked
one of the reference librarians for help. I asked if there were
any books at all on autism. She went over to the card catalog
and scanned it. "I'm sorry, there's nothing here about 'artism.'
Maybe we can try a magazine search on 'artism'?"

If the experience hadn't been so frustrating, I would have
laughed at her calling it "artism." After all, if the boys were
capable of one thing, it was drawing.

Even in the face of all this, I still stubbornly clung to the
belief that Phillip and Stephen only had a language acquisition
problem.

What I needed to do was to explore the language of autism
research. If I had, I would have understood one of the fundamental things about autism. The word itself means "in one's
self." Withdrawal and isolation are common manifestations of
autism, and I saw the twins' silence as the cause of their withdrawal and not another symptom. To me, their silence was the
keystone holding up the walls of their fortress of solitude. Figure out a way to pull words out of them, and you'd also be yank-
ing that keystone out, and the wall would fall.

In my mind, silence was the greatest isolator, and irony of
ironies, because my sons were autistic, I isolated myself in so
many ways!

I did it socially.

I did it emotionally.

In denying the truth about their diagnosis, I isolated myself from the truth. My silence about the issue, my desire to cover it all up, initially isolated me from so many other possibilities. By feeling as if I'd been issued a life sentence, I was relegating myself to a life in solitary confinement.

A war raged within me, with the forces of "my sons are normal" doing battle with the forces of "my sons are special." Both sides waged propaganda campaigns, and my tears fell like leaflets intended to win my own heart and mind.

Three days into kindergarten, Mrs. Andrews had sensed that something was not right with the boys, and she had the school psychologist administer a series of tests. One of them required the boys to draw a picture of themselves. She showed me Stephen's drawing first. It was a competent artist's rendering of a human face with eyes, nose, and mouth. Phillip's was a duplicate of Stephen's drawing. They couldn't have copied from one another since they were separated at the time of the test. I could have chalked it up to a "twin thing," but what seemed even more revealing was the fact that they drew the figures without bodies. Disembodied heads floating in space. Is that how the boys saw themselves? Were they that disconnected, that separate? Was there so much going on in their minds that couldn't be given expression in any way that this was how they saw themselves?

And if the boys were that disconnected, that separate, what did their isolation say about me, the one who I thought probably made them that way?

After diagnosis, the boys were placed in a class for the communicatively handicapped. I wondered then and now how many of us should be placed in that same room. All that well-intentioned placement did for me was to confirm my diagnosis and isolate me further from the truth.

I think that my obsession with getting Phillip and Stephen to communicate effectively was a projection of my own desire to communicate and interact with people. My marriage to Big Steve had long since been over by the time the boys were diagnosed, and even though I wasn't officially divorced, I'd been seeing a man I'd met at one of the accounting offices I worked at. He sent me out on a per diem basis to his clients, and this helped me supplement my meager income.

My boss, Larry Heller, and I spent a lot of time together and drew close. He had what I always wanted for my family and me. His thriving accounting practice offered stability and a clear, certain path to the kind of successful life I'd envisioned for myself many years before. As the relationship developed, we talked about me moving in with him. Because I felt so bad about Big Steve and his inability to work, we were still sharing living quarters.

I told Big Steve that all of that was going to have to change, that we had to move forward with the divorce. As a devout Catholic, that notion was anathema to me, but with Larry in the picture, I knew I had to take that drastic step in order to save my family. I pictured Larry and me married one day, building a new life free of the scraping and struggling that had marked most of my adult years. Larry was extremely generous, and the thought of moving into his fabulous home, having a maid to help out, enjoying outings at his country club, had me almost giddy for the first time in my life.

Three years later, in 1987, Larry and I had our daughter,

Alexandra. A year after that, just barely following the boys' diagnosis, he was out of our lives completely. Larry had never really developed much of a relationship with the boys. I'd hoped that he could be like a father to them, but he was somewhat cold and indifferent. I moved into Larry's house alone. The boys went to live with their father and his parents. I drove from Malibu to their house every day. I couldn't stand to be away from them. The visits with Big Steve and the boys went well. It seemed that everyone had settled into this new routine and new life.

I didn't think that my moving in with Larry was an act of abandonment. Instead, I saw it as a complicated expediency. I cared deeply for Larry, and though he wasn't emotionally generous with my kids, he did help me provide for them. If nothing else, my not having to pay rent or a mortgage meant that the money I was earning would go toward helping feed and clothe the kids. What was the harm in that?

Phillip and Stephen, of course, didn't tell me what they thought or felt. At the age of three, when I first moved in with Larry, neither had spoken a word yet. I suppose that my rationalization factory was running extended shifts because I figured if I was happy, and I was, then they were happy. This was going to be good for all of us. Maybe the change would result in the boys' snapping out of whatever funk it was that had them locked in silence. Maybe they didn't even realize what was going on.

Toward the end of one of my first visits with the boys, as I was preparing to leave, I bent down to say good-bye to Phillip and Stephen. "It's time for me to go. I'll be back tomorrow."

Phillip stood and placed himself between the door and me.

"Mom, you can't leave."

My son's first words, "Mom, you can't leave." He spoke them as clearly as an adult would have.

My throat tightened and I felt as though I were going to be sick to my stomach. I was overjoyed that he had spoken and ended his isolation, but the words stabbed me soul deep.

Phillip was right. I couldn't leave. If Larry wanted to be with me, he had to be with all of us. I was not going to leave my sons.

Richard, Phillip, and Stephen rejoined me, and Larry and I managed to make the arrangement work while living at his place. We were never Brady Bunch blissful, but we managed one day at a time until the A word was handed down from on high.

At first, I didn't know what it was about having a name for the boys' condition that so frightened Larry, but when the diagnosis was formalized, he bailed. In some ways, I respect him for his decision. He was honest. He said that he couldn't deal with being with someone who had autistic sons, saw no real future there. No pills. No treatment. No hope revisited.

Worse, he told me that he didn't think that any man would ever be interested in me again, not with the kind of baggage that I was carrying around. I guess I wasn't the only one putting myself in solitary confinement.

While Larry didn't talk about it directly, I knew that he sided with the doctors I'd spoken to initially. They told me that things would only get worse, that by the age of nine or so, the boys would be so unmanageable that they'd have to be institutionalized.

Even when I tried to do things to break out of my isolation, like finding a good man to share my life with, things blew up in my face. Larry wasn't my only attempt at breaking out of my shell.

The therapist whom I had been seeing for a year also told me, "It's over. Corrine, they lock these kids up in padded cells." If the experts were telling me this, why wasn't I listening? What kind of communicative disorder did I have?

Also, why should I reach out to people if they are going to just hammer me with hurt?

Finally, Larry told me why the label "autism" was the last straw for him. He'd attended UCLA in the sixties and majored in accounting. As an elective one semester he chose a psychology class taught by Dr. Ivar Lovaas. Dr. Lovaas was one of the pioneers of behavioral modification for autistics. Though the condition was rarely diagnosed, he saw that nothing was being done to help these young children, so he devised a treatment plan to train them to respond appropriately to commands. He was a research scientist and wanted to be able to demonstrate the effectiveness of his approach, so he filmed his "experiments." He showed the film in Larry's class.

In it, as Larry described it to me, a young male, named Patient A, was in a straitjacket and helmet. He was twelve years old and had never spoken a word in his life, but he emitted a high-pitched yell continually. The narrator of the film informed the viewers that Patient A was also blind. He had damaged his optic nerve by banging his forehead against walls and floors.

Dr. Lovaas was shown working with the young man. He

held a cattle prod in one hand. Patient A began screaming. Dr. Lovaas told him to stop. He did not. Dr. Lovaas applied the cattle prod until Patient A stopped screaming.

"It works," a beaming Dr. Lovaas said to the camera.

Larry had tears in his eyes when he told me how he sat in that classroom quietly sobbing. When I had returned from UCLA and told him of the diagnosis, he'd immediately flashed back to that morning in 1962, sitting in a darkened classroom watching what seemed to him and many others in the class to be a darkly macabre horror film. He said that he couldn't help but think of Stephen and Phillip as Patients B and C. He imagined them acting out at Braemar Country Club, at school, at birthday parties, at functions and get-togethers with business associates. B and C, and by implication me, didn't fit into the picture he'd formed of his life. He knew that I was committed to helping Stephen and Phillip, that I could never shunt them aside. It was all too much for him. He worried that autism would destroy him in the same way it was going to destroy the boys and me.

Is it any wonder, then, that in my life post-diagnosis, I seldom used the word? Is it any wonder that I withdrew? Here was this man I loved, who told me he loved me, who couldn't stand the thought of my sons being associated with him. Of course, I thought that it was best that we went underground. Of course, given the fragile state of my self-worth, I believed what Larry said about me and any future I had socially and romantically. Of course, I retreated behind the rapidly climbing walls of my fortress of solitude. In the face of what I had been going through, wouldn't the sane thing be to develop a bunker mentality? Lay low and hope the storm blew over?

To add to my figurative isolation of not facing the truth, I literally isolated myself socially. Sure, I would go to work and have the kinds of pleasant but often meaningless exchanges we all have with coworkers and clients. Nothing extended beyond that polite but ultimately unsatisfying connection with others.

Sometimes good things come about as a result of bad things. If before I had been obsessed with finding a "cure" for the boys' silence, a way to end their isolation, after Larry, I redoubled those efforts, but this time with an emphasis on finding out as much as I could about autism.

I didn't hate Larry then or later for what he did. He couldn't help but feel the way he felt. I also couldn't bring myself to hate Dr. Lovaas. I'd not heard of him before Larry told me that story. In truth, Dr. Lovaas was a real pioneer in autism research. First, he was the one who determined that autism was a separate condition not related to schizophrenia or psychosis. He also called into question the wisdom of institutionalizing autistics. What he found out was that institutionalized autistics regressed rather than progressed when placed in "captivity." He was able to prove, through horrific methods like cattle prodding, that once an autistic person learned what an inappropriate behavior was, the learning was permanent, and once the learning started, it accelerated.

We find hope in the strangest places and under the strangest circumstances. When Larry first told me about the film, I was aghast. How could someone do that to another human being, even in the name of science? In my research I discovered that not only was Dr. Lovaas one of the only researchers investigating and treating autism, but he did so even when he could get no funding for his work. He was driven to work with children who'd otherwise been orphaned by society and the medical community.

Though his treatment method for Patient A seemed medieval and torturous, he did, in fact, keep Patient A from doing even greater harm to himself than what the cattle prod inflicted. Patient A stopped banging his head. After six months of behavioral therapy, not only had Patient A stopped harming himself but he was learning words, and he no longer needed to be restrained in a straitjacket. Patient A became a kind of star who was swept up in the professor's trajectory. Dr. Lovaas became a much-sought-after lecturer and teacher. Desperate parents begged him to divulge his training methods and to lend his expertise. He wrote books.

By the time I encountered Dr. Lovaas and his work, he had long since retired. I needed my own Lovaas. I sought out the original but learned that he had stopped teaching, stopped researching. He was very vocal about the fact that he was exhausted. He saw his work as just one leg in a long relay race, and he was looking to pass the baton to other scientists and doctors to do more to investigate this affliction.

With Larry gone, I felt even more alone than before. His statements about no man ever wanting me, and his fears about the social stigma associated with having autistic children, magnified my own concerns and perceptions. People didn't want to be around autistic children.

Whether it was because I was no longer with Larry or because of the twins, I stopped getting invited to social engagements and parties. Phillip and Stephen were invited to one birthday party of a classmate. I screwed up my courage and took them to the bowling alley. While the other kids ran around and had fun slinging the ball down the lane and watching it bounce off the rubber bumpers and into the pins, Stephen and Phillip sat quietly by my side. When it was their turn, I helped each of them pick up a ball and positioned them in the alley, hoping they'd watched and learned. They hadn't. They each dropped the ball on their foot, sat down, and cried. I gathered them up and fled, not bothering to make any apologies or thank the hosts.

Fortunately, I wasn't completely alone. As the saying goes, misery loves company, and sometimes desperation can bring out characteristics in us that we weren't sure we possessed. One day, shortly after the bowling party, I was sitting in the school's parking lot, just having buckled Phillip and Stephen in their seat belts. I saw a woman sitting in another car across the lot from me. I don't know what it was, but I sensed an immediate connection with her. Whether it was the lines of what I interpreted to be sadness that etched themselves around her eyes and mouth, the fact that she was clipping coupons from a Ralph's Market flyer—needing to be frugal with both time and money—or the fact that when she caught my eye, she smiled, I sensed a kinship with her. I don't know if misery actually loves company, but the antennae of those in similar kinds of trouble are particularly attuned to the frequency of distress we emit. I smiled back and then rummaged through the glove compartment, hoping to appear occupied with something other than staring.

I watched out of the corner of my eye to see which child went to her car, hoping that it was someone I'd recognize from Phillip's and Stephen's class. Fortunately for me, I saw her son and recognized him. I'd worked as a classroom aide throughout their kindergarten year and knew a few people in the administrative office. They gave me Robert's last name and phone number. I gave the number a call that same evening, asking for Mrs. Stewart. I explained who I was, that our boys were classmates, that my sons were both in the special education program at school. The words spilled out of me. Then the awful silence that seemed to linger for seconds but was really only an instant was broken.

Connie. She told me to call her Connie and that she was going to be right over, that we should talk face to face. She liked coffee, and could I have a cup waiting for her when she got there?

When Connie arrived, I was again greeted with that warm smile and the sad eyes. I escorted her into the house and into the bedroom where Stephen and Phillip were sitting on the floor, rocking. Her eyes welled with tears, and the lines, like those on a relief map, seemed to stand out more prominently. "Oh, no," I heard her whisper.

Then I knew for certain. She wasn't simply seeing Phillip and Stephen; she was seeing her own son. She told me she was doing everything she could for Robert, running hither and yon, as she put it, to find the cure for his autism. We sat at the kitchen table, she sipping a cup of coffee, me gulping down vast quantities of her words of wisdom. Maybe I hadn't found the book I was looking for, but what I'd read in that parking lot about the woman I now knew as Connie was even better than an account of a successful parent.

I learned that Robert was very passive and quiet. He loved to draw roads. I told her that the twins loved to draw and that roads were one of their specialties. She reached into a shouldcr bag she'd brought with her and pulled out a few loose-leaf pages. I went into a kitchen desk drawer and retrieved a few of Phillip's most recent efforts. We spread them out on the table in front of us and both sat back in shock. If we hadn't known whose were whose, we wouldn't have been able to differentiate them. This was uncanny. Spooky. Hopeful.

You can't imagine what it was like after years of living in denial and silence to hear someone say, "My son draws roads."

"Your son draws roads? My son draws roads! Here, look at these!"

You'd think we'd both produced Nobel Prize winners, the enormity of our relief at finding a kindred spirit and someone who could understand what the other had been through was so great.

You mean, I wasn't completely alone? Connie and her husband became a shoulder to lean and cry on when no one else would make themselves available to me.

I felt even more of a kinship when I drove to visit Connie and Dave at their home in nearby Calabasas. I had Richard and Ali with me along with the twins, and I heard Richard mutter, "What the heck," when we slowed in front of a house whose curb space was littered with mounds of green plastic trash bags. They lay on top of one another and wallowed like sows and piglets. They spilled out of garbage cans, torn and ravaged by birds and other critters. Like me, and like many parents of autistic kids, Connie and Dave had become master jugglers. They were able to make the mortgage payment each month, but Robert's medical bills didn't leave enough money to pay their sanitation charges. Robbing Peter to pay Paul is the way some people put it.

I learned to think of it as robbing Peter to pay Bill. It was a game that Connie and I became intimately familiar with. This was especially true when Dave died of a heart attack, leaving Connie to fend for herself and her son. She managed. She put herself through school, got a degree in special education, and worked in the local school district. Connie was not just a confidante but an inspiration as well. As bleak as things seemed to get, at least we had each other's collected wisdom and hope to draw from. Just the other day as I was beginning the writing of this chapter, I saw a young man who looked familiar doing some shopping at Ralph's. We looked at each other and turned our heads and squinted the way people do when they aren't sure of what they're seeing.

Then I knew that all of Connie's worrying and hoping had paid off. Robert came up to me and extended his hand, saying, "Nice to see you after so long." I recognized the formal diction and precise intonation of a high-functioning autistic person's well-practiced greeting. It was music to my ears. Robert had just graduated from college, was doing a job search, and expected to land something shortly. We said our good-byes, and I told him how proud I was of him, feeling a sense of shared accomplishment for a job well done.

What I find amazing is that Robert knew who I was and also thanked me for some of the work I'd been doing to raise awareness about autism. What was equally amazing to me, even now, is that I have been able to do for others what Connie did for me. I've become a resource that other parents of autistic children can rely on. I can't tell you how good it makes me feel that I'm able to do this, but also how sad it makes me feel that I have to do it—that parents and children still have to suffer because of the same stigma associated with autism. While the media has certainly made people more aware of the condition, again sadly, thanks to the rise in the incidence of autism, I'm not convinced that all the notoriety has translated into the kind of real acceptance of autistics that I hope for and work toward.

In my experience, many of the families who contact me, who have heard me speak at various gatherings, still talk about the similar feelings that I had, including why I felt that I was doing the right thing initially in keeping the diagnosis from everyone. I've already mentioned the guilt and blame component of this. I felt that other people were quick to judge us, and if they could affix an easy-to-apply label to us, I believed their judgments would only get worse. Remember how my therapist responded? Her telling me what "they" do to "them" scared me. I didn't want my twins to be associated with any "them." That was too easy, too dehumanizing. As defensive as I was in talking to Stephen's kindergarten teacher about him not being a "case" but an individual, I was already keenly aware of the negative effects of labeling and categorizing. It was bad enough that the twins would be enrolled in special education, considering what that label said about them and their future prospects.

For a long time, I had known the boys were special—not "riding the small bus to school" special, but borderline geniuses. How else to explain their preternatural ability to put together sophisticated car models, Phillip's penchant for dismantling and reassembling all things mechanical, their love of music, their mastery of reading and basic computation well before an age that is considered "normal." Were they special, or were they normal? And why did those labels matter so much to me and to everyone else?

* * *

AMONG the many things Connie did for me, she told me about a program at the University of California at Santa Barbara (UCSB) she had enrolled Robert in. She'd found my Dr. Lovaas for me. Dr. Robert Koegel, PhD, was the head of the Autism Research Center at UCSB. He'd previously worked at Camarillo Mental Hospital during the dark days of the cruel but effective treatments that Dr. Lovaas pioneered. At our first meeting, he asked us to call him Bob, and so we did. He was a gentle, soft-spoken man, and he explained how he had arrived at the concept of positive behavioral support. He told us about an experience he had at Camarillo when observing the treatment of an autistic man. The patient was bound in a straitjacket and was screaming. Each time he screamed, an orderly hit the patient until the screams stopped. Bob was sickened. He sent the orderlies away and unwrapped a Tootsie Pop. The man was at first suspicious, but he had stopped screaming and sat with his mouth open. Bob fed him the candy. The next day, Bob brought boxes of Tootsie Pops to the hospital.

I'd tried positive reinforcement techniques myself, hoping to coax Stephen to speak or to stop crying by offering him his favorite snacks, toys, coins. Nothing seemed to work. What was this doctor doing that I wasn't?

I asked him, "Am I autistic, too? Am I crazy? Why can't I get him to speak?"

Bob looked at me and then down at his hands as he rubbed his palms gently back and forth. "Corrine, you're not autistic, you're not crazy. You're fine." He reached into his coat pocket and held out a Tootsie Pop.

I took his offering and smiled, feeling unburdened.

To be honest, I'd worried about my sanity and my fitness as a parent. I'd known for some time before the diagnosis that something was wrong with Phillip and Stephen. I hauled them to general practitioners and pediatricians. The boys had been poked and probed and pronounced physically fit. I'd been told to be patient, that they would grow out of whatever phase it was they were in. I'd sat at a family Fourth of July barbecue cringing with embarrassment, shame, and worry when I'd presented my two four-year-old boys with sparklers and they screamed bloody murder instead of beaming with delight like their cousins.

Even at that first evaluation session, I was still dogged by doubt. Stephen and Phillip were placed in the all-too-familiar observation room with toys, puzzles, and games. Phillip sat at a desk and drew, while Stephen retreated to a far corner, his back to the door, assembling Lego building blocks. I took a chair slightly off to the side, ready in case either of the boys slipped into a crying jag. Bob and his fellow doctors stood in the open doorway watching. Every now and then one of the doctors would incline his head toward the others and whisper something. The others would nod or raise their eyebrows or shake their heads. I was drowning in their lack of unanimity.

After a few minutes, Bob stepped forward. "What does Stephen like to eat?"

I thought for a second and was about to speak when I heard a voice coming from behind me. "Pizza."

I turned and there was Stephen, his body now turned toward us, a smile on his face. He clapped his hands. "Cheese pizza."

I was too stunned to make a sound. My son had spoken his

first words. It wasn't "mama" or "dada," but "pizza" was good enough for me.

Through the tears in my eyes, I watched as Bob laughed and tossed a twenty-dollar bill to one of the aides. "Dammit," he shouted, "get this boy a pizza!"

I'd been searching for answers for so long, and as I sat there in that observation room, I was chagrined to realize that not only had I been asking the wrong questions, but I'd been asking them of the wrong people.

I also realized that my son was special, he could speak but maybe had chosen not to, and he was normal. He wanted pizza just as so many other kids do.

It took yet another person to help me actually resolve the special-normal-different issue.

If you would have told me when I was a kid attending Our Lady of the Wayside Church and School that someday one of my closest and dearest friends—a man I'd admire as much as anyone I'd ever met—would be a pot-smoking, ponytailed, homeopathic doctor with a client list that included people like Burt Reynolds, I would have told you the incense from High Mass had had an undesirable effect on you. The truth is that Dr. Don Jeffries was all of those things but so much more. Don started out as a client, but he morphed into a confidant and a quiet champion of the twins' rights to be included in all kinds of social interactions.

To say that Don was beloved by everyone in the Malibu Lakes area and beyond would be an exaggeration. I'm certain that he rubbed a few people the wrong way, but only those who didn't make an attempt to get to know him would feel that this gruffly gregarious, obscenity-spewing character had anything but good intentions. I know this because I was one of those people who was initially put off by him. The two of us couldn't have been any more different in certain regards. I was a strait-laced, uptight Catholic, and Don was a prototypical hippie with an alternative health and spirituality bent.

As a native Californian, I'm well aware of the jokes and the perceptions people have about California and its residents. Though there is a very conservative element in place in the state, when most outsiders think of California, they think of the Hollywood-based liberalism, the countercultural influences of Berkeley and San Francisco, the crunchy granola and flaky sensibilities of goofy-footed Southern California surfers, and the vacuous inanities of Valley Girls. With the exception of the latter, I would say that Don Jeffries embodied most of those stereotypical traits.

Like a lot of successful and creative people I've known, Don's free-spirited nature bled over into his professional life. Trying to untangle the complicated mess of his practice's books wasn't easy, but I liked the challenge of it. I didn't like how Don swore like a sailor on permanent leave from propriety, and we battled constantly on his habit of smoking marijuana in my presence; we debated matters of faith and fact, and he opened my mind to new possibilities and my heart to the wonders of unconditional giving.

In time, my duties transformed from strict accounting to being his right-hand woman, helping to manage some of his real estate investments and generally organizing his financial life. His presence coincided with the positive developments with the twins and my finding my future husband, Doug. The fog was lifting, and much of the light that shone through was the result of Don and Doug.

Don lived in our neighborhood and had a son, Nick, who was about the same age as Phillip and Stephen and attended the same schools as the twins for junior and senior high. Don would make sure to include Stephen and Phillip at Nick's birthday parties, and he always invited all of us to his many dinner parties and other social functions. Don loved to be surrounded by people, and he looked for any reason to host a get-together. With his Hollywood connections, his house would be filled with industry types, stars, and run-of-the-mill folks like my kids and me. In much the same way that Doug was, Don accepted people for who they were and not what label was placed on them. He didn't care if you were on the A list or the Z list; he treated you the same way.

I can remember one party at which Phillip was at the table eating. He still sometimes struggles with his manners. I think that because we had so little food in the house and he still remembers those lean times, he tends to eat way too fast. I remember sitting at the kitchen table with the twins and a few other folks, my ears burning with embarrassment as Phillip shoveled forkful after forkful of pasta into his mouth. I could see a few cringing grimaces on the faces of some of the other guests and was about to grab Phillip and lead him from the table to have another talk with him about his table manners when Don came swooping into the kitchen bearing a huge platter of pasta. He took a look around the table, spotted Phillip, and broke into a big grin. "Jesus Christ on two sticks. I can't believe it. Someone who actually appreciates my cooking. Good for you, Phillip! Let the rest of these calorie-conscious motherfuckers starve themselves. You enjoy, my man!" He heaped another serving onto Phillip's plate and went out into the dining room, leaving behind a chastened but educated group at the table.

In Don's world, there wasn't a single set of manners, just as there wasn't a single type of person he chose to socialize with. Don was all about inclusion, and I appreciated what he did for all of my family more than I can express. I know that in some ways what Don was doing was contradicting what Doug and I were trying to do with the boys. We wanted them to toe the line, to be certain that they spoke their "thank-yous," "yes, ma'ams," and "pleases." We wanted to hold them to the same standard that parents of so-called normal kids did. But we also wanted people to understand that "normal" comes in lots of shapes and sizes, and that the world could accommodate the twins' eccentricities and tics just as it could the eccentricities of those Hollywood types.

A friend recently told me that one of her favorite lines in a book comes from F. Scott Fitzgerald's *The Great Gatsby*. On its opening page, the narrator of the book, Nick Carraway, relates what his father once told him, that the key to a mature understanding of life is to be able to hold two contradictory ideas in your head simultaneously and to believe them both to be true. I don't know if I understood at the time how Don's very existence helped me learn that essential truth. Nor would I have been able to explain so succinctly how that statement encapsulated what I wanted to get people to understand about my twins: that they were differently normal or normally different. I wanted people to understand and tolerate and to not understand and accept, or some combination of all four of those concepts that doesn't even have a single word to describe it.

Any parent of an autistic child will understand the struggle I'm not doing such a good job of describing.

I want people to Don autism.

I'd like it if everybody could embrace, accept, and normalize what is different from what they experience. I want them to be the kind of person that Don was. I want them to know that if it is raining and storming and they see someone like Phillip wandering on the street, they will take him in, hand him a towel, and point him toward the bathroom, where he can close the door and hold his hands up to his ears to drown out the sound of thunder. And when someone calls you on the phone to ask you what's going on, you can honestly say "Nothing" because the boy in your bathroom is there just being and doing who he is—no more and no less. I want people to believe and to live out the truth that Don demonstrated for us so many times: that my boys were remarkably unremarkable, that they were deserving of his time and attention not because of what afflicted them but because they were human beings whose needs and desires should be met.

I hate the fact that the conventions of our language require that I speak of Don Jeffries in the past tense. And not just because those conventions call for past actions to be rendered in that tense. I hate it because one day Don Jeffries was out in his driveway putting up a basketball pole and backboard for his son when he collapsed and died. I don't hate that Don died. It makes me sad, certainly, but not angry or hateful.

Don came to me in a dream the night he died and told me that he wasn't really dead. He said that he now existed at a higher level of energy. I had a difficult time with that concept and asked him if he could explain it all to me more clearly. He went on to say that he was there to do things he couldn't do in his normal existence. That life on my plain couldn't contain the reality he now experienced.

I could have dismissed all that as my overactive imagination. I'd just lost a dear friend and was clearly upset by it, and that's why I had that dream. Rationally I could explain it, but what I couldn't explain was Don's warning and reassurance to me. First, he told me not to get directly involved in the fight that was to come. Second, he told me that things were going to work out for me and Doug and the kids. He wasn't any more specific than that. As things turned out, Don was right on both counts.

Don's death taught me a lot. Phillip was devastated by the loss. Don was someone Phillip could always count on. He was a safety net for Phillip, and when he heard that Don had passed, he got very emotional. I know that a lot of people believe that autistic people aren't capable of forming close emotional connections with others. As the boys grew up and emerged from their silence, I understood more and more how limiting that definition was. I saw how eager they were for contact with other people. I saw the kind of bond that Don and Phillip formed. I saw how Phillip mourned the loss of his friend. Phillip was able to verbalize his shock and sadness. Though the outward manifestation of his grief wasn't the same as what other people expressed, what he was experiencing inside was the same.

Stephen has always been the less verbally expressive of the two, and he approached Don's death, his first real encounter with the death of someone close to him, in a more clinical way. He wanted to know if he would see Don in Heaven. He asked if Don's soul was on its way or was already there. What I found interesting was that their reactions were typical ones that Doug and I or any of Don's other friends might have had. When it comes to most things human, I was coming to realize that "normal," like "autism," exists on a spectrum and is not a definite point on a line. What I also came to realize was that grieving takes so many different forms, that no one awards style points for how we do it; we don't get bonuses for degree of difficulty or anything like that.

I also know that as painful as it was for all of us to lose Don, letting him inside our fortress of solitude was one of the smartest moves I'd ever made. If the twins were to put together a model human being, they'd assemble one just like Don. His ability to include everyone and the lessons he taught me that enabled me to first tolerate, then accept, and then embrace his quirks and his views are among the things I most prize in this life. The way he treated not just the twins but nearly everyone in his life is a path that all of us should follow. Of course, knowing Don like I did, he'd object to that figure of speech. He'd want us to blaze our own trails, but ultimately the destination would be the same, and there'd be a great party going on, and everyone would be included. No one and everyone would be normally different and differently normal.

Chapter Three

Waking Up to Help and Hope

I'M a slow learner. I came to that realization in the last couple of weeks when I sat down to write these chapters. For a long time, I thought of myself as this solitary woman waging a battle on a desolate landscape, surviving on guile and sheer desperation, friendless and alone.

I remember a time when I was in early elementary school. I was at Sunday Mass with my mother and father and my nine siblings. I was usually well behaved, but on this particular morning one of the women sitting in front of us had stood up from kneeling, and her slip had fallen down around her feet. She hadn't even noticed. I would have felt bad for her, but the woman was one of the crankiest in the area and also one of the smuggest. She always seemed to walk around with her nose in the air.

I stifled a giggle behind my hand and nudged my sister in the elbow to alert her to my discovery. She made an exaggerated horrified face, and that set me off into shoulder-heaving spasms that threatened to let my laughter escape. My sister had better control of herself than I did and her facial expression kept alternating between devout and devious. Of course, my mother caught me when I finally snorted out a guffaw, but my sister continued to look angelic. My mother took me roughly by the elbow and led me out of the church.

I thought that when I explained to her what I'd seen, she'd understand, but she was even more upset when she found out I was taking pleasure in someone else's embarrassment. She looked at me sternly, her voice quivering with emotion when she told me that I had embarrassed and shamed her. That our march down the aisle was humiliating. For years, my mother and father had told us all that how we behaved was a reflection on them, that I was their representative out in the world. They also hammered home the point that you are judged by the company you keep.

I would have a lot of explaining to do in confession the next week, I remember her telling me.

From that day on, I was even more keenly aware of how important it was to behave well outside the home. The twins' public outbursts drew more attention to me than I wanted, making me feel as though we were all specimens under a very watchful and unforgiving microscope. Their spoiling of those cereal boxes in the grocery store was just one in a series of episodes I wanted to forget and avoid repeat performances of.

It's interesting to me now that I didn't ask questions like:

Why couldn't people reserve their judgment until they'd walked a mile in my shoes? What happened to giving people the benefit of the doubt?

The only thing I really doubted was myself and my suitability as a parent, especially my ability to control my twins and their crying and screaming. I've seen the looks that fellow airline passengers give parents whose children cry. Try doubling and tripling the intensity of those looks when your autistic child acts out. That's what I lived with on a daily basis, and since I couldn't predict what would set them off and was so tired of being made to feel like a bad mother, I did retreat. Staying behind closed doors seemed far easier than subjecting myself and the twins to whatever reaction they would get from others.

In truth, as I said before, I was alone a lot of the time by choice and by circumstance. As a natural outgrowth of being the parent of an autistic child, you develop a kind of "us against them" mentality anyway. It was hard to go to the grocery store and see parents with "normal" children and not feel a bit of envy for their good fortune and a little resentment about the hand I'd been dealt. It's hard to feel hopeful about acceptance when your local librarian doesn't even know what autism is, and when the man you love says explicitly that the company he keeps would neither appreciate nor accept the twins for who they are. It's hard not to feel alone and isolated when your own family can't quite understand or deal with your kids and the situation you've found yourself in. Out of sight and out of mind is certainly true, but you could extend that statement to out of sight, out of mind, and out of guilt.

I think that my siblings used geography as an excuse, since

we were separated by distance. However, we were also divided by something less tangible but more difficult to overcome—the gulf between their experiences and mine. It's kind of a chicken and egg dilemma. Did they not understand since I wasn't sharing my story with them, or were they not listening because they didn't want to hear and I stopped trying? Knowing that they grew up hearing the same lesson about the importance of proper behavior, I was loath to say too much to them about the twins and just how difficult they could sometimes be. The twins' failings were my failings, and the less my family members knew about them the better I might appear in their mind's eye. It was hard, but when I asked them for money or to otherwise help me with the kids and they didn't come through, it was partly my fault for not communicating to them how dire our situation was.

In retrospect, I see now that there were people in my life who helped me a great deal. Connie and Don were our angels. And Stephen and Phillip's paternal grandparents, Mary and Richard, were devoted to all my kids, and my mom and dad did the best they could to understand what I was dealing with, based on the limited information I was giving them. As frustrated as I was in the early year with doctors who failed to correctly diagnose the twins' autism, I can see now that they were ignorant of the condition and not malicious or malingering. If they had known more about autism, if the world had had a better understanding of it, then they would have come to my aid much earlier on.

Sometimes it takes someone with more of a beginner's mind to really understand and to see clearly. Those doctors had their years of schooling and past cases that in some sense limited their thinking. A neighborhood girl, Dana, didn't have all that data and learning to blind her; instead, she based her interactions and impressions on what her heart told her.

Phillip and Stephen met Dana when they were six years old. To this day, Phillip remembers that she had bright brown eyes and beautiful blond hair. He also told me that her skin was tawny and she was smart, and he wondered why she was in his class.

Phillip also told me that they met while eating lunch. Dana came up to Stephen and Phillip and said, "Hi. You should use a napkin." Then she plopped down between them. She pulled off some of her orange slices and gave some to Stephen and Phillip and told them to eat them. At that point, groceries were scarce around our house. I don't know if she could tell the boys were hungry by the way they eyed that orange or if she was just being polite. Phillip came home from school that day and told me how she'd handed them paper napkins. At that point, we were still working very hard on hygiene.

After that, Dana ate lunch with them every day. I got daily reports about the "nice girl." About thirty days later Phillip finally asked her what her name was. It took Stephen a full year to say a single word to her. The twins were doing very well in school, but as Phillip put it, "Our social graces needed improvement."

That was where Dana helped the most. She would tell them when not to say inappropriate things or when not to cry. Phillip was habitually late getting to the bus, and without Dana intervening by telling the bus driver to wait, I would have had to schlep him to school. We started depending on her for many things.

In talking about his experience with Dana, Phillip once said, "I never really believed in guardian angels until the time she left. I thought she would always be there. But like an angel, she flew away. From the hundreds of times I cried, these were the first real tears of sorrow."

The boys struggled a bit when Dana transferred schools.

I'm the one who told Phillip and Stephen that Dana was their guardian angel. I got to know Dana and her parents fairly well. Dana had suffered some kind of brain injury that produced problems with her short-term memory. Her mom and dad were divorced but still living together. Whenever I saw Dana together with the twins, she would chat and chat and chat. Stephen wouldn't say anything, but Phillip would talk to her a bit. His face would light up. Because Dana's parents lived so close to school, the twins would go home for lunch with Dana. They could avoid the teasing and harassment that way. Dana or her mom would call me if there was ever a problem with Stephen and Phillip being picked on or hurt by the other kids.

One day I got a call from Ward Thompson, the school's principal. I was expecting the worst. I liked Ward, and I knew he had a good heart. He also had a booming voice that I imagined frightened some of the smaller kids. I'd heard him come down hard on some of them, his voice rattling through the walls of his office. This time there was none of that imposing menace in his tone. I could imagine him with his great horsey grin, sitting at his desk with his arms folded over the top of his head, the phone pinched between his cheek and shoulder. "Corrine, you've got to tell the boys not to start fights. I can't have them beating up other kids."

Even with the mirth in his voice so clearly obvious, I couldn't believe what I was hearing. Phillip and Stephen were never violent. I'd strictly enforced the rule that they not raise their hands in anger against anyone. Ward laughed openly and told me the story.

Dana was being picked on by a group of boys. They were giving her a hard time because she was in special education classes. Phillip and Stephen, who'd just watched the movie *Rocky* on video for the first time the previous weekend, saw and heard what was going on and came to her rescue. Ward didn't know exactly what they said or did, but he told me there was some kind of dustup on the playground, and one of the monitors had to break it up. From what the monitor told Ward, Phillip and Stephen were giving as good as they got. Some clothes were torn and a nose bloodied and a lip or two swollen, but he wasn't going to discipline any of the kids, just send them back to a neutral corner and let the parents have a talk with them. I promised I would.

I sat the twins on their beds; they looked so downcast it nearly broke my heart. Neither of them liked disappointing me, especially Stephen, who was so hard on himself for any perceived shortcoming or failure.

"Phillip. Stephen. I just want you to know how proud I am of you. Dana is a good friend, and you did the right thing. I know what I've said about fighting and how I don't like it, but sometimes doing the wrong thing is the right thing to do.

Knowing when is part of growing up and coming into your own as a man. Thank you."

What often frustrates people about dealing with autistics is their flattened affect, their lack of a pronounced emotional response. I'd grown accustomed to that, and while we didn't experience the family sitcom ending—a hug and restatement of the value of the lesson learned—we did savor that small triumph. We celebrated at dinner. I opened a second can of Dinty Moore stew and added a few fresh potatoes and carrots. The metallic taste of the can of generic fruit punch drink let me know it was a fine vintage, that I wouldn't always have to look back on things with the taste of sour grapes in my mouth.

In junior high, Dana moved up north with her mom, who had remarried. Like the boys, I felt as if I'd lost a good friend. In truth, I hadn't lost her at all. Not only do we all have such fond memories of her, but we still keep in touch, and Dana comes and visits us every now and again. Phillip lights up every time he sees her, and Stephen's shy smile speaks volumes about his affection for her. She's a mom now with a baby daughter of her own. Though Phillip said that he didn't do too well after Dana left, the truth is, because she took an interest in Phillip, he learned what good or better or best friends means. Maybe we were just getting by financially at that point, but we were doing it with a little help from our friends.

Among the people I counted as friends were Dr. Robert Koegel and his wife, Dr. Lynne Koegel. I can't tell you that they saved my life, but they did release me from the prison, self-imposed and otherwise, that I believed I had been placed in immediately after the diagnosis. Life hadn't been the proverbial bed of roses before that, but having a name to give to the disorder that limited the twins' speech and connection to the rest of the world gave me a focus that I needed. By reaching out to Connie and revealing to her the truth of their condition, I'd been amply rewarded with the lead that took me to Dr. Koegel's office and Stephen's breakthrough.

Being the slow learner that I am, I didn't extrapolate from that success that I could benefit—and the boys could likely benefit—from being more forthcoming about their condition. Back then, I didn't view the situation that way. I still felt that I could open the door a crack, take a peek around its edge, let in a likely sympathetic soul, swear her or him to secrecy, and then furtively slam the door shut again.

Another entirely sympathetic soul was Dr. Bernard Rimland. Dr. Rimland was one of the early pioneers in autism research. In 1956, when his son, Mark, was born, a diagnosis of autism was extremely rare. A research psychologist himself, Dr. Rimland admitted that he had not even come across the word "autism" in any of his previous studies. When Mark's development veered from the normal track, Dr. Rimland had his son evaluated, and it was determined that Mark was autistic. Dr. Rimland then made it his life's mission to understand the condition. Prior to Dr. Rimland and his work in studying autism, the prevailing theory of the nature of the disorder was that it was a result of the so-called refrigerator mother. University of Chicago professor Bruno Bettelheim was the major proponent of the theory that cold and distant mothers who couldn't easily bond with their children were the cause of autism in infants.

Dr. Rimland was the first researcher to seriously counter

that theory. He believed, and it is accepted wisdom today, that autism was a neurologically based disorder. Dr. Rimland was based in San Diego, where he founded the Autism Research Institute in 1967. Prior to that, he established the Autism Society of America in 1965. I met Dr. Rimland toward the end of his distinguished career. What I loved about him was that though he was one of the world's leading experts in the field, he still took the time to answer phone calls and provide support to parents like me. I was sad when he passed away in 2006 but deeply grateful that he had done so much work in the field. Though he became a somewhat controversial figure because of his belief that some inoculations that children routinely receive—those containing traces of mercury—were responsible for the rise in the incidence of autism, he did so much to bring attention to the issues and engaged in so much valuable research that I couldn't possibly say a bad word about him.

In working with Phillip and Stephen, Dr. Rimland touted the benefits of dimethylglycine (DMG). DMG is a nutrient, like vitamin B6 and magnesium. Dr. Rimland and others' research showed that DMG was effective in strengthening the immune system. Many autistics have a dysfunctional immune system and also suffer from seizures. Though it has not been proven definitively that DMG helps autistic children, Dr. Rimland's research studies demonstrated that many autistic individuals showed improvement in behavior when they took at least 125 milligrams of DMG a day and worked up slowly to as much as 500 milligrams a day.

I was reluctant to get Phillip started on any kind of "drug" treatment therapy. Though it was a very safe thing for him to take, and inexpensive as well, I wasn't at the point where I wanted to rely on chemicals. Eventually, I took Dr. Rimland's advice and gave the boys DMG (and later the only way to control Phillip's Tourette's was with drugs), but I didn't stick with the program religiously, so I never saw any real changes. I was grasping at straws, I suppose, but I was just so grateful to have someone in addition to Dr. Koegel to talk to, someone else who was offering support and guidance and hope.

Maybe it was because Larry had told me about Dr. Lovaas and the horrible kinds of treatments that autistics were subjected to, or maybe it was a combination of my own fear and uncertainty about what the school district might do, but I didn't tell anyone immediately that Phillip and Stephen had been diagnosed as autistic. Something told me that it was better for me to learn as much as I could, get them into Dr. Koegel's program, and then let the truth be told when the boys were much better. And I did expect that they would improve dramatically. I don't know if I expected a "cure," since I'm not certain exactly what that would mean or look like in terms of their behavior, but I did allow myself to hope that Stephen's saying "pizza" would be just the start of a long menu of choices available to the two of them.

I also know that in the back of my mind, I suspected that the school personnel and the world at large weren't ready to accept autistic people into the mainstream of our culture. I knew that according to the Individuals with Disabilities Education Act (IDEA), my kids were guaranteed by law a free and appropriate education (FAPE) in the least restrictive environment possible.

Under the terms of the act, Phillip and Stephen should have

been placed in a school environment with nondisabled peers to the greatest extent possible. I can see now that I was operating in vague and contradictory territory, but at the time I didn't see it. If I told the school that Phillip and Stephen were diagnosed with autism, a disability, they would have been covered by the provisions of the IDEA. By not letting the school know that they were diagnosed as autistic, I didn't have the law on my side, but I was assuming that without the formal diagnosis, they would be treated like every other student. Without the label of "disabled," which I later learned was one that Stephen and Phillip both despised, I was forcing the school to treat the twins like every other student. To me, that meant that they would be in the least restrictive environment, and they would be with their peers.

I can't stress enough how much it mattered to me that the twins be with other people. I knew that they were intelligent. I didn't need anyone to administer a test to tell me that they could read at or above grade level. To be honest, I don't remember reading to them a whole lot, but I'm certain I did. I just don't have a strong recollection of those shared experiences. What I do remember is Stephen and Phillip spending hours quietly engaged in reading and drawing. We had an old set of the World Book Encyclopedia. I can still picture the red-gone-to-nearly-brown covers and the fake-gold embossed lettering on the spine of each volume. I can't remember if the set came from my family or Big Steve's, but I do know the boys loved it. One of the features of the edition we had was a series of pages that were made of some kind of clear plastic-like substance. These special pages were a series of overlays—peel back the first page of the overlays on the human body and the muscular system was revealed. Peel back the next layers and the digestive system or the circulatory system or the skeletal system was revealed, in four-color illustrations. Another set of the overlays revealed the intricacies of the internal combustion engine, the human eye, and other assorted concepts.

I knew that Phillip and Stephen could read and write, because not only would they copy the various drawings in exacting detail but they would label the parts. In some cases, they would take entries that didn't have overlays and create their own drawings and labels based on what they read. I didn't spend a lot of time with them doing reading readiness exercises—teaching them the alphabet and getting them to sound out words and repeat after me—nor did I do a lot with them to develop number literacy. They just seemed to have it.

Given their intellectual gifts, it was hard for me to classify them as disabled, and I despaired at the notion that they should be treated that way. Today, I understand that the school's administration and staff were ill prepared to deal with my sons and their needs. Back then, I was more fearful than understanding. I can remember having seen David Lynch's film *The Elephant Man*. To some, it may have been a kind of horror film, but to me it was a representation of what I feared the twins' lives would be like.

The movie tells the story of a young Englishman in the late nineteenth century who is horribly disfigured and put on display in a carnival freak show. A doctor discovers his existence and arranges to have him presented in a kind of medical/scientific show-and-tell. What stayed with me long after I saw it was the scene depicting the end of the so-called Elephant Man being on display as a medical curiosity, when he is back on the streets and heading back to his life with his cruel caretaker. One of the doctor's assistants turns to the physician and asks, "Do you think he's an idiot?" (Here he is using the word in its formerly technical sense of a label for someone with a low IQ.)

Dr. Treves, the man who had put the Elephant Man on display, says, "For his sake, I certainly hope so." Treves couldn't bear the thought that the Elephant Man knew what was wrong with him and was intelligent enough to understand how people viewed him. Better, in Treves's mind, that he be a dumb beast than a human being with feelings and desires. As it turned out, the Elephant Man, whose real name was John Merrick, was actually quiet intelligent and a dignified, sensitive soul who was keenly aware of how he had been mistreated by nature and society.

I worried that people would view Phillip and Stephen in the same way that those in Victorian England viewed the fictional and real-life Elephant Man. Once the stigma of the word "disabled" was applied to Stephen and Phillip, would they be considered nothing more than freaks? Would people assume that because they were autistic, they were incapable of thought, of intellectual achievement and advancement?

In my limited experience and exposure to the concept of autism, I knew more people than not who associated autism with retardation. Would I be severely limiting the boys' opportunities and future by letting the school know about their diagnosis? At the time, it occurred to me that I had two options in this regard. I could fight to educate everyone about the nature of autism and the kinds of treatments the boys were receiving and have them demonstrate their intellectual potential, or I could hide behind the claim that it was their speech problems that caused most of their developmental delays.

I stuck to the second of those, and Stephen and Phillip remained in kindergarten at the Chaparral Elementary School. On weekends and in the afternoons after they were released from kindergarten, I would take them up to Santa Barbara to work with Dr. Bob.

Taking the 101 freeway to see Dr. Bob was like taking valium. I could just feel the tension easing its grip on my shoulders. I felt as if I could open my mouth easily instead of having to forcefully disengage the lock on my stress-ravaged jaw muscles. With Bob and his staff, I didn't have to pretend, didn't have to lie. Not only were my kids being taught but I was being taught how to teach and how to interact with them. Everything about the work we did at the Autism Research Center (ARC) at UCSB felt positive. Many days, Lynne Koegel would greet us in the parking lot. She'd wrap the boys in an embrace and tell them how glad she was to see them again. She'd lead them each by the hand down the sidewalk, chatting away with them like they were her old chums from grad school stopping by for a visit. Phillip would tentatively put an arm around her, while Stephen stood stiffly.

I know that Lynne did this to lessen the boys' anxiety, but the overflow of her generous spirit washed over me and soothed me as well. I reveled in being in a place where hope seemed to flow through the ventilation shafts along with the air-conditioning. The basic premise of the work that the Koegels were doing with autistic kids was both miles apart and right next door to what Dr. Lovaas had been doing twenty years previously. It was all based on conditioning and reinforcement; however, instead of using negative reinforcement like electric shock treatments, they used positive reinforcement. Instead of punishing their students for wrong behavior in order to extinguish it, they rewarded their subjects for correct behavior in order to nurture it. That all sounds simple enough in theory, but in practice it did work. What required a lot of labor and patience was being willing to reward the behaviors over and over again. While Phillip and Stephen were both intellectually bright, when it came to learning to communicate and function socially in an appropriate manner, they were slow learners. We would have to repeat the same instructions and information literally dozens of times until they would remember the appropriate responses and behaviors and produce them when asked.

While this type of positive reinforcement and training could become monotonous for the instructor/coach, in the early stages of working with the Koegels, the novelty of seeing the boys focusing and engaging with a variety of people besides me never wore off. The boys were rewarded with a coin for successfully engaging and speaking. At the end of the session, they would be led to a store on campus, where they could purchase the candy and snacks of their choice with the money they'd earned that day. Even the staff at the store contributed to the good feelings we had during our time at the ARC. They had grown used to having autistic kids as clients, and if any of the kids acted out inappropriately, they didn't give them horrified looks or angry glares. This was all part of the normal course of events in their day, and they were sure to reward Phillip and Stephen with genuine smiles and expressions of pleasure at both having met them and being thanked.

Some of what the boys were learning made me think of the ARC as the AFS—the Autism Finishing School. Manners and appropriate behavior were a large part of the curriculum. For Stephen and Phillip, that meant making eye contact with whoever was speaking to them, responding to questions, and generally learning what it meant to interact socially with other people. This wasn't always easy for them, and they did their fair share of crying and screaming, but it seemed to me that each week they were getting better and better. While Stephen wasn't developing into a chatty TV-talk-show-host type, he was speaking more and more. Phillip had always been more gregarious by nature, and the difference in his communication was a matter of quality and not quantity. Whereas prior to working with the Koegels he was prone to responding with non sequiturs and illogic, he was now able to sustain a traceable conversation for a few moments at a time.

I was being trained in the Koegels' methodology and putting it into practice at home whenever I could. Getting Stephen and Phillip to ask for what they wanted as a snack or wanted to drink with their meal was a major accomplishment. It was sometimes difficult to stick with the program and get them to answer beyond pointing, nodding, or some other nonverbal means, but I counted even that kind of interaction as a victory. As the second half of their kindergarten year was beginning, I was feeling like we were finally making progress. That's when I got the call.

Chaparral's social worker reached me in the early evening. She told me that she needed me to attend an emergency meeting the next morning that involved Stephen and Phillip. She couldn't go into any detail, but it was imperative that I be there. She spoke the word "imperative" like she was a factory machine stamping out a part. The amount of pressure she placed on the word unsettled me. I told her I would be there, and made arrangements at work to go in late and stay beyond my usual time to make up for my absence. The next morning, I drove the kids to Chaparral and accompanied them inside the building. The administrative offices were a glass-walled section just off the main entrance. I presented myself to the secretary. She knew me from work there as a part-time classroom aide, and I saw her pupils widen and then narrow when I greeted her by name. Brushing back a strand of her curly red hair, she said, "They're expecting you." No "Hello." No "How are you?"

I followed her down a short hallway to a conference room. Her short high ponytail scampered ahead of me like a squirrel. She opened the door for me and stepped aside. Seated at a rectangular desk were the principal, the boys' teacher, the school social worker, and a man I didn't recognize but who introduced himself as the Las Virgenes School District's superintendent. He offered his hand and then pointed toward the one empty seat.

After a few brief introductory remarks, and thanks and apologies for the inconvenience, the principal got to the point. "As I'm sure you know, Mrs. Morgan, the law stipulates that we have an obligation to investigate any matters that may appear suspicious. We don't want you to think that we are making accusations; we are simply trying to protect your children. It's imperative you keep that in mind."

That word again. And "stipulates," what was going on with that? Was this a tryout for *Jeopardy*? I looked around the room. Every one of them held my gaze with an expression that ranged from indifferent to accusatory.

The speech therapist pushed himself back from the desk and steepled his fingers. "Mrs. Morgan, several of the staff have noticed and pointed out to me behaviors in Stephen and Phillip that have prompted us to call you in this morning." He spread his hands wide to indicate everyone in the room. "Stephen and Phillip cry quite a bit, as I'm sure you know. At first we attributed this to the usual adjustment period, separation anxiety, that sort of thing."

He paused, looking at me expectantly.

I shrugged. "They do cry. Yes."

"What we've noticed is that they frequently cry when it is time for the bathroom break. Whenever a toilet flushes, they get very agitated, cry, scream, and otherwise act out. If this were a one-time incident, we might have simply noted it and moved on. However..." He let the word sit there and drift, like a fly fisherman settling his bait on the surface of the water. I felt a bead of sweat drip down from my underarm and slide along the edge of my bra. I knew what they were implying, and I was faced with another of those hard choices. In my mind, a series of expressions ran rampant: the jig was up, the cat was out of the bag, my goose was cooked. Deciding that the hard place was a safer landing spot than the rock, I said, "My boys have been tested and identified as autistic. The loud noise of the toilet flushing triggers their crying. Like many autistic children, they have acutely sensitive hearing. Loud noises irritate them."

In the faces of some of my accusers, I saw relief ease the tension around their eyes and mouths. In others, I saw their censure turn to pity or, if not full-blown amazement, then certainly surprise. It was as if I'd taken the Etch-A-Sketch and given it a bit of shake and distorted but not obliterated their view.

The meeting didn't last much longer.

They were glad I'd told them about the assessment, said that what I told them made sense and that they would no longer pursue the child abuse angle. I left the meeting feeling a bit relieved. I wouldn't have to pretend and lie anymore—at least not when dealing with the school. I would still have to live with other people's lingering suspicions that my kids weren't being well cared for.

ONE Saturday night, when Phillip and Stephen were in the fourth grade, I was sitting at home watching television. Ali lay dozing on the couch. I'd covered her with an afghan Big Steve's mother had knit for me. I was only half paying attention to the movie. I'd settled in for a quiet night at home, reveling in being able to sit in front of the television in a pair of old sweatpants and an oversize long-sleeved T-shirt I must have worn at some point when I was painting the house. I'd indulged myself, pouring a glass of a fruity German wine my former in-laws had given me when I dropped the boys off with them earlier that afternoon. This was my version of girls' night out: me, Ali, and a glass of Liebfraumilch. I had threaded my bra through one arm of my shirt when I heard a pounding at our front door. It had been so long since anyone had come to the house invited or uninvited that I was immediately on edge. Though it was only seven thirty in the evening, I felt as though I'd received one of those four-in-the-morning phone calls that can only bring bad news.

Glass in hand, I made my way to the door. When I opened it, I was surprised to see one of the county's social workers, a man who often wouldn't return my calls or set up the meetings I requested. I'd seen him around the school at various times. Standing there with him outside my door, I remember being struck by something. Outside the elementary school with its foreshortened furniture and knee-height water fountains, he seemed of normal size, almost diminutive in comparison to the ogre-like image I had of him. I was nearly so preoccupied with those thoughts that it didn't register with me at first how odd it was that he was standing there flanked by two policemen. I sputtered some kind of greeting, and he responded with a curt request to come inside the house. At first I thought maybe he'd had a minor car accident somewhere nearby and needed me to vouch for him.

His eyes wandered all over the room. I'd been involved in enough real estate transactions to recognize when someone was appraising, and this was clearly the case. Fortunately, the house was neat and tidy. The two police officers, both men, stood in what I've come to refer to as penis protection mode—their interlocked hands resting in front of their groins. After an uncomfortable few moments of silence, the social worker assumed the position—who did these guys think I was, some kind of ninja warrior bent on destroying their reproductive capabilities?— and he cleared his throat and nodded. "Mrs. Morgan, we've received some reports that Phillip has sores all over his body. On his exposed skin. Is he here? We'd like to see him."

"Phillip is at his grandparents' house tonight." I was as calm as it's possible to be with two policemen and a social worker in your house investigating a report of possible child abuse. I knew about the sores on Phillip's body. He had eczema, and I'd taken him to the doctor and we'd been applying various salves and ointments to try to keep it under control. I explained all this to the men, and then added that Phillip was autistic.

I watched as the social worker's tense face and posture visibly relaxed. He even tucked his hands inside his pants pockets, checking to be certain that I'd done no damage with my witchy ways, I guessed. He smiled, "Yes, I understand. I used to work with a lot of autistic kids. When I was with the county." He turned toward the two officers. "It's very common for autistic kids to have eczema. I don't know why exactly, maybe their high level of anxiety or whatever, but that would explain the sores."

The two officers nodded and pursed their lips. I got the feeling they would rather be anywhere but here. I would have preferred they be anywhere but in my home as well. I folded my arms across my chest, conscious of my bra hanging loosely inside my shirt. I was about to excuse myself to go to the bathroom to restrap it when the social worker spoke again.

"We have this report on file, and so we have to follow through. I'm sure you understand."

I did understand. I knew that the school's teachers were just doing their jobs. I'd been made aware that they held monthly meetings and discussed students who they thought might be abused or neglected, targeting mainly low-income families whose kids appeared in school in dirty or torn clothes, who didn't seem to be bathing regularly, that kind of thing. I was hurt that someone had suspected me of neglect or abuse but was simultaneously grateful that someone was also paying enough attention to my kids to notice them. However, I'd say that at the time the embarrassment and resentment were winning out over the gratitude.

"Do what you have to do," I told them.

The social worker was very apologetic. He sat on the couch next to Ali, and I sat on the other side of her. He took her hand and held it while he pushed up the sleeve of her pajamas with the other. She looked at me, her eyes wide in a mix of curiosity and fear. I told her it was okay and smoothed my hand over her hair. He checked her legs as well, and satisfied that there was no sign of bruising, he apologized again and again. My heart had gone out to my daughter, so there was no place left in it to consider how awful his job must have been, the kind of heart-breaking things he had witnessed.

All the apologies were a prelude to another request. They wanted the address of where Phillip and Stephen were staying. They had to check them out as well, to verify what they were being told.

"You can't just go over there. You scared the crap out of me showing up with the police. They're older people. You'll give them a heart attack."

"You have to understand, Mrs. Morgan. If we call people ahead of time, they can cover things up. Surprise visits are effective."

"Well, you already know what's going on here. I'll give you the address, but I will call them first to let them know what's going on."

"That's against policy, ma'am," one of the officers said.

"That's fine. That's fine." The social worker put his hand on the arm of the officer who'd spoken and led him toward the door. "I'll take care of this."

The two officers left.

A little more of the gratitude elbowed its way past the anger and humiliation. The social worker sat at the kitchen table while I made the call.

Big Steve's parents were shocked and saddened, of course, but I got them to focus on the idea that it was Phillip's eczema that had aroused suspicion. It was all a mistake, a misunderstanding, and it had been cleared up, but policy and all that necessitated this visit.

"You mean inspection," Richard said.

"Well, yes." I'd never heard such a pointed tone from him before and was taken aback by it.

"I wonder sometimes just what goes through the minds of these people."

I felt relieved that his anger wasn't directed toward me but toward the authorities.

I never told Richard and Mary about the other visits that were to follow this one. Subsequent reports of suspicions of neglect resulted in more visits from social workers. I remember one who came in and saw how neat the place was, how comfortable and at ease the kids were. She said, "There're no signs of abuse here. What are these people thinking?"

Then she opened the refrigerator, and she audibly gasped. "What do you do for food around here?"

Her comment stabbed me. Richard was constantly asking why we didn't have more to eat, moaning (rightfully so) about the meager meals I was serving. Plain pasta just wasn't covering it, no matter how much salt and pepper and margarine we put on it.

"Don't you have anybody who could help out? Where's the rest of your family? Do they know what's going on?"

I would tell my mother now and then that I was broke. That clothing and feeding the kids was next to impossible. My parents would give me a few dollars, but that didn't do much to offset the problems I was having. At the time I was angry with my family for abandoning me, but I realize now that I wasn't very good at asking for help. I would call my parents or one of my siblings and say I was having a hard time. I wasn't any clearer than that. I was too tired and too ashamed to go into detail. I often mixed up my problems with relationships with the reality of the twins' diagnosis. I simply wore out my family's sympathy, and I wasn't able to be there for them when they struggled with their own issues. If I had said, "Listen, the county social worker showed up at my door and said that my kids are dressed like bums, they're underfed, and they're being categorized as neglected," maybe they would have responded more forcefully.

I couldn't be that direct. I was feeling humiliated and neglected enough myself that I couldn't heap that embarrassment and admission of failure on top of it.

Whether it was a result of my naiveté or a faulty synapse or two, when my mind was rambling over all the clichéd expressions in that abuse investigation meeting at Chaparral, one of them escaped me: opening Pandora's box. By the time I got home, I wondered just what effect my revealing the boys' diagnosis would have on us all. I didn't have long to wait.

A few days after the meeting, when the twins were in kindergarden class, I got a call to attend another session at school. This time, no "imperatives" were uttered. I was invited, and they would be pleased and hoped it wouldn't be an inconvenience for me. I'm usually pretty good at being able to sniff out insincerity and pity, and in this case, I detected neither. We were going to discuss Stephen's and Phillip's education. I made the same arrangements as before with my boss and found myself a week later back in the "aquarium" off the lobby. The secretary said, "Corrine, how are you doing? Can I get you a coffee?" I could have sweetened the drink with her smile and disposed of the stirrer in her dimples. I thanked her and sat down in one of the chairs next to another mother, who eyed me suspiciously. After a few minutes' wait, it was the same walk down the hall to the same conference room, but this time my secretary buddy walked along beside me, laying her hand gently on my forearm when she excused herself after ushering me in.

This was the same crew as before, minus the boys' teacher, but their lithium must have kicked in. They were all smiles and cat-that-ate-the-canary smugness.

This time, the principal did most of the speaking. After a few warm-up remarks, he said, "We've spent a great deal of time and expended a number of resources to determine what is the best course of action to take with Stephen and Phillip. I believe that we've arrived at the best decision for them, for you, and for the other students here. I want to assure you that the program that we've set up for Phillip and Stephen will be minimally disruptive and will cost you nothing."

I wasn't sure why cost had anything to do with it, but if they were going to lay out extra cash for tutors or special counselors, I was all for it.

"Go on."

"We have made arrangements to have Stephen and Phillip transported, again at no cost to you, to the Camarillo Mental Hospital. There, they will receive their treatment and instruction. At the conclusion of their day, we will bus them back to Chaparral. They can then get home via the same route as they have been."

Everyone in the room, except me of course, sat back looking very pleased, as though the wisdom of Solomon had just been dispensed. Instead of being in a state of awe, I was thinking, "Aw shit. Not this. No way."

I'm usually a very meek and amiable person. I don't know where I drew my strength from, but I stood up and said, my voice at first quivering with rage and indignation and then with a jolt of adrenaline-fueled anger, "You know what? You can't do this. I've done my reading. I know what my kids' rights are. You are not going to bus them forty-five minutes each way every day to a *mental hospital* and call that an educational program. You just want them out of your sight, don't you? You just want to be able to pass the buck, to shirk your responsibilities to do something for my kids and pawn them off on someone else. Out of sight, out of mind, is that it? Well, you must be out of your minds. I know what the Lanterman Act says about what my kids are entitled to. I know what the federal legislation states, and I will go all the way to the Supreme Court if I have to, to keep you from doing this to my kids."

I don't think I was aware of how worked up I was, but when the superintendent stood up and yelled at me to sit down, I had a pretty good idea of how loud I'd gotten. "Mrs. Morgan, I will not sit here and be threatened by any parent of any student, regardless of the circumstances."

I cited him chapter and verse, kept referring to the least restrictive environment, and hammered on the word "rights" enough times that I think they realized it was *imperative* that they not go ahead with their plan.

I'm a child of the 1960s. I know all about "the man." I know all about the military industrial complex. I know all about corporate America, bureaucratic bumbling, nabobs of negativism, and all the rest. Even I was surprised to learn that not only did the administration come to their collective senses and not impose what I believed to be a death sentence on Phillip and Stephen, but they decided that it made better sense to bring in someone from the ARC to do staff development work with the teachers. This would be the first training the teachers and staff would have in dealing with autistic kids, and if it took me standing up and shouting and threatening, then it was well worth the damage to my vocal cords and to my reputation. If

I was going to be considered a troublemaker, then at least it was going to be in the name of a good cause.

In the fairy-tale version of this story, everyone lives happily every after. Stephen and Phillip come out of their shells, the teachers all recognize the value of the training they received, and the autistic are welcomed into the warm and loving embrace of Chaparral Elementary School staff and students. As a result, the Las Virgenes School District becomes a beacon of enlightenment for the education of autistic children in the mainstream educational environment. Read me that bedtime story over and over, please. That's one wish I'd really like to see granted. I'll tell you more about these issues later. For now, I just want you to be aware that while letting people in and speaking the truth about the twins' autism was a good thing, I still had to do battle with the uninformed and the uncooperative. At least I was out in the open, and at least I had some allies both inside and outside the educational system.

One night in 1994, without realizing it or initially wanting to, I would add another very important member to Team Morgan—my husband, Doug Thomas.

A girlfriend of mine, Jill, decided that she was tired of me spending so much time working or caring for the kids. She invited me to go with her to a bar in Malibu. I told her that I didn't want to go. I didn't have a sitter for the kids, it was a Tuesday night and I had to work the next day, and I really had no interest in going to a bar. I enjoyed an occasional glass of wine, but I didn't drink beer or mixed drinks. She kept urging me to go, but I can be stubborn, and I finally won out. A few hours later, I got a call from Jill. She'd gone to the bar by herself and knew she was in no shape to drive home. She asked me if I could pick her up. While I wasn't that eager to go out, I was glad that she had done the responsible thing and not driven under the influence. I told her that I would be right there.

Since I was just going to pick up my friend, I didn't bother to change out of my play clothes—an old pair of jeans and an oversize button-down man's shirt. Since I was going to be gone only a short while, I left fourteen-year-old Richard in charge of the younger kids and headed over to Murph's. You can tell a lot from a name, and I knew it wasn't some kind of yuppie bar with racks of wineglasses suspended from the ceiling and a bartender in a tuxedo shirt and enough product in his hair to create an oil slick that would stretch all the way out to the Channel Islands. I knew that there were still a few holdout establishments that longtime locals patronized and the moneyed set either vilified as eyesores and blights or lusted after as prime real estate for developing.

I parked my car in a pool of red, blue, and yellow neon, a combination of Bud Light, Budweiser, and Miller Genuine Draft signs. I tried to peer through their collective glare and the main window to see if I could catch Jill's attention. When I couldn't, I walked inside. The place was about what you might expect— a long wooden bar at which a half-dozen people sat beneath halos of smoke, and from the jukebox in the corner, Sheryl Crow declared that all she wanted to do was have some fun. From a darkened booth, I saw lit ends of cigarettes skitter through the air like fireflies. Jill was nowhere to be seen. I stood in the middle of the bar waiting. I figured Jill was in the bathroom and all I had to do was wait a few minutes and we'd be on our way.

A few seconds later, I felt a hand touching my elbow. I started, surprised at being touched. I turned and saw a man smiling at me. He had a pleasant face and a warm engaging smile, and he apologized for startling me.

"Are you looking for someone?"

I rolled my eyes, waiting for the punch line to this obvious and no doubt groanable pickup line that would make me want to punch the smug grin that would replace the earnest smile. When that line didn't come, I was thrown a bit off balance.

"I just thought maybe I could help is all. You looked a little dazed when you walked in here. My name is Doug."

He held his hand out to me, and something told me I could let my guard down a bit with this guy. "I'm Corrine. And yes, I'm here looking for a friend of mine. If you'll excuse me."

That was about as far as I was willing to let anybody get beyond my defenses. I took a few steps away from Doug. From my new vantage point, I could see that Jill was one of the firefly holders at the booth. I walked over toward her. Seeing me, Jill gave me a big drunk girl wave over. She looked like she was at the head of a cavalry unit and was signaling her troops to charge. She introduced me around to everyone and said that she just wanted to finish her drink and then we could leave. She made sure to point out to everyone that I was her ride, her truly oldest, dearest, and most trusted friend. I'd been in this kind of situation before, when someone else's Hennessy-fueled hyperbole had me cringing just a bit at the well-intentioned but obvious insincerity of it all. My antennae were tuned to any hints of that kind of thing. Part of the reason for my sensitivity was that my staunchly Catholic genes were twitching. I'm not against drinking, but I was brought up to believe that the people we meet in bars belong in one category, an admittedly lower category than the people we meet at work, at church, or someplace else.

I realize it's a bit absurd to base a judgment of someone on the circumstances of where we meet them instead of on some impression of what kind of person they are, but that's the truth of my initial assessment of people in bars. If they are at a bar, they are there to drink, not in and of itself a bad thing, but the activities people engage in when drinking too much are what really concern me.

All this is to explain what I did next. Doug, the man who'd greeted me initially, had drifted over and moored alongside me. The nautical language is intentional. I didn't turn to face him; I simply saw him out of the corner of my eye. He seemed to be bobbing like an anchored boat being subjected to the rise and fall of a distant ship's wake. Nothing too severe, just a gentle but clearly perceptible change in pitch and yaw.

For the second time in a span of just a few minutes, I felt his hand on my arm. "Hi. I see you found your friend. Can I get you something?"

All those forces that had my defenses up and on high alert had me so tense, I snapped, "Yes, you can. You can get away from me. You don't want anything to do with me. I've got four kids. Two of them are autistic. You don't want any part of my life."

I saw him blink his eyes rapidly for a couple of seconds, like he'd stuck his head out the window of a moving car. He quickly recovered. "You've got kids. That's great. What are their names?"

I thought this guy must be the most sincerely desperate or desperately sincere man I'd ever met. I wasn't exactly wearing club clothes, my hair was a mess, I didn't have on a molecule of makeup, I probably smelled like the fried bologna I'd made for dinner, and he stood there asking me a question that was socially appropriate and designed to either disregard or transform my anger into something more positive.

I told him my kids' names, and we spent the next fifteen minutes chatting. Doug was a charmer, but not the dangerous sort. He had, and has, a knack for talking to people in a way that immediately puts them at ease. I guess that's a product of his background and the varied experiences he's had. He also made it clear that he was actually listening to what I had to say. Most people I've encountered in conversational situations look like they are formulating what they are going to say next instead of really listening to what I have to say. I can see through the transparent current of interest they're exhibiting and view the machinations going on in their brains as they figure out and mentally rehearse their next comments. It's almost as if I can see the first words forming on their lips the whole time I'm speaking. With Doug, there was none of that "hurry up and finish what you have to say because you're going to love what you're going to hear about me next" kind of false attention. He seemed to really want to know more about me and what I thought.

Ever since Larry, I'd been leery of relationships. I could still hear his harsh words about my desirability as an echo to whatever of came out of any man's mouth. I could still hear that with Doug, and even when he said, "I'd love to take all of you guys out fishing," Larry's "With your family, no man will ever be interested in you again" came bouncing back off the walls. Something inside me decided that I had to stop those echoes from dictating the course of my life. I told Doug that sounded great and told myself that I was agreeing more because the boys needed to have a man in their lives than I did. Our first outing was a success. Richard has always been a bit shy, certainly not as shy as Stephen but still reticent around people he doesn't know well. Doug seemed to win him over, not through any kind of apparent effort but by treating him like he was just any other person he happened to bump into on the street.

What impressed me was how Doug treated Stephen and Phillip. He knew about their condition, but he didn't do the always frustrating slow talk–baby talk thing with them. I know that people are often just trying to be nice, but when they mindlessly and effusively praise the twins for doing the simplest things (Wow, good for you. You opened the car door all by yourself!), my hackles rise. Doug did none of that. A couple of times he asked the boys if they needed help in switching lures or repositioning the bobber on their line, but other than that, he talked to them as if they were the young adults they were. He treated them like they were twelve-year-olds, and that's exactly what they wanted and needed.

Our trip to Castaic Lake was a great first step for all of us. Phillip was his usual vocal self, and even though the twitching and other physical manifestations of his Tourette's syndrome were present, Doug didn't respond too strongly to anything that Phillip said or did.

I would come to understand better why Doug was so easy-going and accepting of the twins and me. We were a somewhat ragtag bunch, but Doug had been judged and dismissed as a little bit odd often enough himself to recognize that surface appearances are often deceiving. I think that, given his background, it's no wonder he found work in Hollywood as a scene painter and set-construction guy. He worked in a deceptive world, and being behind the scenes so much, he had no illusions that what seemed magical was anything but the product of hard work.

I don't want to leave you with the impression that Doug thought of the family as a rescue mission, a task he could undertake to make himself feel better about the direction his life was taking and to establish a legacy to leave behind. I also don't want you to think that I chose Doug and eventually married him because I was on my own rescue mission. I know that there are people out there who do those kinds of things, but I'm not one of them.

Neither of us was in a place, financially speaking, where we could rescue anybody. On our second date, Doug and I went to a restaurant called the Place. It was a pleasant little family-run eatery near Malibu Lakes. Its décor was as unpretentious as its name. The five of us and Doug all crowded into a booth— Doug always wanted to include the kids on our dates—and we ordered two steaks. That's all we could afford, and we'd split the meat, the baked potatoes, and the vegetable sides among the six of us. I sat there listening to Doug regaling the kids with a story about Bruce Willis and Cybil Shepard and some work he'd done on the set of the TV show *Moonlighting*. The kids were too young to remember the show, but the boys had all seen Bruce Willis in *Die Hard*, so they were listening intently.

When the waitress came to our table, she set a plate down in front of Richard, then Phillip, then Stephen. I looked at her and said, "There's some mistake. This isn't our order. We only asked for two dinners."

She kept setting plates down until there was one in front of each of us. "We had a mix-up back in the kitchen, and these all got cooked. We don't want them to go to waste."

Before I could say anything else, she had turned on her heel and headed back into the kitchen. I knew that there was no mistake. I'd been in the Place a few times before with the kids, and the staff there was always extra kind to us. I appreciated the fact that they made the effort not just to feed us but to not make it feel like we were charity cases. This happened on more than one occasion, and each time it did, I felt grateful to know that such kind people existed.

In a way, that's how I felt about Doug and how I think he felt about me. We weren't capable of rescuing each other. I don't think either of us had it in us to do that. Working together, and with the proverbial kindness of strangers to assist us, we could get by. We could start to enjoy ourselves a bit more. I was at an age when I'd abandoned any thoughts of my life being a fairy tale. I had thought that Larry was the prince who was going to sweep me off my feet, love my kids as much as I did, and provide us all with a life we'd only previously dreamed of. I walked into my relationship with Doug about as clear-eyed as I ever have. I was grateful that he saw us at our worst and our best and accepted both. Sure, I was hoping for some escape from the conditions we lived under, hoping that the progress the twins were making would continue and that the evidence of Phillip's developing Tourette's syndrome and obsessive-compulsive disorder were red herrings, but I had no hope or desire that Doug was going to toss us a lifeline and pull us out of the morass we were in. We were all in quicksand, and I'd seen enough movies to know that the more you struggled against it, the quicker it sucked you down. With Doug, I was learning my first lessons about surrender.

Believe me, if someone had come up to me and told me that I was being given a second chance, that I could have time turned back and my sons could be born without autism, I would have taken that deal whatever it cost me. I'd do that not because it would relieve me of the burdens I had but because it would relieve Stephen and Phillip of some of the troubles they faced.

Doug knows as well as I do that there are some rewards that come from overcoming obstacles and meeting challenges. I took on the task of raising autistic kids and later raising awareness about autism because I had no choice. There's the line about some people having heroism thrust on them, and although I don't really think of myself as heroic, the statement applies in a certain sense to me. In Doug's case, he chose to join us. I can't fully speak for him, but from what he's told me, he saw something in me that attracted him. He wasn't attracted to the idea of autistic kids; he just accepted that if he wanted the one thing, me, then he'd have to take on the other. That's a big deal, a whole lot to take on, and the fact that he accepted us for what we were—didn't try to change us, didn't try to paint this mountain and make it into something it wasn't—speaks volumes about him as a person. Whatever transformation Doug needed to make in his own life he made independent of all of us. He was willing to take a fearless step into the unknown, to delve into the mysteries of what life was like with autistic kids.

I guess because of Doug and so many other people who were willing to reach out to me, I was also learning not to fear so many unknowns and mysteries, coming to understand that letting people into my life could sometimes be painful but mostly beneficial. Since that time, I've come to realize that I wouldn't have been able to fully understand what the benefits were if not for the pain. Most things come at a cost to us, even things that are freely given, like love and acceptance. That's another of those contradictions, I know, but as it was just then beginning to dawn on me at about the time of Stephen's Miracle Run, life with autism is about as contradictory as it can be.

One of the other ways I would eventually expand my understanding was by realizing after the Miracle Run—and after all the publicity that Stephen got locally—that I owed something to the community and that my mission in life was to expand understanding of autism beyond just the local schools the twins attended. If so many people were willing to reach out to me, I could do the same.

SHORTLY after the Miracle Run cross-country season ended, I got a call from a Reverend James of the Born Again Baptist Church in East Los Angeles. He told me that he'd heard about Stephen, that he was a runner himself back in the day, and that he'd been in the Olympics and earned gold. He wanted us all to come to speak to his autism support group. Reverend James spoke with such power that I couldn't help but listen and obey his every word. It was as if I were hearing the voice of God through this man—that is, if God sounded like James Brown. We agreed on a date and time three weeks later.

I told Stephen a little bit about Reverend James and his being a runner. Stephen was intrigued. The day of the meeting, his curiosity had been transformed into eagerness. He was ready two hours before we were scheduled to leave. Phillip needed to be bribed to go. I told him that he could bring his guitar and his music books. We'd gotten Phillip a guitar for his fourteenth birthday. I showed him a couple of chords, and my father, who played the mandolin, helped him out as well when we visited my parents in Chatsworth, California. Phillip didn't need much urging or instruction. He seemed to have an innate ability. Though we eventually got him a teacher, just picking and strumming on his own, Phillip was soon composing songs. I don't know if there is a factual or scientific basis for this, but in my experience, many people with autism have some kind of talent for music. I also know about the connection between mathematics and music, and since both twins excel in math, it doesn't surprise me that they both have musical ability. Stephen plays the guitar and takes lessons as well, but Phillip is much more passionate about it. If it weren't for his guitar playing, I don't know what Phillip would have done. His OCD and Tourette's symptoms were barely contained. That day of the meeting with Reverend James, I knew Phillip was especially exhausted and despairing. I also knew he was having an okay day when I could hear him playing and singing.

Phillip loves the music of the sixties and early seventies,

especially Crosby, Stills, Nash, and Young. When he isn't playing music, he's listening to it. I think that given his heightened aural sensitivity, being able to control the volume has a soothing effect on him. In any case, getting him to go along with us to speak at the autism support group required me to tell him he could bring his guitar.

The first thing we heard when we got to the Born Again Baptist Church was the sound of an organ. Being raised Catholic, I was used to the sonorous, almost funereal sound of organ music coming from a church. What we heard as we approached the church sounded nothing like what I would have associated with a house of worship. The church itself was not what I'd expected. I had envisioned a minor variation on the traditional white clapboard structure with a steeple. I knew that we were in East L.A., in a very urban environment, but I'd never been in a storefront church before. More accurately, I'd never been in a converted movie theater church before. It was probably all our imaginations, but Doug sniffed the air and said, "Do you smell popcorn?" The fact was, we all did.

The sounds of the organ began to pick up in pace and volume and were soon joined by the thumping tympani of drums and an electric bass. A few seconds later a tambourine filled in the empty spaces of the soundscape. I was concerned that this would be too much for Stephen and for Phillip especially, since we were in one of those cycles when we couldn't get Phillip's med levels right. I needn't have worried. Phillip stood for a second and raised his head and then tilted it to the side. He reminded me of a dog sniffing the air, checking to see if any other canines were in the area. He smiled and tromped down the inclined aisle and stood in front of the choir with a huge smile plastered on his face.

Seeing Phillip so eager to perform was a real delight. I remembered the early days, when the twins were both so completely in their own world. Now, they were both eager to share their experiences and perceptions with other people. I knew that my own shyness would have prevented me from getting up and speaking to a group of strangers, but there were my autistic boys—the ones who were expected to remain almost completely antisocial—about to take part in what my newly hipster son Phillip called his "gig."

We'd arrived a little early and must have walked in on choir practice. The assembled singers weren't wearing their robes, but they were in full throat and swaying and clapping and making a joyful noise. A soloist stepped forward and belted out the words to what I later learned was a song called "Long as I Got Jesus." The first verse was all about the bad things that had gone on in the singer's life, a wailing tale of woe and strife. Then the whole choir came in on the chorus, and you knew just from the increase in tempo that things were going to be okay, as they sang, "Long, long, long as I got Jesus, I don't need nobody else." As the song continued, they sang about Jesus as a load sharer and a burden bearer. We all stood there mesmerized by the passionate beauty of the singing. We leaned against the raised stage and enjoyed the last few minutes of their show.

Then a man came up to us and introduced himself as the Reverend James. His closely cropped hair was receding, and his exposed scalp gleamed from the overhead lights. I could believe that he'd been an Olympic athlete. His shoulders threatened to swallow his neck and head. He wore a tight-fitting black knit short-sleeved turtleneck. It seemed so tight on him that it was squeezing the excess flesh out of the sleeves. His arms were as big as my thighs, and the veins stood out on his coal dark skin like rivers on a relief map. His high-wattage smile instantly made us feel welcome, and he ushered us to an area opposite the choir, where chairs had been arranged in a circle.

"I'm so glad you got to hear a little bit of our choir this evening."

We all talked over one another, singing our praises.

Reverend James smiled that smile of his and excused himself for a moment. He spoke with the choir director and then with Phillip. Phillip trailed after the reverend as he made his way back toward us. In a few minutes, we were joined by about twenty or so members of the congregation, each of whom walked up to us to introduce themselves. When they settled into their seats or stood behind the circle of chairs, Reverend James formally introduced us. Stephen spoke first.

"Hello. My name is Stephen Morgan, and I am autistic." He paused, and I noticed one woman was already daubing at her cheek with a tissue.

Stephen continued, "And one day, I'm going to run in the Olympics." He turned and looked over at his new hero, the Reverend James. The reverend nodded his leonine head, then bowed from the waist. "All right, then," he said, "make it happen."

Stephen spent a few minutes telling everyone about his

workout schedule. As he was close to winding up, he said, "It's hard, but I never give up."

"Hallelujah!" One of the women stood up and raised her arms to the heavens. In a moment, two others joined her. Stephen stepped forward. His face lost its usual speech-giving seriousness. With a smile as wide as a church door, he said, "And I say 'hallelujah,' too."

Everyone started laughing, stomping their feet, clapping their hands, and falling all over themselves and each other. The reaction was infectious, and we soon joined them.

The rest of the evening was an informal chat. I think we got far more than we gave that night. I don't think I'd ever had so many people tell me in so many ways that God was blessing us all and that they would keep us in their prayers as I did that night. We were a long ways from Agoura Hills, but I never felt so at home as I did that night on Martin Luther King Jr. Boulevard and the Born Again Baptist Church.

That incident helped me overcome some of my fears, not just about the stigma associated with autism but my own personal fears of speaking in public. As I said before, whenever we faced a problem, we took baby steps at first. Seeing how Stephen managed to communicate such a positive message despite his autism made me realize that I had no excuse for not accepting an invitation to speak at the Simi Valley Mothers of Autistics support group.

The invitation came a few weeks after the original *L.A. Daily News* piece ran about Stephen's cross-country success in December 1998. Doug accompanied me to the nearby town of

Tarzana, and I was very nervous. I didn't like speaking to large groups, but my fears melted away as we walked into the New Moon Chinese Restaurant. In the back corner of the restaurant sat a group of six overweight women, who immediately recognized us from the photographs that ran with the interview and beckoned us to the table. Doug being Doug, he sat down and started chatting away. I sat there and watched as platter after platter of food arrived at the table and the women dug in.

As they ate, they shared their stories. It became very clear to me why these women were as heavy as they were. They were so stressed-out, so despairing, that the only comfort in their lives was food. In fact, when one woman started talking about her eating issues, the rest of them chimed in and confessed that they knew they were damaging their health by gaining so much weight but they felt powerless to stop. It was sad and surreal to be sitting there with them, but I was entirely empathetic. While I didn't overeat or succumb to any other kind of addiction, I could understand how they turned to this unhealthy behavior as a way to cope. My coping mechanism was cutting myself off from others. None of us there had dealt with our children's condition in the most appropriate manner possible. One woman sobbed as she told about her travails with her eight-year-old son who still did not speak, and mutilated himself by biting his arms and legs and banging his head against floors and walls. The whole time she spoke, she continued putting forkful after forkful of moo shu pork onto the pancakes and passing them around the table.

That was the first time I realized that the parents of autistic kids needed care almost as much as their children did. Over time, I would eventually deliver a message to the caretakers that they needed to take better care of themselves. If they didn't, they would be of no use to their kids. I'd seen marriages ripped apart by autism and, of course, had seen my own relationship with Larry fail as a result of the autism diagnosis. I knew of parents who descended into all kinds of acting-out behaviors—drinking, drugs, running up huge credit card debt, promiscuity—the whole gamut of self-destructive things that people engage in when they are too overwhelmed and feel guilt and shame as the parents of autistic kids. That night in Tarzana, we talked and laughed and shared, and professed our faith in the goodness of fortune cookies. If we didn't get a fortune we wanted, we asked the waitstaff for another cookie. They were glad to oblige, and the giggling band shared a no-holds-barred night of camaraderie and compassion. I had worried needlessly about getting up in front of a group and sharing my wisdom and insights. What those women wanted wasn't someone to listen to but someone to listen to them.

Shortly after that meeting, we got a call from a woman representing the Westlake Mothers Autism Support Group. Just so you don't think I'm expressing my bias, here is how Wikipedia describes Westlake Village, California: "This city located in the Conejo Valley is known for its affluence and secluded character, and is considered one of the wealthier communities in the Greater Los Angeles Area." I've detailed only a few of our exploits in public speaking, but our trip to East L.A. and the Born Again Baptist Church was more the norm. We weren't used to being invited by the big shots.

When the Westlake Village representative tried to entice us

by saying that they'd picked out a very fine restaurant, Piatto Ristorante, to host the event, we were anything but enticed. We were Denny's kinds of folks, and our only previous experience with a support group meeting at a restaurant was one of our most memorable and likely to be the exact opposite of what the Westlake Village experience was going to be.

I didn't imagine that the Westlake Village group would be as warm and welcoming or as willing to just sit and chat. They were paying for our services as speakers by providing us with a lovely meal. Doug and I put on our Sunday best, which most likely put us somewhere around Tuesday midmorning in the wardrobe week of our hosts. We climbed in the Suburban and headed to posh Westlake Village. Once we found the restaurant, we saw that there was valet parking, and Doug said, "What the heck. Let's live large." We smiled as we rolled past slot after slot of one luxury import after another. The parking attendant was courteous, and we felt a little bad about being so presumptuous.

We weren't really expecting checkered tablecloths and candles stuck in bottles of Chianti, but we weren't prepared for the first impression the interior of Piatto Ristorante presented us with. The stucco walls were the color of roasted red peppers, and the off-white leather chairs looked like they had come from the sitting room of a Bel Air mansion. The waitresses wore strapless little black dresses, and the waiters were attired in black suits with shirts the color of the walls. As we stood waiting for the maître d', men clad in Armani suits and women in Joan and David shoes strolled past us.

I leaned into Doug. "We are definitely in the wrong place, wrong time, wrong world."

Doug shrugged his shoulders. "Maybe they meant for us to meet them at Pizza Ristorante. Easy enough mistake."

Frazzled autistic parents confusing the name of the meeting place? I could buy that. Maybe some emergency had come up; maybe they'd tried to reach us at home; maybe a lot of things. I gave the name of the woman who had contacted me to the maître d', and he nodded and said, "Right this way."

Our hostess introduced Doug and me around the table full of men with martinis and women with designer purses. I was growing accustomed to being thought of as the twins' mom and not as Corrine. Everyone was very cordial, and filled us in on what they knew about Stephen and Phillip, the runner and the musician, respectively. They'd read all the articles, they'd seen the news broadcasts, and they were eager to learn more. Before we got too far along, we all ordered. Salads for the ladies; the richest, creamiest pasta dishes for Doug and me.

While we waited, Doug started off by saying he wasn't sure what they wanted to know. I started in on one of our classic stories about Stephen not knowing where he was supposed to go to volunteer for a race. Doug took over halfway through, and by the time he got to the punch line, I sensed a change in the mood. They were laughing; some trying to politely hide it, others just letting it rip. Next I started in on a story of Phillip going on the Internet to look for people who would join his band. Late one night I answered the phone and heard an angry voice rising up from deep in the bowels of Texas. The man was demanding to speak to Phillip. When I told him my son was asleep, he grunted something and then said, "Your son! Ma'am, how old is the boy?"

"Seventeen."

"Good God Damn, Marlene!" I heard a ruckus on the other end of the line. "It's bad enough you want to run around behind my back, but you're gonna get your ass arrested for it."

Eventually I straightened things out with Tex, explaining that all the voice mail messages asking for his wife to meet with someone and to come to L.A. were the product of a teenage boy's rock and roll fantasies. Phillip was looking for a singer, not a lover.

Whether it was the martinis or our charm that disarmed them, I'll never know, but that story had all the Westlake parents laughing and high-fiving one another. As the meal went on, they requested more. I alternated between funny and sad, horrific and hilarious.

The Westlake Village couples shared a few stories of their own, some that had me in stitches, some that had me in tears, stories of torment and triumph—sometimes both of those simultaneously. I wasn't the only one who ended up crying that night. After the first few stories Doug and I shared, while we ate, I stopped and asked myself what my problem was.

These people were really no different from me. The circumstances of our lives were different in some regards, but what united us was the struggle we had in raising autistic children. By the end of the evening, I'd come to the conclusion that the Tarzana ladies and the Westlake Village parents weren't so different at all. They were both trying to escape something—one group behind platters of food, the other behind wool suits and Italian leather shoes. Who was I to judge? How long had I been in hiding? How long had I hid behind my fear and a belief that the haves and the have-nots always get treated according to their particular lot? We were all caretakers who needed to take better care of ourselves.

I felt bad about spending so much time thinking that I was better than those in the neighboring communities I referred to as yuppies because I wasn't the one who thought I was better than someone like me.

Autism didn't discriminate. It didn't pick and choose whom to plague and whom to pass over. Whether you lived in a gated community or a ghetto, it would find you; it knew the tricks to infiltrate the one and wasn't afraid of the other. Line all our kids up in a row, put the same tests in front of them, and you wouldn't be able to tell which one came from which side of the divide that I'd imagined for so long had separated us.

We stayed until closing time. I even indulged myself with a glass and a half of white wine—not the "correct" drink to pair with pasta, I realize, but it seemed appropriate to go against the grain, to mix things up a bit, to defy expectation. As Doug would say, "We kept it autistic," and we were rewarded for our efforts with a full heart.

If I was nervous about addressing small groups of autistic parents, imagine my trepidation when Hollywood came calling.

As a result of all the publicity that Stephen and Phillip received in the L.A. media, we were eventually approached by several different agents and other people in the entertainment business. They wanted to talk to us about the possibility of developing our story into a movie. At first, I was really hesitant to get involved. What would all this mean, and how would exposing ourselves to public scrutiny impact our lives? Would the movie exploit our situation and ultimately our cause? Even though I was willing to go out and spread the word about autism to groups of autistic parents, I wasn't sure that I was ready to let the whole world witness what our lives were like and have them question our motives for getting a dialogue started.

Of course, eventually the financial necessity won out over any qualms I had. We were paid a small initial fee of $5,000 by a woman named Beverlee Dean for the rights to our life story. We were thinking, if nothing else, that the money would help fund the boys' and Ali's college educations. We doubted anything would ever happen on the movie front, and if it did, we imagined that reaching and educating a larger audience would offset any personal feelings of embarrassment or exposure.

A month or so after signing on with Beverlee as our agent, she called to let me know that she had set up another meeting. This one was with a manager she'd met at a poker night a mutual friend hosted. The man's name was Joel Gotler, and he worked at the Artist's Management Group (AMG). At the time, I had no idea that AMG was one of the leading Hollywood agencies, and the name Michael Ovitz didn't mean a thing to me. Later I would come to understand that he was one of the most powerful men in Hollywood, first as the founder of AMG and later in several other capacities. I didn't understand the difference between an agent (Beverlee) and a manager (Joel Gotler) and didn't bother to ask. All I knew was that this man was someone who could help us get a movie made, and therefore he was someone we had to impress.

Once again, we loaded up the truck and headed to Beverly

Hills, the world of swimming pools and movie stars. When the kids first heard that we'd been contacted about selling our story to Hollywood, they had difficulty containing their excitement. Phillip and Stephen both thought they were going to be rich. In fact, I think they had both mentally begun spending their enormous fortune on video games; cars they weren't able to drive; and guitars, amplifiers, big-screen televisions, and nearly every other electronic gadget under the sun. Ali and Richard were equally thrilled, but a bit more pragmatic. They were hoping that we'd no longer have to worry about making ends meet, that there would be a steady and abundant supply of food and clothes.

Though I wanted to rein in the twins' enthusiasm, I knew I had to let them dream. I also wished Ali and Richard had more elaborate desires. I suspected that having autistic brothers had taken its toll on them, had made them more realistic, but that knowledge didn't give me any comfort. It was as if their capacity to expect the best had been diminished, the sharp edge of their imagination dulled, their vision of what might be possible foreshortened. Still, despite their less grandiose plans, they were excited about the opportunity.

We didn't take long to get ready. Stephen put on a pair of track pants and a T-shirt. Phillip dressed in a hand-me-down polo shirt from Doug. Somehow between the time he put it on and we got into the car, he managed to get a spaghetti stain all along its front. Richard was probably the most laid back of us all, clad in a pair of jeans and a sport shirt. For his part, my husband sported a mismatched suit jacket and pants, which he bottomed off with a pair of his work boots. Ali put on her best junior high chorus T-shirt, while I searched in vain to find a scarf to hide the vast expanse of my dark roots. With our vehicle registration paid and our insurance up to date, we were set. We were going to Hollywood!

The offices of AMG were unlike anything I was used to being in. It was as if we'd stepped out of our rustic ramshackle home into the pages of *Architectural Digest*. Joel's assistant greeted us, and she looked like she had just stepped out of the pages of *Vogue*. I thought that if this was someone who worked *behind* the scenes, just imagine how beautiful the people in front of the camera must be. We were led to a conference room. We took our seats around an enormous oval table and sank into the supple leather chairs. Phillip immediately began rocking his chair and Stephen scooted his up to the window to enjoy the view of the Hollywood hills and the valley beyond. I had stressed to everyone for a day in advance of the meeting how important it was that even if we didn't dress normally, we should act normally. That meant being on our best and most polite behavior. For Phillip, that meant no outbursts or verbal tics; for Stephen, that meant making eye contact, stating he was pleased to meet them, and thanking them for this opportunity. I knew I had nothing to worry about with Richard and Ali. I knew we were like billboards advertising how out of place we were, but we could at least mitigate that first impression by acting as if we knew what the heck we were doing there. As Doug had said, "Even if you've never done this kind of meet and greet, you can at least fake it like you have."

In a moment, we were joined by Joel and several of his associates, whose names went in one ear and immediately out the other. Joel was a distinguished-looking man in what I estimated to be his mid-forties. His appearance was deceiving. He carried himself with an effusively enthusiastic manner that had him alternating between sedate and needing to be sedated. After the introduction, a few awkward moments ensued. They wanted us to tell our story, and I started in. I was nervous, and stammered over a few brief remarks about Stephen's Miracle Run. He was still seated by the window, with his back to the rest of us. That distracted me, and I lost my place in the story.

"I'm hungry," Phillip stated, filling the void of silence.

"Well, we'll have to do something about that." Joel asked his assistant to get some snacks. She returned a moment later with a bowl of Goldfish Crackers. Phillip dipped into it and extracted a handful. If we were there to pitch a nature special on grizzly bears and their feasting on salmon returning to their spawning grounds, we were off to a great start. I sat and stared at my shoes.

"Where's the pizza?" Phillip asked, between and through a mouthful of severed Goldfish heads.

I looked up to see Doug clutching his chest, feigning a heart attack. I knew he was as nervous as I was. We couldn't help but feel we were being judged—that was the point of this meeting, after all—and our anxiety levels had risen throughout the day. Now, to have your kids behaving like they'd never been fed wasn't exactly how we'd envisioned the meeting proceeding. I had gradually grown accustomed to the idea that when we were in public, people were going to judge us. Whether or not Stephen and Phillip were autistic, that was going to happen. We lived in a place where most people had a lot of money and dressed like it. We didn't. We lived in a place where people drove cars that reflected their status. Their status was high; our status was low.

It was more difficult for me to accept that people were judging us because of the twins' condition. Over time, and particularly when the twins were finishing high school, that sense of being judged had diminished. For the most part, you would have thought that the boys were different but not disabled, that they lacked social polish—not that they had no social finish on them at all.

Still, this meeting was an entirely different animal. We weren't just being judged as normal or abnormal; we were being judged as worthy or unworthy. Would these people be willing to risk their professional reputations and millions of dollars on telling the story of our family? Would we prove worthy enough in their estimation so that our financial hardships could be wiped out? It was one thing to be judged while sitting in a movie theater with Phillip tic-ing away, but it was another to fall short of someone's expectations about whether you were worthy of *being* a movie. The possible financial boon loomed large.

Thankfully, Joel took charge before things spun dangerously out of control. He asked each of us in turn to describe how we lived, what our daily lives were like, how we had managed all those years. When it was Stephen's turn, he stood up, looked Joel squarely in the eyes, and said, "I'm going to the Olympics."

Joel leaned back in his chair and splayed his legs and arms. "I love it!"

He looked around the room at his associates. "Get TV in here! Get motion picture in here! Hell, get Robin in here!

Where is he? Anyone know? Get me Robin Williams right now. He'd be an idiot not to do this story."

I was sitting there wide-eyed and my mouth gaping. Doug was grinning like he was the village idiot, when all of a sudden, Phillip was seized by a physical tic that had him jumping and jiving in his seat. Every eye in the room was on him, and when his body stilled, he looked around at all of us, his brows furrowed in consternation. "Can I have more Goldfish?"

The room exploded with laughter and excited conversation. I couldn't keep track of what everyone was saying, but I recognized enthusiasm and a positive response. Over the tangle of voices and laughter, I heard the strains of a harmonica. Oh, shit. Phillip was at it again. We let him bring his harmonica, thinking it would serve as a kind of security blanket for him. Only when I looked at Phillip, he was chewing on Goldfish and mumbling something. I looked around to see where the music was coming from.

It was Joel. He was playing "Swing Low, Sweet Chariot." After he went through the first verse, Phillip joined him.

Later, when we were all back in the Suburban, Richard asked, "Do you think they liked us?"

"Oh, they liked us. They really liked us," I said. I looked in the rearview mirror at the smiling faces of my family. Phillip squirmed a bit and then produced a handful of Goldfish crumbs from his pants pocket. He held them out to his siblings. Ali's "Eww!" and Richard's scrunched-faced look of disgust were all the reply he needed. He shrugged and brought his hand to his mouth. Stephen looked at Phillip and smiled briefly before returning to his contemplation of the scene that rolled past.

They liked us, I thought again. They really liked us.

Get me Sally Field. She'd be an idiot not to do this story.

From not wanting to let the twins' teachers and other school personnel know about their diagnosis to "keeping it autistic" in a high-powered Hollywood mover and shaker's office is quite a journey, I know. That we could find some measure of acceptance in both places just by being ourselves was an enormous revelation. When you spend so much time in hiding, you lose a sense of who you really are. The bunker mentality you develop produces a kind of groupthink. I was proud of the work we were all doing with autism support groups, but we had to expand beyond that tight circle to the larger world outside of autism.

That didn't mean that we had to stop keeping it autistic. To the contrary, by keeping it autistic, we enlarged for ourselves, and hopefully for others, what it meant to have autism in one's life. By exposing ourselves to more and different sets of social interactions, we were helping the twins overcome the major deficit they had to deal with—their lack of social skills. We could have spent thousands of hours at home, talking ourselves blue in the face tutoring Phillip and Stephen about what Phillip referred to as "social graces," but unless the boys were out there in the real world, observing and learning for themselves, I don't believe they would have truly learned anything.

If I hadn't gotten out there and met Connie, Don, Doug, and all the other people who helped me better manage this thing called autism, I don't know if Phillip and Stephen would have been able to achieve everything they have so far and will in the future. I had to realize my own limitations in order to remove some of the limitations on the twins.

If nothing else, making the transition from recluse to advocate demonstrates the power of letting people into your life. For so many years, I insisted on going it alone and yet hated the loneliness and isolation that such a decision enforced. Looking back now, I realize how much of my life was lived amid the tension between opposing forces. Sometimes that tension lay within me, but other times the imagined "us against them" dichotomy became real.

I don't regret not opening up to everyone immediately, despite the headaches and heartaches that decision caused. In some ways I think I had to experience isolation, which allowed me the time and space to imagine what Phillip and Stephen were experiencing in their closed autistic world. By doing that, I got as close to being in their shoes as I ever could as an outsider in their world. And that allowed me to become fiercely devoted to the idea that they would not be denied the opportunity to be out in the world and among other people. If my experiences in my fortress of solitude hadn't been painful, I might have kept them in there with me. Like I said, I'm a slow learner, but as any parent might wish, my kids have benefited from my experiences and mistakes.

I don't want to leave you with the impression that opening yourself to the world by having your life story told in a television movie, by writing a book, or by telling your story to everyone you meet is going to lead you to bliss. It's not. There are still people out there who won't understand, who will judge, who will stare or turn away. The thing is, though, that that's their choice. By finally opening up and admitting the truth, I was able to make choosing one of the priorities in my life and, more important, in the lives of Phillip and Stephen. I can't control the choices that people make and how they respond to me or to them. All I can ever do is control how I react to their reactions. That doesn't mean that I don't get angry or frustrated sometimes; it just means that anger and frustration aren't my automatic default.

And to tell you the truth, I am stronger because of those judgmental looks, the stares, and the whispers. I had to develop a few calluses to toughen me for the work ahead. If I had reached out too soon and too often, I might not have been able to do the work that was necessary. I might not have been able to fight for my boys or their rights. Of course, one of the problems with forming calluses is that it makes it harder to feel not just the pain but any other sensation. For a while, I became comfortably numb, and because of that, I almost missed out on a life-changing moment. It took Stephen's Miracle Run to bring me out of that stupor. That's the thing—you can't let yourself become numb. Maybe talking about your story or hearing the experiences of others will be what keeps you strong and hopeful. But you have to be ready for it.

I no longer think of myself as judge, jury, and jailer of my life or my children's lives. I was finally able to let go and strike a balance between protecting and preventing.

Chapter Four

A Matter of Choice—
Learning to Pick My Battles

SINCE becoming an advocate for autistic children and families, I'm often asked about my decision to keep my kids in public schools. The answer is both simple and complex. The financial reality is that I couldn't afford to send the kids to a private school with programs for kids with special needs. I know that I could have pressed the school district to send Phillip and Stephen to a special program for kids with learning disabilities and other forms of special needs. In many ways, however, my first experience with the school district's efforts to provide an appropriate alternative education for the boys scared and scarred me. Their initial offer to send them off to a mental hospital so far from home clearly wasn't my idea of what the boys needed. Having them shuttled off to another location was an "out of sight, out of mind" solution that might have been easier for the school administrators but certainly wasn't going to do the boys much good.

With that as my initial experience in what the school district considered a suitable alternative, I thought it best to stick with the regular public school special education program. I'd clearly and emphatically expressed my opinion on the matter; in fact, I'd insisted that I get my way through threats, but that was out of character for me. I don't know if it was sheer desperation that prompted me to stand up so boldly to them, but it worked.

In general, though, I believe that the "walk softly and carry a big stick" approach is best. I knew that I couldn't continually antagonize the faculty, staff, and administration. I guess that learning I had allies in my personal life made me better understand that there's strength in numbers. If I could find people within the school system whom I could count on as being on my side, I'd be much better off dropping my absolute "us" against "them" mentality. Put another way, I realized that I needed more members on the "us" team in order for the fight to be fair.

As I said in the introduction, learning to be fierce but fair was one of the most important lessons I had to learn. I don't know if it is because I am a product of the 1960s, but the concept of fairness has always figured prominently in my life. I was an awkward youngster and an even more awkward adolescent, so I had to endure more than a little bit of teasing and abuse from classmates and peers. I could put up with that, but what bothered me far more than the taunting I received was the taunting I saw directed at my classmates and others. While

I could suffer in silence when I was mistreated, it tore me up inside to see anyone else put through what I considered to be torture. My feelings of outrage weren't confined to seeing other kids abused but animals as well.

Back then I wasn't always able to stand up for myself or for my peers; I think the pent-up frustration of those experiences served me well as the mother of twin autistic sons. Even though I'd allowed Larry to walk out on me and say some horrible things to me, I did fight back. Though we'd never been officially married, we'd been together long enough that I was able to file one of the first of the so-called palimony suits in California. I didn't really have the money to hire a lawyer, but I found a way to scrape enough together. What was right was right, and I was going to do everything I could to make sure that Ali and I were treated fairly.

As with many women, a lot of my insecurities and other issues surface in my romantic relationships, as they did with Larry. I was able to gain some measure of what I felt I deserved after the fact with him, but I certainly hadn't been proactive. I vowed that I would do better next time or avoid a next time completely. My relationship with Doug came as a complete surprise to me.

To cloud up matters even more, as time progressed and Doug and I grew closer, I had some real doubts about him and his suitability as a mate. In time, Doug asked me to move in with him. He had a place up on the hillside overlooking Malibu Lake. It was really little more than a cabin back then, what the Realtor in me would have referred to in a listing as "charming" and "rustic" and a bit of a fixer-upper to be sure. I suppose the same adjectives could have been applied to Doug and, truth be told, to me. In that sense, we made a good match.

I'd been seeing a therapist for a while, and when I told her about Doug, she was a bit skeptical, wondering if I was in a good enough place in my life that I could make sound judgments about men and relationships. In some ways, her words echoed my own thoughts. I didn't have a great track record when it came to selecting men. I'd come to doubt my own judgment, but something in my heart told me this time, with Doug, was different. Besides, I wouldn't be my mother's daughter if the therapist's words didn't get my back up a bit. I can be as stubborn as anyone when I want to be. I didn't let her dictate what I was going to do, but when I realized something about Doug and mentioned my suspicions to her, I knew I had to act.

Doug was working and doing well, but money was still tight. Each night when he came home from work, he would have a few beers. I didn't really see anything wrong with that at first, but over time, I noticed that six-packs, twelve-packs, and cases of beer were coming in and going out of the house with great regularity. I couldn't always say the same thing about the quantity and quality of the food that was entering and leaving the house. No matter how tight things were financially, we managed to have enough alcohol around to keep Doug's habit met. When I told my therapist about Doug's drinking, she told me that he was likely an alcoholic. I knew about Doug's drug-taking past, and when my therapist said that about Doug, all those visions of what kind of men you meet in bars that had been etched into my brain came to life in full Technicolor.

Oh my God. I was living with an alcoholic. I was exposing

myself and my kids to someone who could ruin our lives with his problem. I'd never been around drinkers myself, so my definition of what was normal or acceptable was so skewed from most people's sense of things that it took an outsider like my therapist to clue me in. I was disappointed in my failure to recognize what was going on and to trust my gut enough to have spoken up sooner. I'd commented on Doug's drinking a few times, dropped hints, but I was too timid and too unsure of myself to really confront him. Now my therapist was telling me that I had to. She was only reinforcing what I already knew. That didn't make it any easier.

What also contributed to not making things easier was that Doug was one of the kindest and most genuine people I'd ever met. Only a few months after we'd been seeing each other, Doug had done one of the nicest things any person had ever done for me up to that point. We'd met in the fall, and when the Christmas holiday rolled around, he was at the house I was renting. He commented on the absence of decorations. I told him that Larry had won them in the settlement of our palimony suit. He didn't celebrate the holiday himself, but for some reason he wanted them all. I couldn't afford a few presents and decorations, so we were going to go without a tree or any lights strung on the outside of the house.

I came home from work the next evening, and the house was ablaze with lights. A few evergreen trees that fronted the property were also spiraled in glowing bulbs. A few plywood cutouts of reindeer, a Santa Claus, and illuminated angels surrounding a crèche sat in the yard. A wreath hung from the front door, and a scotch pine tree stood leaning against the house, waiting to be brought inside. I found out from the kids that when they got home from school, Doug was on a ladder stringing lights. I was touched and a little chagrined. I knew he didn't have a lot of money either, and for him to go out and buy all this had to be a burden he didn't need to take on. When I thanked him, he relieved me of my worries. He'd gone home the night before and taken all the decorations and displays he'd had at his place down and brought them over to my place. He told me Christmas was for kids and family, and it didn't make any sense for him to have things up at his place where only he and maybe a neighbor or two could enjoy them.

After all we had shared, it would be painful to ask Doug to leave the house and, therefore, my life. However, I focused on the fact that I would be doing what I needed to do to protect my kids. I was concerned about Doug driving them anywhere, not knowing what state he was in. I knew that sometimes he drank in the morning, and who knew what went on at work or after. I knew the crews on the sets were hard-living, hard-drinking, party-boy types, who worked long hours and whose down-time mostly consisted of them downing drinks. I was upset with myself for not recognizing sooner or wanting to admit to myself the full extent of his drinking problem, for not seeing that some of Doug's charm, his outgoing and glib nature, was alcohol fueled. He was a great storyteller because he spent a lot of time in bars, listening to and sharing stories.

I took the Band-Aid approach when I got home from the therapist. I immediately went to Doug and told him that I had had enough of his drinking and that I wanted him out. I had enough to contend with, and the additional worry and fear his drinking produced in me were just too much to handle. I'd like to think I articulated it that clearly and dispassionately, but I know I didn't. I don't remember the exact words we exchanged, but the discussion got quite heated. All the kids were home, and as much as I knew that loud noises bothered the twins, and that seeing two adults arguing wasn't good for any of them, Doug and I both got emotional.

Stephen and Richard were both crying. Neither of them wanted Doug to leave. How could I do this to them? Boys need a man around, and I'd screwed up again and brought the wrong man around. Well, not the *wrong* man, but one who was broken in a way that I alone couldn't fix.

Standing in the kitchen of Doug's house, my bare feet digging into the weathered rough-hewn oak floor, my face red with anger and embarrassment and disappointment and sadness, I experienced a moment that most mothers would be unlikely to describe as transcendent. From out of the corner of my eye, I saw Phillip stand up and take a few steps toward us. "I'm on my mom's side," he declared. "You're a bum. You should get the hell out of here." He planted his feet and pointed toward the door like an archer lining up his arrow.

With the exception of Stephen's quiet sniffling, the room was silent. Doug raised his hands like he was being arrested. He nodded a few times and backed out of the room. This was his place; we were the ones who should have gotten the hell out of there, but he left for the night.

When you live with autism, you find your victories wherever you can. Having your preteen son step up and defend you like Phillip did was one of those good-bad autism moments. Up to that point, I'd never heard Phillip swear. He'd used the word "Hell" in talking about the geographical opposite of "Heaven," but he'd never used the word in anger. He'd never voiced his opinion and his belief in me in that way before. I knew Phillip loved me, just as I knew the other kids did, but this brave act to defend my honor left me with a lump in my throat the size of a potato. Sure, I was upset about what had taken place between Doug and me, and I was upset with myself for causing such an emotional scene that resulted in Phillip's outburst, but I was also pretty damned proud to see my son standing up for me.

The irony of the whole situation didn't really hit home until the next morning. I had enjoyed having Doug around because he was able to teach the boys what it took to be a man in ways that I as a woman simply couldn't. The success of those efforts was demonstrated most clearly by having Phillip remove that same man from the house. There was something archetypal and mythic about the whole thing, but I couldn't and didn't want to consider all the implications of it. I simply wanted to enjoy the fact that out of the misery of my confrontation with Doug, Phillip had experienced one of those pivotal transformative moments from childhood to adolescence.

Fortunately for all of us, the eviction only lasted a few days. Doug and I talked things over, and he agreed to stop drinking. He went to AA a few times, but basically quit cold turkey all on his own. He hasn't had a drink since. I find that remarkable, and I'm proud of him for doing it and proud of myself for the small role I played in making it happen. Even in the first few months of Doug's sobriety, I noticed a change in him and in me. I was certainly more relaxed, since I had one less thing to worry about, but I also felt better about myself for demanding what I knew to be right. Again, I was learning that some good things could happen if I opened my mouth and communicated. Granted, I could have taken a more adult and better communicative approach than throwing him out and calling it quits, but I didn't have very many examples of good communication to draw from. I'd handle things differently today, but back then, speaking up at all was a big deal. A few months after we resolved the drinking issue, on Valentine's Day 1995, Doug proposed. We married on New Year's Eve of that year and remain happy together today.

Along with the obvious change in my relationship with Doug, I noticed a long-lasting change in Phillip. After confronting Doug, Phillip began talking even more. This wasn't his usual chatter; instead, he became much more expressive about his emotions. It seemed as though he felt freer to tell us what he was really thinking and experiencing. For a long time I suspected that the boys had far richer emotional lives than what they ever expressed to me. The incident with Doug gave me my first real insight into the depth and genuineness of those emotions. Hearing Phillip say he was on my side made up for any token of affection, any Hallmark mementos, flowers, or boxes of candy I might have received if the boys hadn't been autistic and had known to shower me with such. I don't know if Phillip understood that he was being heroic, but I knew he was.

Phillip's standing up for me and becoming more expressive emotionally helped me better understand that they were progressing, if not at the "normal" rate then at their own pace.

For so long, I'd wanted them to keep up developmentally and educationally. Recognizing that they were progressing at their own rate was the first crack in the mirror image of other kids I compared them to. It would take some time, but eventually I'd fully understand how arbitrary some of those externally imposed timelines and checklists of behaviors and achievement are. When I looked at my own experiences, I saw that I hadn't exactly conformed to the norm, either. I was still learning a lot about how to deal with people and situations, so it was unrealistic for me to expect that Stephen and Phillip were on par with their classmates and age group.

I see a definite parallel between their education and maturation and my own. I had to confront so many unknowns and mysteries myself.

As the parent of a child with any kind of special need, I think you become more sensitive to the limitations that other people want to place on your kids. I'm sure parents of so-called normal kids experience some of this, but I don't think they do so as acutely. At first, I saw these limitations as most people do—things that would prevent, restrict, or prohibit them from doing certain things. The issues, then, were more black and white.

I've since come to think that the limitations are more like differences than prohibitions. It isn't so much that Phillip and Stephen can't do certain things because of their autism, but that they will do those things and experience life in a way that is different from what most people do and experience. It's not my role in this life to decide for anybody what is right or wrong, better or worse. It's my job to understand, and now I'm hoping to make other people understand that while autistic children and adults do experience the world in ways that are different from the norm, that doesn't mean that they shouldn't be allowed to have the same opportunities as other kids and adults.

Simply put, we must give autistic kids the chance to do the things that every nonautistic kid gets the chance to do by creating as nonrestrictive an environment as possible. Don't say, "Because we know that Stephen or Phillip won't experience this event in the same way as most of the other children, we don't believe that they should have the opportunity to be a part of that event."

What riles me about that attitude, which I did adopt on too many occasions, is that no two people ever experience anything in exactly the same way. I realize that there are certain parameters that create the boundaries of normal, and we need those for a society to function, but we're not talking about autistic kids like Phillip and Stephen doing something illegal or immoral. I am also highly sensitive to the idea that the boys' opportunities shouldn't interfere with the opportunities of other kids. I know that at times they were disruptive in class, especially when they were very young and the transition to school was so difficult for them. As they got older, those disruptions weren't a factor. On the one hand, I didn't want other kids' lives and experiences to be encroached on unnecessarily by the twins; on the other hand, I didn't want my kids to be shortchanged in any way because of other people and their perceptions of how a distraction might be defined.

All this is to say that I firmly believe that it was important, and not just financially expedient, for the twins to go to a mainstream school. I realize that in some cases of very low functioning autistic children, this isn't possible. I also understand that for some parents, homeschooling is preferable. Whenever I'm asked about homeschooling, my response is that if it is at all possible to avoid homeschooling, then parents should opt for mainstream schools, be they private or public. More than anything else, I believe that our exposing of Phillip and Stephen to many different people, experiences, and settings contributed to their overcoming the major deficit that autistics face—their different approach to social interaction.

You will have to face some obstacles when trying to get your autistic kids to be able to fully participate in class or school activities. For example, in the first grade, all the parents were invited to an assembly. Each of the grade levels was going to perform a song. I was thrilled. Even at that age, Phillip loved music. The assembly started with the fourth graders. They paraded on stage and stood in rows while the music teacher led them in a rendition of some song I've long since forgotten the name of. Proud parents snapped photos. The same thing happened for the third and second graders. When the first graders marched onto the auditorium stage, I craned my neck to see around the abundantly tall man in front of me, and tried to see where Stephen and Phillip were. Even if no one had been in front of me, I wouldn't have been able to spot my sons.

They weren't up there.

Someone in his or her infinite wisdom either decided to exclude or had simply failed to include the special education students. I decided to do something about that. I can play the guitar and sing a little, so I called the school to ask if anyone objected to my coming to the special education classes to teach music.

I had a great time doing that, and I know the kids appreciated it. They even got to perform in front of the whole school at their own assembly. Ideally, they wouldn't have had to opt for separate but equal treatment, but at least it was a start. The other thing that I learned from this experience is that instead of just complaining, I offered a solution. Even better, I was able to provide the solution to the school at no cost to them. I've worked with enough people over the years in a variety of situations—professionally, personally, and as an advocate for autistics—to know that complaints eventually deafen ears. Solutions open minds and offer you entrée into places you might not otherwise gain access to.

Unfortunately, this attitude toward inclusion didn't carry over from first grade into second grade. In the second grade, the boys weren't allowed to attend several field trips. Instead, they had to sit in the office for four hours while their peers enjoyed some kind of enrichment activity. I was told that the twins needed to complete their regular classwork, but I suspected that something else motivated that decision.

I suppose that it was a question of how much time and attention the school could focus on the twins; I understood then and now that public education has its limitations for most students. I figured that if the school wasn't always going to go out of its way to make sure my sons were treated fairly, then the least they could do was to make sure that Phillip and Stephen were treated humanely. Because they failed the fair and equitable test, I was suspicious that they weren't doing everything they could to ensure that the boys were safe physically and emotionally. For that reason, I frequently left work to spy on the boys. I knew that they had recess at ten thirty in the morning, and I would take a break and do a drive-by to check on them.

The recess area was just off the parking lot, a stone and pea gravel rectangle with a few pieces of playground equipment and at the far end basketball hoops with backboards made from some kind of steel mesh. The basketball court was where most of the older boys hung out, as far as they could get from the playground equipment and all the associations with being a kid. Watching the interactions of all the kids, or lack of interaction in some cases, I was reminded of the Venn diagrams I had to create in high school algebra. We had to draw circles that contained all the possible answers to some problem. Sometimes the circles overlapped, including one set or even an individual number inside more than one circle so that those numbers were a subset of the other numbers in the adjacent circle. While the grade levels and the genders weren't segregated into discrete groups, I did notice that other groups formed and staked out a specific territory, like those numbers in a single circle. Only occasionally would the circles overlap and members from different groups commingle.

I would see Phillip standing on the edge of one or another of those circles, his face expectant, hopeful. He'd take a few tentative steps into one of the circles, be subsumed into it, and then he'd be shot out of it, his expression changed to panic-stricken. At first, I couldn't tell what had forced him out of the interior, but over time I witnessed enough repetitions of the same set of actions to see some of the boys pushing him, slapping at him, their laughter and derision a potent fuel combusting and sending Phillip careening out of their orbit. I'd try to note the faces and clothes of the ones physically coming into contact with Phillip, but it was often difficult to distinguish one pair of shorts or jeans and T-shirt or surfer shirt from another. I'd call

the school and speak with the principal or his assistant to let
them know that Phillip was being bullied and they needed to
be more vigilant. I also reported that the older boys were stealing the twins' jackets and tossing them on the school's roof.
Nothing came of my reports, except I learned how kind and
patient the janitors were.

As the year progressed, my understanding of the situation
advanced. I no longer mentally pictured those Venn diagrams;
instead, I saw Phillip as a virus attacking and then being repelled
by a cell. He could penetrate the membrane only briefly before
being shunted away. In my mind, Phillip wasn't harmful like a
virus, but I assumed that's what those kids thought. Phillip was
something foreign and posed a kind of threat, more dangerous
than girl cooties or some such thing. I saw in Phillip's desire to
belong and subsequent rejection his future writ large. Gregarious by nature but crippled by his inability to express himself flu-
ently and understand the subtle nuisances of elementary school
social mores, Phillip was eternally the frustrated wannabe.

If Phillip was a pesky invading organism within the body of
his peers, then Stephen was a comet, or asteroid, or some other
bit of space junk that sometimes randomly and sometimes in a
fixed orbit passed by that body of peers at a great distance. He
would frequently be found seated at or sidling along the fence
that bounded the periphery of the recess area. I'd sometimes see
him walking with his fingers lightly brushing the chain link, as
though he were playing some vast stringed instrument. I liked
to imagine that he was picking up some vibration, some pleasant sound that soothed his agitated nerves.

Phillip would tell me that he would frequently be sent out

into the hallway with his desk to spend class time separated from his classmates. He was disruptive, I knew, his more frequent and boisterous vocalizations both a disturbance and an omen. Later, when he was diagnosed with Tourette's syndrome, I wasn't surprised but merely saddened by the additional burden he would have to bear. Though some people found Stephen's silence disquieting and alien, it served him well in class. As long as he was quiet, he could blend into the bland background, be as unnoticeable and inoffensive as the beige walls. Eventually, I would find out that Stephen was crying and getting as agitated as Phillip was—he just didn't tell me about the incidents that incited him.

At the end of second grade, the administrators decided that it was best to separate Phillip and Stephen. They felt that the boys were mimicking one another and that if one acted out, the other would repeat and amplify the behavior. They were too disruptive together, and having two autistic boys in a single class was too much for any one teacher to handle. To put them in separate classes at the same school likely wouldn't work, either. They'd know that the other was nearby, and their awareness of being separated would be more acute, their anxiety heightened. In my heart and mind, I knew this was wrong, but I was so exhausted from working two jobs; trying to intervene in ensuring their safety; calling to request meetings; having those meetings repeatedly put off, canceled, rescheduled; and generally feeling like Sisyphus pushing that rock up the hill that I agreed to the switch.

The twins had not been separated for more than a few hours at a time their entire lives, and they did have the kind of bond that most twins have. They always seemed calmer and more at ease when they were together, but my perceptions seemed out of line with what the teachers and administrators were telling me. I thought a change in venue might do Stephen some good, stimulate him in a way. Without Phillip around to be his voice, he might become more expressive himself.

Autistic people are very much driven by routine, so I had to weigh the negative influence of disruption against the fresh-start benefits. What surprised me was that Phillip seemed to fare much worse than Stephen. One day I got a call that Phillip was crying and screaming and clearly out of control. I had to leave work to go pick him up. I assumed he was in his classroom, so I walked down the hallway and asked a student at random if he knew where Phillip Morgan's class was. The young boy took a step back from me and screwed his face up in disgust. "That kid? Yeah, I know where is. There's something really wrong with that freak."

I felt like I'd been slapped. My cheeks flushed, and I rocked back on my heels. Fighting tears, I walked down the hall in the direction the boy had pointed. Why such anger? I know that I was hypersensitive and protective of the twins, but there was a note of genuinely vehement disgust in that boy's tone that shocked me. If he could direct such a strong emotional reaction toward me, a stranger, what might he be capable of saying or doing to Phillip? As much as I was concerned about the quality of the education they were receiving, I was even more worried about their safety.

If it hadn't been for Stephen's very positive experience at White Oak Elementary School under the care of his second grade teacher, Jill Johnson, I might have given up entirely on the idea of public schooling for the twins.

Jill possessed the traits necessary to be a successful special education teacher—patience and determination—but she also had a degree of empathy and compassion that far exceeded those other traits. Jill was a nurturer, and Stephen thrived under her watchful eye. Even though he was only officially in her classroom in the second grade, she took Stephen under her wing and allowed him to spend time in her classroom before, at times during, and after school in grades third through fifth. What Jill demonstrated, more than anyone else had to that point, was that with the application of a more liberal dose of nurturing, autistic kids like Stephen could succeed academically and not be a distraction or nuisance. She showed that by reaching out to Stephen, he was willing and able to extend his hand in return. From the beginning, Stephen was an excellent student. He was probably more demanding of himself than the so-called experts were. Every semester, each of the twins received an Individualized Education Program (IEP) that laid out the goals the staff had for him based on their evaluation of his performance and data gathered from other assessment instruments.

Looking back now, I realize that I could have, and probably should have, done more to make Stephen's and Phillip's time in school more valuable. I'd receive copies of their IEPs and was often horrified by what I saw there: "By the end of the year, Stephen will be able to write and correctly punctuate a complex sentence." Well, I knew that Stephen could already do that. I'd read some of the things he'd written that weren't part of his schoolwork, and they demonstrated a mastery of language and a degree of imagination that were well beyond his chronological age and grade level.

I struggled with the notion of just letting this underestimation of his and Phillip's skills pass. In retrospect, I should have been more tenacious about challenging the presumptions made. One of the reasons I let the IEPs stand as written was that I didn't have enough confidence in my own abilities to challenge them—that slow-learner thing came creeping in again. After all, these people were the professionals, the ones with the degrees in education, and I was a single working mother with a degree in accountancy.

I realize now that I was perfectly capable of holding those people accountable, but another factor weighed heavily on my decisions. I was exhausted—from having to work two jobs just to keep the family fed to monitoring the twins' safety—and I wasn't able to be the most passionate advocate for my kids' education as I would have liked to be. That would have been like taking on another full-time job, and I just didn't have it in me.

Also contributing to that exhaustion was the constant nagging of self-doubt about my capabilities as a mother. I was a bit naive back then, but I wasn't so innocent to believe that my kids were being teased solely because of their autism. I knew that the upper-middle-class Agoura Hills kids my children attended school with dressed much nicer than my kids did. The only designer label duds we managed to afford were hand-me-downs that we scrounged up on a shopping trip to the Goodwill Thrift Store.

I also understood that one of the hallmarks of many autistic individuals is that they tend not to be scrupulous about their grooming and hygiene. We struggled with both those issues with Stephen and Phillip, and even today they both have written reminders that prompt them to shave daily, brush their teeth, and perform other routine tasks that most of us don't need reminding of. I was acutely aware of their fashion and hygiene shortcomings back then, but I was smart enough to realize that I had to pick my battles. I could have spent valuable hours each morning making certain that every article of clothing the boys wore was wrinkle-free, fresh smelling, and suitably au courant to suit the taste and sensibilities of their peers.

It was either let it go, or use the money I spent on food, just enough mind you to keep them from going hungry each night, to make certain that they were shod in the latest from Vans or Nike or whatever brand was the current "in" shoe. I know that sounds a bit bitter, but maybe you'll understand the dilemma I faced better when you consider that I was more concerned about being certain that the boys were speaking and learning as well as their physical health than I was about their appearance. Believe me, I understood that proper grooming and hygiene were essential social skills, and I did what I could to assist them in learning those fundamentals. That said, I had to keep things in perspective. That wasn't always easy.

I also came to realize that there were some battles that weren't worth fighting, and I'd have to redefine what "winning" meant for the boys and for me.

Believe me, it wasn't always an easy decision. I've told you about the teasing, the jacket stealing, and the like. As the boys made progress, some of those troubles still cropped up. I keep returning to this point about participation and inclusion because I think it is crucial to understand that the belief that autistic people choose to isolate themselves from others is, based on my experiences with the boys, a myth. Phillip's experiences help to shed some light on this issue and how complicated it all gets.

He wanted to play on the local youth league soccer team. He saw that many of his classmates and peers were playing, and he came to me to say that he wanted to join the team. Verbalizing his desires was an important step, as was his wanting to be included with a group, so I wanted to honor his wish. I learned who the coach was and called him. As I usually did, I thought it important to be the teacher in this case. I didn't want Phillip to show up at practice and have his behavior or demeanor surprise the coach. I didn't think it was fair to Phillip or to the coach. I explained who I was and why I was calling. I filled him in a little bit on how Phillip's autism might affect him and how he might sometimes behave. I didn't paint a rosy or a bleak picture. I told him as honestly as I could what he might see and hear from Phillip. The coach listened patiently, asked a few other questions about Phillip, very neutral demographic data-type questions—height, weight, age—before he told me that he didn't think it was a good idea that Phillip play. He made a move toward suggesting the issue of liability and insurance and all that, but I cut him off. I knew that wasn't the issue at all, simply a convenient excuse he could use to make his decision look as if it weren't personal but rather a school policy.

I didn't want Phillip to be associated with someone like that anyway. Phillip was about eight or nine at the time, and I don't think his presence would have been a distraction or a detriment to the team. I have no way of knowing if this guy was a gung-ho, win-at-any-cost kind of coach, but to my mind, with eight- or nine-year-olds, soccer is not a life-or-death proposition. You let the kids run around and have some fun. I didn't dwell on that rejection for too long. I didn't really have the time or energy to fight that same battle on yet another front.

Phillip also wanted to join the Cub Scouts. The den leader was genuinely sympathetic to our desire to have Phillip be included. When he asked about overnight camping trips and what accommodations would have to be made, we both realized that given Phillip's need for routine and his fears of lightning, loud noises, and other things, it probably wasn't wise for him to go on those trips without someone to supervise him directly. I couldn't possibly take on that task in addition to everything else, so I declined to enroll him. That seemed to be the reasonable thing to do.

Later, Stephen wanted to join the Scouts, and I took him to the troop in Tarzana, about twenty miles south of Malibu Lake. The troop leader took a look at Stephen, took a look at me, asked Stephen a few questions to which he offered no response, and then told me that my son wouldn't be a "good fit." I'd heard that term before when an employer was talking about a potential employee or when a homebuyer decided against a particular home, but this was the Scouts we were talking about. All-American virtues and morals and upstanding citizenry and all that. I got the "I wouldn't stand in your way, but if he were my son..." line and could see the rest of the handwriting and hand wringing on the wall. I walked away—in my mind, a reasonable response to an unreasonable reaction.

One of the great things about dealing with rejection is that you learn to be adaptable and self-reliant—both things that the Scouts teach. Instead of being formally enrolled in any of the programs, I, and later Doug, created our own Scouting program for the boys. They learned how to tie knots, build a campfire, canoe, and behave ethically. That was all good and fine, but I still really believed that learning those things in a vacuum, without the socializing aspects of having their fellow Scouts around them, diminished their experience in some way. Still, what we learned was to be flexible, and when we couldn't get others to help us, we would take on the tasks ourselves. Scouting is all about becoming self-reliant and trustworthy, and in those situations when we sensed we couldn't really trust others, we trusted ourselves to come up with alternative solutions.

In retrospect, I realize I could have raised a big stink and gotten Phillip and Stephen accepted into soccer, the Cub Scouts, and other programs. That's the thing, though. I could have *gotten them accepted*. That doesn't mean that the other boys or the adults running the program would have accepted them as truly part of the group. I couldn't force people to make the choices I wanted them to make; all I could do was try to provide the twins with all the opportunities I could and make other arrangements when the cost-benefit ratio wasn't in their favor.

Put another way, I could have won a lot of battles like these, but the casualty count would have been too high. In that sense, I wouldn't really have been winning anything.

Somehow we muddled through it all. By the time Stephen and Phillip entered Canyon Middle School, what once felt like a crisis now seemed normal. Human beings are amazingly adaptable and malleable, and the pounding we'd all taken seemed to have collectively beaten us into a tempered sword. If I'd known back then what a plowshare was, maybe I could have thought of us in even more biblical terms. All I know is that I felt like a draft horse, tugging a heavy plow behind me. I didn't yet know what kind of yield the crop I'd planted would produce. I just struggled on, hoping the plagues that were visited upon us would cease, that somehow we'd make it to the promised land. Little did I know that in ways large and small, our story would have, if not a Hollywood ending, then certainly a Hollywood middle.

Before we got to Hollywood, however, we'd have to deal with high school. Unfortunately, we discovered a recurring pattern of infrequent but frustrating instances of exclusion.

Agoura High did not want its special education students to take the SAT test. I was told that it wouldn't be appropriate for Stephen or Phillip to take it. When pressed for a further explanation of the reasons behind this, I was given vague statements about blows to their self-esteem, the adverse effects of taking a test in a high-pressure high-stakes environment, and a few other things that seemed to fly in the face of Stephen's success in the classroom. I could understand that Stephen's past history of taking less-than-excellent results very poorly might mean he'd act out inappropriately. When I placed that possibility and whatever damage that might do to his self-esteem on one side of the scale and placed the damage being done if he wasn't being encouraged to go to college and take *the* test that admissions officers used to grant or deny entrance to their institutions, I saw far more harm in the latter than in the former. I tried to find out some information on how I could sign them up for the test, but that proved difficult and time consuming. Also, self-doubt crept in. What if taking the test and not doing well not only prevented them from getting into a college or university but also made them doubt their own abilities? Stephen's refuse-to-quit attitude was wonderful, but the high standards he set for himself were also another obstacle he had to overcome.

Ultimately, what convinced me that I was tilting at another windmill was attending College Night at the high school. I'd learned about it indirectly from a colleague. None of Stephen's or Phillip's teachers or their guidance counselor had suggested we attend. I knew that getting angry and ranting and raving (never my style) at being snubbed wouldn't do us any good, so I just showed up. Lots of colleges and universities sent representatives to the school. They were all seated at different tables in the library and the cafeteria. They had identification placards tented in front of them, and glossy four-color brochures set in neat stacks showing their smiling diverse students at various locations on campus. I thought it was wonderful that such a wide array of the human species was attending each of the schools. The representative wheelchair-bound or white-cane-carrying student was pictured there as well, a fully integrated member of the student body with the same "so happy to be here" smile as the nondisabled students.

Parents and students were lined up near each of the tables, waiting to ask questions of the representatives. Stephen and I got in one of the shorter lines. Chapman University was a smaller liberal arts college in Orange, California. Its brochure touted its small class sizes and personalized attention. The campus recruiter was a licorice black young woman with braided and bejeweled hair. As she spoke with the parent in front of me, I could hear her lilting African accent. When it was my turn, I introduced myself and shook her hand. I told her that I only had one question: What kind of accommodations does the school make to assist autistic students? Immediately her face became a mask of panic. She quickly shed that and replaced it with a smile. I figured she was embarrassed to admit that she didn't know the answer.

"I don't believe we have any special programs for them."

"I don't mean special programs. I mean what do you do to help monitor their progress, help them to fit in socially."

"As far as I know, the question has never come up before."

I thanked her and got in line at a half-dozen other tables during the course of the evening. Each time I asked a variation of the same question, and each time I got a variation of the same look of panicked puzzlement and chagrin. As far as I was able to determine, none of these schools had even considered the possibility that autistic students might be enrolling. They made accommodations for all kinds of physical impairments but had never been confronted with this kind of disability before. Each of the people I spoke with was very gracious and asked the appropriate questions about Stephen and marveled at his ability and success. They wished me well, handed me a brochure, and said that I could contact the student services people to get further information.

I was used to having to blaze certain trails, and as discouraging as it was not to be able to have a ready-made program that I could slot Stephen and Phillip into, I was glad to be checked back into Reality Hotel. We'd been enjoying so much success on so many fronts that bumping up against this kind of barrier produced a familiarly uncomfortable sensation. It also made me realize that without SAT scores, it would be almost impossible for a college or university to evaluate Stephens' or Phillip's candidacy for admission. If they didn't have the kinds of programs that would help acclimatize the twins to life on a college campus, even if the boys did live at home and attend one nearby, they'd still require some kind of provisions to ease their transition and integration into the mainstream. Knowing that the SAT issue was just one of a series we'd have to face in order to get them into college, I dropped my pursuit of alternative testing solutions. I never, however, gave up on the idea of them attending college.

They'd both expressed a strong desire to go. In fact, I don't think they ever considered any other option but attending college. I'd gone, their biological father had gone, and we placed a high value on education. Richard had joined the Navy partially because of the educational benefits he received. The question was, were any of us really prepared at that point in time to do everything it would take to make that eventuality an immediate reality?

One of the most important lessons we had to learn along the way was that we should never do anything to thwart the twins' ambitions. I've often been asked if Stephen wanted to run on his own or if that was something we encouraged (and what I really think was being implied was that we'd forced him). The answer is unequivocally that Stephen developed that interest on his own. All you have to do is take a look at Doug or me, or any other members of the family, to know that a rigorous sport like cross-country running or even track isn't something we are involved in ourselves. I had to learn a lot about running and nutrition and other related aspects of fitness long after Stephen undertook his mission. Similarly, we never discouraged either Phillip or Stephen from attempting things they thought they'd enjoy. Before settling on cross-country, Stephen had tried working on dance committees and joining the political debate club. Phillip came to his interest in music on his own, and he had his own forays into other areas as well.

While we'd never support or advocate efforts to do anything dangerous or inevitably harmful, we've given the boys the freedom to choose their interests and pursuits in the same way we did with Richard and Ali. We always had financial constraints to be concerned with, but we would sacrifice in other areas in order to make up for any shortfall caused by our kids' pursuit of some interest. We supported Stephen's and Phillip's desire, their right, to do all the things their nonautistic peers did.

I'll admit that we probably weren't as well prepared and on top of every issue regarding their attending college as we might have been. Thanks to all kinds of grants and scholarships, I managed to get a college degree. I knew the kinds of resources out there and available to students like me. I tried to do some fact-finding about support for the boys, but knowing that the environment they'd be entering into might not be the best for them or the most welcoming, we backed off on our pursuit down those avenues. Here's where the real lesson came in.

As much as we wanted Phillip and Stephen to fit in and to have the same kinds of experiences as any other teen, we realized after a while that they didn't have to do everything according to the same timetable as their peers. We could have the same expectation—they will go to college—but that didn't mean that they had to enroll right after finishing high school, get a degree in four years, and start work in their chosen field immediately upon graduation. That might be the norm, but that didn't mean it was realistic for the twins.

I remember a conversation I had with one of Phillip and Stephen's teachers. We were just talking about education generally and not about special education students. She said that based on her experience, too many kids went to college without really being ready for it academically or even socially. They weren't mature enough. They were just rolling along the assembly line, urged on by the school and their parents to fill in a slot. Then they got to college, did the whole partying thing, and put themselves at risk academically. Some flunked out, some got not-so-politely asked to leave, but the majority muddled through the transition and eventually turned things around and graduated. She thought the system was inefficient and harmful to a lot of kids.

She didn't like the kind of arbitrary "you must do this by then" guidelines and expectations that were being placed on kids. She said she also saw a similar phenomenon in high school. Because kids had to be there, they didn't really put forth the effort they might if they really wanted and needed to be there. I think that because Stephen and Phillip knew the kind of effort it took to get them into the public schools, because they wanted to prove they belonged, they were more highly motivated than most.

I'm not an expert on the educational system for mainstream kids, but what this teacher was saying made sense to me in terms of not forcing the issue of timelines. We all had to learn to be patient and let things come to us at the appropriate moment and not get too anxious if they didn't. I think it's inter-esting that much of our thinking about college and the boys' future coincided with our education about the film industry.

We had to learn to be patient with that process as well; we had to understand that no exact timeline existed to measure the progress of the project from concept to screen. There was what we all hoped for, and there was reality. I think that for any par-ent of an autistic child, it's coming to understand that the devel-opmental delays that I experienced with Stephen and Phillip (their not talking until much later) are the new normal. Find-ing that difficult balance between acceptance and resignation took me a long, long time. If nothing else, I hope that relat-ing our experiences will help parents struggling with the diag-nosis understand that many of the guideposts that we come to measure development are arbitrary, especially once autistic kids move into their teens.

I understand and agree that certain markers—language acquisition, crawling and walking—have certain age parame-ters associated with them. I don't disagree with that. There's sound research to back up the desirability of having your child meet those "deadlines." But what I had to keep in mind is that those weren't really deadlines at all. I couldn't stumble into the pitfalls of rigid thinking. The boys were exceptional in the strictest and loosest interpretations of the word. They were exceptions to the rules. One of the delicate dances we all had to learn the steps to was how to accommodate those elements of their condition that made them exceptions to the rule and yet not base our judgments or expectations of them completely out-side the norms established for nonautistic kids. I don't have any easy answers for parents. I can't put large footprints down on the floor showing the exact steps to take. That would be contradictory to my belief in being flexible. All I can do is relate to you our experiences, missteps and all, and let you decide how you feel most comfortable moving forward.

For several reasons, including a mixed stew of those above, we didn't pursue getting Phillip and Stephen into college the summer following their graduation from high school. We needed to do a bit more homework. The twins were accepting more speaking engagements and helping with the planning of the fundraising race hosted by the autism awareness foundation we had just formed, and we all needed a bit of a break from everything. We would regroup, give the boys some time to adjust to the idea of no longer being in the familiar environment of high school, and examine their options. As much as we sometimes had to battle with the public school system, it was a question of dealing with the devil we knew versus the devil we didn't.

One of the other hallelujahs in our life was a tutor who came to our home. Her name was Barbara Mona, and she was employed by the Las Virgenes School District. I was incredibly grateful for her presence in our house. Phillip missed quite a few days of school. There were times when he had taken so much Haldol and Thorazine to treat his symptoms that we could barely rouse him from his sleep. The first time Ms. Mona showed up, Phillip hadn't been in class for a couple of days. She brought all his books, papers, and even pens. They sat down at the table, and as soon as they did, Phillip's tics kicked in. We'd grown so accustomed to them that we didn't really notice. I had gotten home from work and was in the kitchen fixing dinner, and I looked over to see Ms. Mona sitting there with Stephen while tears ran down her cheeks.

I took a few steps toward her, my heart aching. She kept teaching until one tear landed on the notebook she'd set in front of the two of them. "Oops! Phillip, I'm sorry. I have a small cold." She reached into her purse and took out a package of tissues.

"Open your history book to page 145 and begin reading to me."

Phillip started reading, his head tossing from side to side and bobbing up and down. Ms. Mona sat wiping her eyes and blowing her nose. She came over every other day to work with Phillip. We bought her a flowery box of tissues and set it on the table for her before she arrived.

One day, Phillip woke up sneezing, with a runny nose and a slight fever. "I think I caught Ms. Mona's cold." This was one time I was grateful that Phillip's autism made it difficult for him to accurately read some social cues.

In time, Ms. Mona asked me if it would be okay if she took Phillip out to lunch. This was in the summer just before Phillip started his senior year. The district paid Ms. Mona to work with Phillip even when school wasn't in session. I was concerned about letting Phillip go with her, but Phillip's pleading eyes made my decision easy. She would let Phillip pick the place. She said that lunch out was a reward for his hard work. I knew that Ms. Mona had a hidden agenda besides wanting to motivate Phillip to work hard. Agoura Hills had gotten to know Stephen through his running; she wanted people to get to know Phillip Morgan. She wanted them to see him, tics and all.

Just as Phillip's senior year was about to begin, Ms. Mona

made an announcement. "Phillip is ready for his last year in school. It's time for him to get a job. I've found one for him at the Agoura Hills Library."

I nearly fell out of my chair. Was this woman nuts? A library? Wasn't that a place where people went to read, to study, to find a quiet place? How did she expect a kid with Tourette's syndrome not to create an enormous spectacle of himself and disturb all the patrons? Phillip, of course, was thrilled with the idea. He loved the library, and getting paid to spend time there was a double bonus. Still, I didn't want to subject him to the disappointment of getting the job and then being told in a day or so that it wasn't working out. Better to let him be disappointed without the failure added in.

I caved in. Again. Phillip went to work after school. On day two, I was at home when the phone rang. I looked at the clock. Phillip would have been at the library for an hour or so. My heart sank. This was it. I picked up the phone, fully prepared for the inevitable.

"This is Mrs. Stevenson at the library. I'm calling about Phillip. Is it possible for him to work an hour or two more today?"

I paused. No, I choked.

"You want him to work overtime?"

"Yes. We really love our Phillip."

I'd spent years living with Phillip and his tics and screams and his occasional slaps to his own face. I also knew he had a heart of gold, so the rest didn't matter.

"So do I," I said. "So do I. Sure, he can stay." I thanked her for the call and then sat on the floor in the kitchen with my back against the refrigerator. Tears were streaming down my face. I got up and retrieved Ms. Mona's tissue box. I guess I'd caught whatever it was she had.

I had someone else to thank for Phillip working at the library. She was a part of the Transition Program. Many of the special education students were placed in jobs throughout the community as a way to give them real world experience. Sandy Moshin worked closely with Phillip, and she prepared him for every phase of the process—from the job interview to appropriate dress to punctuality. I knew what kinds of challenges she faced, and Phillip faced, and it was marvelous that the program achieved its intended outcome. Phillip not only earned money, had greater exposure to a wide variety of people and situations, but, most important, felt so much better about himself. I knew in theory that not sheltering and isolating the kids was the best thing that I could do, and the Transition Program at Agoura High, Ms. Mona, and the staff at the Agoura Hills Public Library showed me a way that this could be done and have it benefit everyone. It would have been easy for any of us to say that this task was too difficult, but no one did, and I'm extremely grateful for that.

Neither Phillip nor I saw that job as a be-all and end-all for him. He had hopes that spanned far beyond the confines of a library's shelves, magazine racks, and study carrels. Other than being with a supportive group of people and being exposed to the rigors of reporting on time and being held accountable for duties to be performed (all valuable and essential skills, I'd like to stress), the Transition Program had some gaping holes in it. Only as the twins got older and developed a taste for self-reliance that exceeded their abilities to live independently did

the gap between their desires and their capabilities really confront us in a meaningful way. From the very basics of transportation issues to the more complex issues of selecting a potential
major to choosing and registering for classes, the tasks involved
in securing a higher education were more complex. To have
thrown the twins into that without sufficient preparation would
have been disastrous. My focus had been divided, and that contributed to the sense that we all needed to take a step back and
survey the field.

I can't tell you how freeing it was to know that we were taking this time-out, not because we weren't behaving properly
and were being sent to sit in the hallway but because we decided
we needed the time. College could wait; the local junior colleges and universities weren't going anywhere. We all knew in
our hearts that Phillip and Stephen were going somewhere, but
only when it was right for them.

We'd store up some energy, plan a little more strategically,
and resume our roles as advocates for what was right and what
was fair.

Chapter Five

Refining Your Instincts

A friend of mine lives in a somewhat wooded area in northern California's Sierra Nevada. He has several dogs that he allows to roam free on the acreage he owns, where a lot of wildlife—bears, elk, deer, mountain lions, foxes, and coyotes—also traverse his property. He's often mentioned that he feels comfortable knowing that the dogs are around and serve as a wonderful alarm system. He's been able to distinguish their barks, and now knows that when he hears a certain pitch and rapidity, a bear or mountain lion is in the area. Another type of bark lets him know that they have spotted some prey.

While chatting recently, he mentioned that the Animal Control Officer had stopped by to issue a warning to him. While his dogs could be off leash on his property, they couldn't roam freely on the public land that bordered his place. My friend asked why, and the officer said it was to protect the wildlife. In fact, it was the Animal Control Officer's duty to decide if a dog was posing a threat to a wild animal, and at his discretion, he could shoot a dog threatening wildlife even if it was on private property.

My friend was aghast at the thought of his dogs being shot, and even more troubled by what the local wildlife service was doing. He said that the deer and to a lesser extent the elk were as close to domesticated as could be. They had no fear of humans because of the bans on hunting and other public policies put in place to protect them. The policy of protecting the wildlife from dogs seemed to him, and to me, to be a disruption or reversal of the natural order of things. Dogs weren't supposed to do what their instincts told them to do, and wild animals were losing their instinctive fear of predators. The whole predator-prey thing and who was protecting what from whom was all murky and didn't seem to be serving anyone's purposes.

My friend wanted to protect his dogs, but leashing them up wouldn't be right—his dogs wouldn't want to be tied up. He felt conflicted, and I empathized with him. It is so difficult as a parent, let alone as the parent of an autistic child, to want to protect children while at the same time letting them go and be free to experience life. To be honest, this has perhaps been the most difficult thing for me, and I was pulled in many directions and stretched nearly to my breaking point.

A part of growing up involves learning painful lessons. When the boys were younger, I was far more watchful over them. As I told you, I often went to school to observe them and to see how they were being treated outside the classroom. I had to make some tough decisions about their involvement in Scouts and other activities. I think that most parents loosen the reins a bit as their kids get older and demonstrate their ability to make good choices. With Stephen and Phillip, I employed the same method, but the standards I used were likely far different from what parents of nonautistic kids develop and use. Again, the truth is that I had to ignore the timetables that had been well established by the boys' peers and their families and figure out as we went along what was appropriate and beneficial for them to do, regardless of what age they were chronologically.

This tug-of-war any parent of an autistic or special needs child has to engage in goes beyond simply saying no to things that are harmful and yes to things that are safe. The deeper issue was my concern about wanting my kids to be treated like everyone else while still having other people (as well as me) recognize that they did have some special needs and that some accommodations would need to be made based on them. The most difficult thing to get other people to understand was that making accommodations for them didn't meant they were limited—only different.

I don't know if this tension will ever ease, since, even today, with the twins in their mid-twenties, we're preparing them to live independently in their own apartment. We still have to walk that tightrope between the opposing poles of limited and different, justifiable accommodations and advantageous exceptions, and protecting and interfering.

What's most painful for me to remember is the times when I was either overzealous in my protecting them, and thereby prevented them from experiencing something valuable (those cases are, thankfully, rare), or skewed in my own expectations regarding special and normal.

Stephen's success on the cross-country team eventually earned him a lot of notoriety. I became much more involved in his athletic pursuits as a result, but I was still very much a newbie when it came to sports in general and high school athletics specifically. I learned what a dual meet was (one school vs. another), a triangular (three schools facing off), an invitational (multiple schools competing), and a PR (personal record, or an individual's best time in running a particular distance). What I needed to learn was that even my vision was sometimes clouded by Stephen's diagnosis and that other people were more clear-eyed about him and his athletic abilities than I was.

What was also gratifying is that the frosh-soph team Stephen was a part of went undefeated during the dual meets against the other teams in their league. Stephen's success paralleled that of the team. He was the top finisher among Agoura's runners in each of those dual meets. Assuming that he was the water boy and not a fully participating team member was just the beginning of my vision being corrected. Maybe because the cross-country coaches didn't know his past they could perceive him with a beginner's mind. Maybe that's what I needed to do—to change my focus from the past to the present.

At the end of the season, Stephen attended the team's award-night banquet. I was extremely proud of what Stephen had accomplished, so I invited my mother and father to attend the banquet with me, Stephen, Phillip, and Doug. My parents had been there from the beginning, when I'd expressed such grave doubts about the boys' future. I wanted them to see how far we'd all come. It meant a great deal to me and to Stephen that they'd be there with us.

I was still struggling with the notion of how our family fit in, though. I've said over and over that Agoura was a somewhat wealthy town, and though I'd gotten to know some of the parents, I was still laboring under the assumption that we were what they would have considered if not poor white trash, then at least poor white recyclables. We'd been used once and could likely serve a purpose again at some point with the right investment and equipment. So, with that attitude lingering in the back of my mind, we made our way to the Willow School. The cafeteria was festooned with crepe paper and balloons in the Chargers' blue and gold. We sat at a table near the rest of the frosh-soph team, and after we went to the buffet table and took our seats again, another couple with their son was seated with us. I didn't recognize the boy, but he said hello to Stephen. My son didn't respond verbally, but he did nod. Doug, ever the gregarious one, introduced us. The Perrams and their son, Tim, seemed very nice, and we all chatted and ate. I kept glancing down self-consciously to see if I had any stains on my blouse or if a button had come undone.

After we ate, Coach Duley got up and made a few remarks. Maybe it was Coach Duley's mustache that gave me the impression at first that he was a stern man. He had thick wavy hair, and a full mustache that reminded me of two pocket combs angling away from an aquiline nose. His deep, pleasant voice was rough around the edges, and when I'd heard him barking out commands and encouragement during a race, I was certain his tone was able to cut five to ten seconds off everyone's finishing time. While he recapped the season and thanked the parents, I kept looking over at Stephen. His eyes were riveted on the coach. I'd never seen him so attentive to someone speaking in public like this before.

After his general remarks, Coach Duley started talking about each team individually. He and Coach Andrews worked with both the boys' and the girls' teams, so with two girls' squads and three boys' groups, he had a lot of ground to cover. I was surprised that when he finished with his recap and had introduced all the team members, he said that he was now going to present awards in three categories. He began by announcing the most inspirational boy and girl. When I heard the word "inspirational," I immediately thought of Stephen. I mean, here he was a kid in special education, an autistic, and he'd led his team with the best time in every meet. What could be more inspirational than that?

My heart sank a bit when Stephen's name wasn't called. Bless him, Stephen seemed unfazed by the whole thing. He added his applause to the ovation the winner, Jeff Louie, received. Mentally, I began preparing my consoling remarks to Stephen. He gave his best and that was what was important. He should be proud of what he'd accomplished, and that was its own reward. Coach Duley said that the next presentation was for the most valuable runner on the frosh-soph team. Tim Perram said loud enough for all of us at the table to hear, "Bulldog gets it."

I wondered which of the boys had earned that nickname, and then I remembered that Stephen would practice on a high hill in Malibu Creek State Park along Bulldog Road. Was he the only one who ran there? I couldn't get much further than that because the next thing I knew Tim Perram was on his feet, whistling and stomping. Doug was making nearly as loud of a ruckus as Tim was. I looked at Doug, and he could read my confusion in my expression.

"MVP. Stephen's the most valuable on the team."

Stephen ran up to the coach, his face beaming. Everyone at the banquet was standing and applauding. Word had spread through the tightly knit running community about Stephen's condition. This outpouring of appreciation and admiration for what he'd accomplished was nearly overwhelming. Parents were furiously snapping pictures, and we all enjoyed that movie moment when the hero is blinded by flashes and his "gosh, isn't this something, who'd have thought a kid like me could do so much" smile is captured forever. The thing was, I knew in that moment that the one person who thought it was all possible was Stephen. I had to laugh at myself. I was overjoyed, and any thoughts of consoling Stephen were now ridiculously unnecessary. I had to think of things to keep myself from crying. He didn't get the award I'd expected, but he got the one that he deserved and that I think really reflected Coach Duley's attitude. As Coach Duley would later tell me, he didn't realize at first that Stephen was autistic, and he treated Stephen just like the rest of the kids, expecting the same results from him. He was rewarded with Stephen's tireless efforts, which produced great results. Stephen wasn't being singled out for being different or special but for being a remarkably strong contributor—the one who was the most valuable to the team's success.

I wanted the moment to linger, to be shot in Hollywoodesque slow motion, but before I had much of a chance to think the whole experience through, Coach Duley was on to the next award.

The rest of the banquet was a blur and remains so. Maybe I'm shallow, but it felt so good to see other people recognizing my son's efforts. I was proud of him for lots of reasons, but this was different. It didn't make up for every perceived slight I felt, every sidelong disapproving glance, every bit of bullying, but I did feel vindicated in my belief in him. This wasn't him being encouraged and supported for being the courageous disabled kid; this was him being rewarded and recognized for his achievements, his skills, his successes. Though I'd sold him short in thinking that he was the team's water boy, I think I'd sold myself short even more. I was the one who didn't have the faith in myself to let my son succeed. Sure I'd hoped, but until the Miracle Run and that award-night banquet, I hadn't truly believed.

Later that night, long after Stephen and everyone else had gone to bed, I sat in the family room thinking about what I'd witnessed that night and the two months leading up to it. All those mornings when Stephen woke up at what Doug referred to as "O dark early" had paid off. Stephen had been inspired by Stallone and Schwarzenegger, and his underdog-will-triumph mentality had taken him to the top. I'd seen what was possible—not in any kind of fantasy realm but in reality. Having a tangible reward like that meant a lot to me, and I know that it meant a lot to Stephen. What I discovered next may have meant even more. The coaches had handed out a comb-bound packet with all of the results from the season. I still have the 1998 Charger Cross-Country Yearbook. Its laminated cover is a bit scratched and scuffed, the four corners of each page are somewhat turned up, but the Agoura High Charger is still galloping full speed, his knight clinging to him. That night I flipped through its pages and read the inscriptions Stephen's teammates wrote.

Laurel wrote about how much Stephen had improved over the course of the year. Shannon, Jeff, and Kevin echoed one another's sentiments, commenting on how fast he was, encouraging him to keep working hard, and told him they were looking forward to seeing him on the track team in the spring. What meant the most to me were the words Tim Perram wrote:

Morgan—
You're ~~chure~~ sure fast.
Congradulations on F/S MVP
It's been cool eatting lunch w/ you.
Keep up the training.
You're a good friend and a cool guy.

I don't know where Tim Perram is today. I do know that the very next year, Tim was selected as the most inspirational athlete for that season. I didn't get to cast a vote, but I certainly would have if given the opportunity. As much as the MVP award meant to Stephen and to us, the fact that he had a friend like Tim, someone who sat at lunch with him, who saw, or maybe even better didn't see, Stephen's autism and saw the "cool guy" beneath all that was so unbelievably rewarding. I don't know this for certain, but based on how Stephen and Phillip had been treated in the past, I imagined that it couldn't have been very easy for Tim to have chosen to sit with my son. I imagine that he was the subject of some teasing, but he chose to ignore it.

Jeff, another of Stephen's teammates, wrote, "You run fast and don't feel pain." I don't think I knew enough about running back then to really understand what a compliment that was.

I've since come to understand more about running and the type of person it takes to really succeed at it. In the world of high school sports, cross-country and track athletes are pretty close to the bottom of the totem pole. They don't earn the kinds of accolades or adulation that football players, basketball players, and, to a certain extent, baseball players earn.

Coach Duley built up a great program, and both the local and the L.A. papers recognized the kind of success Agoura High enjoyed, but even so, that recognition was small compared to the coverage the other big three sports received. It takes someone who is very inner directed, someone who sets goals and is satisfied internally with achieving them, to be a good runner. There's not a lot of glory in cross-country, but there certainly is a lot of physical pain. Unlike in contact sports, the pain is mostly self-inflicted. Running as fast as you can over a 3.5-mile course when your breath is coming in ragged gulps, your lungs are burning, and the muscles in your legs are being drawn tight isn't easy.

When I saw Stephen run, I didn't see pain etched across his face. In some ways, he made it look effortless. I knew that he had the ability to go someplace else in his mind, to find a fixed point in the distance that he could stride toward. Running made concrete for me, and I think for him, the kind of effort it was taking for him to just live his life with autism. No one would have blamed him if he had retreated completely inside a shell or thrown his hands up and said, "This is too hard. This hurts too much. I just want to lie down now and not feel bad about all this."

I asked him once about the pain, and he said, "It's my choice." I didn't press him for more details because I liked how vague his answer was. I may be projecting here, but as his mother, I think he meant he had been the one who decided to join cross-country. He was the one who decided to rise early every morning and run six miles before school. He was the one who chose to push himself during all those races. It moved me—he wasn't the one who chose to have autism, but he was the one who chose to use the skills he had.

Stephen still never considered himself inspirational, but he always thought of himself as valuable. If not *the* most valuable, still valuable nonetheless. What was important to him was contributing to a team's winning. He liked the "individual within the team" concept. He could succeed on his own terms and also be part of a group effort.

Along with his award, Stephen earned something else— the acceptance of his teammates. I'd seen some of that change occurring even before the media learned about Stephen. For example, one day after practice, Stephen was walking to the car and one of his teammates said, "Hey, Morgan, we're going to McDonald's. You wanna go?"

Stephen looked back at his teammate and then at me, his eyes pleading. I still wasn't so good with the letting go, so I said to him, "I'll drive you."

Stephen told his buddy that he'd meet them over there. I handed him a few dollars, dropped him off, and pulled into a parking space to wait for him. I couldn't resist the temptation to observe them. I angled the rearview mirror so that I could see them through the big plate-glass windows. All the boys were seated in a couple of booths. Of course, I couldn't hear what they were saying, but I could tell that they were having a good time joking with one another. A few times, I could see all their heads pivot toward one guy. They'd settle for a moment, and then they'd all rock back away from the center laughing. Stephen isn't good with jokes. He deals with the world in a very literal way, and jokes often rely on some play on words or other linguistic trick. Over time, he's learned to take his cues from other people.

That evening, I saw him carefully watching the expressions and reactions of his teammates. When they laughed, he'd start laughing, just a beat or so behind the others but joining in none-theless. I have to admit I wished that he could have understood the joke himself, or been the one telling it, but I can't deny that I felt a real lightness of heart as I sat there watching my son hanging out with his friends. I took as much pleasure in that as I did in all the column inches of newspaper coverage he received. For most par-ents, having your kid going to a local burger joint or wherever with friends isn't a big deal. It becomes commonplace after a while, a kind of emotional fast food for the kids and them—not really sat-isfying but seemingly always there at every turn. For Stephen and for me, this was emotional haute cuisine. I was so grateful for it all. Every bit of it seemed miraculous to me.

But even now in relating this story, I can see that I was will-ing to let go but still hovering a bit. Sure, my going to McDon-ald's had a practical value—he would need a ride home—but I was still not completely sure that I could just let him go on his own. What if he was being set up for a fall? What if instead of enjoying the camaraderie with his teammates, someone was playing a practical joke on him? I wish that I didn't have to think that way, but my protective instincts were still in place. I did the best I could to serve his interests by letting him go and not making it obvious that I was out there hovering, and I also served his best interests by being there to intervene in case something went wrong.

Letting go was still incredibly hard for me. After Stephen's first year in cross-country, I became the supervolunteer for the team. I did want to contribute to the team's success, but I was still so worried about Stephen that I felt I had to be there to make sure he was okay. I knew that it was important for him to experience this success independent of Doug and me, but I had to weigh that against my fears that some harm could come to him. So I tried to figure out a way to watch him without making it obvious to everyone else on the team that Morgan's Mom (everybody on the track and cross-country teams called Stephen by his last name) was there. So, I ran the snack bar at the home meets, helped with timing the runners at track and cross-country races, and assisted Coach Duley in ordering uniforms and T-shirts. I even traveled with the team to San Diego for a meet and camped out with them.

Why would I go to such lengths to keep an eye on Stephen? Was I just an overbearing mother who couldn't let go? The truth is that for as much success as Stephen was enjoying in the meets, and as much as he was progressing at school, I would still hear from time to time about incidents that had bad results and could have been prevented. Like when the team traveled up to Mammoth, the ski area north of Los Angeles, for a training session. The coaches took them all out to a lunch spot, they each ordered, but Stephen did not. He went without lunch because no one was there to watch out for him.

Then there was the time during his junior year when Southern California was hit with a rare early-fall rainstorm. Coach Duley wasn't about to cancel practice, even when the sky was being split by thunder and lightning. I'm not blaming Coach Duley for his decision, because he didn't realize that Stephen's sensitivity to loud noises would trigger a strong reaction. I showed up at school that day at the usual time of six o'clock and no Stephen. Deep in my heart, I knew Stephen was in trouble. I thought of the rain, the thunder, the lightning. To the twins, it would be as if a freight train were bearing down on them and their shoes were caught in the railroad ties. Their whole bodies would shake.

I got out of the car and found Coach Duley and told him that Stephen wasn't around. A few of the members of the team helped me search. One of the girls from the team found Stephen huddled under a small overhang at the far end of the school. She was empathetic and tried to soothe him, but Coach Duley was upset. How could this kid run off and be so afraid and skip a workout? This was one of those times when Coach Duley's desire to treat Stephen like everyone else became a good/bad thing. He didn't understand the level of hypersensitivity autistics have to loud noises. He didn't want to make excuses for Stephen skipping a workout. I started to explain, but I could see in his eyes that I was only making things worse, so I stopped.

The quandary that most parents of autistic kids face is similar to mine. You want both things—for them to be treated equally and accepted but to have the occasional exception made for their condition. For a while after that incident, I rode behind the team as they ran through the neighborhoods near the school. The kids were used to seeing me around, so they just figured this was one more of my volunteer duties. I tried to be inconspicuous, but at the time I was driving an enormous white Chevrolet Suburban, so I was about as difficult to ignore as Moby Dick. The kids assumed I was a support vehicle, there in case any of them got a cramp, turned an ankle, or otherwise needed assistance.

I'd done something similar when Stephen was in middle school and wanted to go to a dance.

In February of seventh grade, Stephen told me that he wanted to attend the Valentine's Day dance. My heart skipped a beat, and I wasn't sure what to say or do. I was frightened for him. I can still remember those heartbreaking moments I experienced as a kid on Valentine's Day. It seemed as though one's own self-worth was being calculated and put on display on February 14. If the pile of cards and candies on your desk was smaller than the other kids' piles, you knew where you stood. Let me take that back; you probably already knew where you stood, but you didn't have such visible evidence of your standing in the world placed in front of you. I knew that a dance and card exchanges weren't the same, but they were neighbors—gossipy, spiteful ones at that.

Another part of me, the part I only let out occasionally, was jumping for joy. Stephen was always the shyer of the two boys, and the fact that he told me what he wanted, and what he wanted was to attend a social function, was a cause for celebration. Still, those nagging doubts about how he would be treated and how that treatment would affect him had my mind racing. It was as if someone had presented me with a problem in differential calculus or I had a complicated set of books in front of me that required I do a fast accounting of whether or not the debits outweighed the credits. I pulled the stall out of the mother's bag of tricks. Instead of responding immediately, I said, "We'll see."

I didn't go to see Stephen's principal, Wolf Thompson, but I did speak with him. I liked Wolf. He was one of the good guys, as evidenced by his reaction to Stephen and Phillip coming to Dana's defense. Wolf was a straight shooter, and when he told me that he thought Stephen would be fine, he confirmed what I was already inclined to believe. Stephen should go to the dance. In the days leading up to the big night, I probably wore a millimeter off my rosary beads. I told my mother about Stephen going, and I'm sure she lit enough candles in her church to raise the temperature in the place several degrees. Stephen, God love him, seemed unaffected by it all.

I pressed a pair of pants and a shirt for him. He shrugged off my offer to help him with his hair, but I noticed that he took a longer shower than normal. Doug and I drove him to the school. Doug had spent a few hours with him during the course of the week instructing him on how to ask a girl to dance, shared a few of his experiences with girls, and generally tried to put Stephen (but in reality me) at ease. Stephen nodded, blinked, and furrowed his brow in concentration during Doug's dating-data download. "I understand," was about all Stephen would say in return.

I guess that any parent would be nervous and excited about sending their child off to their first big school dance. I was a little surprised that it was Stephen and not Phillip we were sending off. Phillip was always more outgoing, but Stephen was the one who always seemed to find a way to surprise us by revealing some new dimension of his personality. The strong, silent, mysterious type, that Stephen! He was the one who challenged my protective side more than Phillip. I have to admit that some of my concern was how Stephen's behavior would reflect on me and, to a lesser extent, on Doug. We'd worked hard to get the boys into a routine and a comfort zone, and I hated to see anything happen to disrupt the delicate equilibrium we'd established. That said, I was just as proud that Stephen had chosen to take this leap of faith in himself and in his classmates. Maybe all my attempts at clutching him and Phillip close in a protective embrace had chafed him just enough to make him want to take flight.

While I felt I'd done as much as I possibly could to control how Stephen would behave at the dance, I knew I couldn't control two other things: what he would be thinking and feeling, and how the other kids would treat him. Another lesson for me in letting go, I suppose, but at the time Stephen's dance experience didn't feel so much like a lesson as a penance. When Doug and I dropped him off at the school and we watched him grow smaller until the main entrance of the school seemed to swallow him up, I felt like I was in Purgatory—I'd find out in a couple of hours if Stephen and I would be in Heaven or Hell.

Rather than drive back home, we waited in the parking lot. As sorely tempted as I was to go inside to take a peek at how things were going, I resisted. No seventh grader wants his mother showing up at a school dance to check up on him, and I knew Stephen was no exception. He deserved the right to experience this event free of my interference. That sentiment didn't prevent me from getting out of the car to stretch my legs and to take a casual stroll. From a distance of about a hundred yards, I could see through the windows of the cafeteria. The usual ugly fluorescence was replaced by a few theater lights hanging from the poles that normally held up the volleyball nets. Red and white balloons and streamers festooned the walls and cascaded from the ceiling. At the end of the cafeteria closest to my position, I could see a heart-shaped-balloon-bedecked trellis. Occasionally, a couple would stand under the trellis arm in arm. A teacher dressed in a suit would step up and say a few words to bless their union. The photographer's flash would catch the happy couple in a typical teenage pose—the girl with a broad smile stretched widely across her face, her head canted toward her beau's; the boy standing stock-still, his facial expression an attempt to mask his discomfort, lust, or whatever other feelings he was denying.

I didn't see Stephen at all, and I wondered if he had found someone with whom he could pose. I didn't dwell on the question for long. I returned to the car. Doug and I sat and listened to the radio, reminisced a bit about our school dances, and wondered how many others of our generation had slow-danced across one gymnasium floor or another to "Stairway to Heaven."

The two hours passed more quickly than I had anticipated. I saw Wolf talking with a few students and parents near the entrance to the school. I walked up to him, and he gave me a big thumbs-up and assured me that all had gone well. "He'll be out in a minute. He had a good time, I think. I saw him being a bit of a wallflower, but you could tell he was enjoying just being there." I thanked Wolf, and when Stephen came out of the school, I could see what he meant.

Stephen's emotional states can sometimes be difficult to read unless you know him well. He's not particularly demonstrative, but I could tell by how unlined his face was, how he walked toward me with his eyes looking up and not down at his shoes or at the few feet of sidewalk just in front of him, that he was happy. He let me drape my arm around his shoulder and walk him back to the car. In early spring, the air in Southern California takes on a particularly pleasant fragrance of citrus and rose. I exhaled deeply and breathed in as much of that scent as I could. Stephen looked up at me and smiled and nodded. There was no need to say more.

Doug's "Hey, buddy. How'd it go?" fractured our brief reverie, and Stephen's "It was good" sounded and felt like a benediction. As we drove home through the dark, we all sat in silence. Stephen rested his arm on the ledge of his open window, his hair dancing in the wind. I didn't need a stairway to climb to this Heaven; I was already there.

I was beginning to understand the importance of letting go. I didn't have to be right there beside him, making sure that he wasn't getting hurt. I couldn't define for him what his experience should have been like. No one else should do that to him, either. Wolf didn't have to tell me that Stephen spent most of his time on the periphery—that he watched but didn't dance, serving instead as a witness, however unobserved and unasked, to the dozens of pseudonuptials conducted that night. He was there on his own terms, doing what he wanted, having the experience that meant something to him, something that none of us could define or guide for him.

I could look at his smile and find it wonderful, but I couldn't judge him and his experience and deem them worthy or unworthy. All I could do was let him go and let him decide for himself what risks were worth taking, what rewards were worth garnering.

We were all fortunate that there were people in our lives who never treated Phillip and Stephen as autistic or different, who didn't lower their level of expectation because of what some specialist had written on a piece of paper. But I didn't always think we were fortunate that Big Steve's parents, Richard and Mary, had that attitude.

For several summers when the boys were between the ages of eight and fourteen, I would send them to their paternal grandparents for two weeks. I was always apprehensive about doing that, not because I didn't trust Richard and Mary but because I was a worrywart. They really didn't believe the boys were autistic, which in some ways was a good thing. They allowed the boys more freedom to do things than I was capable of giving them.

I didn't learn about the following incident until Phillip came home and told me the story. Their grandparents took them on a trip to Yosemite National Park when the twins were fourteen. One day, they suggested the boys go alone on a five-mile round-trip hike. Phillip couldn't really remember the details about the hike, but Stephen, who is fascinated with maps and directions and has a nearly savant-like ability to remember routes, did. He said that they started at a trailhead just above the Tuolumne Meadows Group Campground. Their final destination was Elizabeth Lake. From the campground, the trail climbed steadily to the glacier-carved lake at the base of Unicorn Peak. By this time, Stephen had begun his physical fitness training, and the hike was fairly easy for him. It proved a bit too strenuous for Phillip, who got to the lake but didn't want to go any farther—including back to the campsite. They hadn't brought any food or water with them, and Phillip was "starving and dehydrated." He knew enough not to drink from the lake without boiling the water or filtering it.

He wasn't sure what to do, but "I knew I couldn't take another step without something." Phillip can be dramatic when it serves his best interests. Stephen, his imagination fueled by the *Rocky* movies, his recent fascination with Arnold Schwarzenegger (he'd seen *Conan the Barbarian* and knew that Arnold had books on weight training and bodybuilding—in fact, in one of the rare instances of him requesting something, he'd pointed out one of those books in a store and said, "Please get that for me"), and his concern for his twin's safety and comfort, told Phillip to stay put. Stephen then took off at a run back to Mary and Richard to retrieve food and water for him. He'd then run back to the lake to save the day.

Stephen did exactly that. Except when he got back to the lake, instead of finding a bedraggled and bereft Phillip, he found him sitting happily among a group of German tourists, munching on a sandwich and sipping iced tea. I wish that I could have gotten Stephen to comment on how he felt when he saw Phillip no longer in need of being rescued, but he simply said that what he did wasn't hard.

I love that story now, but at the time I was a little freaked out by it—only because of all the what-ifs that ran through my mind.

I particularly like the story because even though they are twins, and they are both autistic, they are individuals. They have their own ways of solving problems and getting what they want and need. Phillip told me that he informed the Germans that he was autistic, that he had OCD and Tourette's syndrome, and that he was having a bad day because he was hungry and thirsty. He laid it all out on the line as directly and simply as he could. Stephen took a different route, literally and figuratively, but the important thing I learned is that no matter what, the boys were more capable of managing on their own than I was of managing my fears at that point. It was going to take some time and effort for me to get to the point where I could just send them off.

In ways large and small, I had been doing that all along, but I could still see no end to my feeling protective of them. As any parent knows, wanting to protect your children from harm, wanting them to succeed, helping to fulfill their dreams, is part and parcel of raising kids. And as any parent of a teenager will likely tell you, it gets harder instead of easier, the issues more complex, the emotional stakes higher.

In any teen's life, two rites of passage stand out: first love and getting a driver's license. As complicated as both those matters can be, when you factor autism into the equation, you have to have a mastery of higher math and a grasp of the chemistry of the volatile emotions of teenagers firmly in your mind.

Although I had mixed feelings about them falling in love, I firmly believed that Stephen and Phillip had the right to apply for and to try to get their driver's licenses. If they passed the written and the driving tests, demonstrating the competency that any other citizen possessed, then why not?

On the other hand, I had some pretty good why-nots in mind. The anxiety level they both exhibited in new situations, especially when exposed to things like loud noises, would potentially make them a danger to themselves and to other drivers. All the medications that Phillip was on and the unpredictable interactions among those drugs didn't make him a good candidate for driving. When I stacked those reasons up against their strong desire to drive, and what more potent symbol of a teen's freedom and independence exists than driving, I was torn. I didn't want to be the one to stand in the way of their dream being fulfilled. To give you a better idea of how much driving meant to him, Phillip had written a song aptly titled "The DMV Song." I didn't like to ever play favorites, but I could reasonably imagine Stephen being able to earn his license. With Phillip, I thought the odds were stacked against him.

On one occasion, I took them both to the DMV office. I turned them loose after telling them which line to stand in. I sat in a waiting area with my fingers crossed, hoping that they'd both fail the written test. I knew that would greatly disappoint them both, but failing on their own was better than me not allowing them to do something they wanted so badly to do. The first time Phillip took the written test, I could see that he was struggling. I don't know if it was nerves or what, but I could read the panic in his eyes as he scanned the questions. That surprised me since they had both studied very hard for the test. When Phillip completed his test and brought it to the clerk, he kind of shuffled up and looked as though he was about to collapse within himself. It took a few moments for him to get his score, and when he was called back up, it was clear that he hadn't passed. I breathed a deep sigh of relief. Stephen had already passed the written portion of the exam and was in line to take the vision test. I now only had one to worry about.

Then I noticed that the clerk had taken Phillip aside. I didn't want to make a scene, so I stood up and inched my way closer to where the pair was standing. The clerk, obviously very sympathetic to Phillip's plight, was asking him a series of really basic questions about driving. The next thing I knew, he was shaking Phillip's hand and congratulating him for passing the written test. I couldn't believe it. It was a nice gesture, but all I could think of was that he was hoping that Phillip wouldn't make it past some of the other hurdles he had yet to face.

As it turned out, neither of the boys passed the driving portion of the exam. I was so relieved. They both vowed to work harder and to pass the next time. As bad as I felt rooting against my sons, I knew that in the end their not getting to drive was a good thing. I would hate for them to do harm to themselves and to another driver or pedestrian. Balancing what is right for them with the needs of the larger community is an ongoing task.

I believe that someday they will both be able to drive. Quite a few high-functioning autistics do, and I feel that once the twins mature a little more and learn to deal better with loud noises and such, they will be good drivers. One thing is for sure: they would never get lost. Stephen especially is like a human Global Positioning Satellite. I'm not fond of driving, and I frequently get lost, but if Stephen or Phillip is in the car with me, I never have to worry about finding my way. It is uncanny how we can be traveling in some unfamiliar place and they always manage to get me back on the road to home.

The twins still talk about getting their licenses, and I think that one day they will. They just have to be patient, a virtue whose importance we all became acutely aware of throughout the years.

As for that other major adolescent rite of passage—first love— I knew I wouldn't be able to have the proverbial birds and the bees discussion with Stephen and Phillip. I knew that my nervousness and awkward attempts to communicate with them about reproduction and sexual intimacy would send the wrong signal to them. If I stuttered and stammered, hemmed and hawed, turned beet red and blanched at any of their questions I thought were too frank, all I would do was add to their confusion. I also knew that I owed it to them and to my daughter to make certain they received the proper information about sexual matters. There is a five-year age difference between Ali and the twins, they have different fathers, and though there was never any suggestion of inappropriate conduct on their part, I was paranoid about custody issues due to my previous experiences with child welfare folks.

For that reason, I sent the boys to a psychologist when they were about to enter their teens. The boys had received some instruction at school about reproduction, mostly a very clinical, very scientific parts-and-process inventory that had little to do with their real world concerns. I wanted them to go to someone who could speak with them on their level about all kinds of matters that I would have never been able to bring up: nocturnal emissions, masturbation, intercourse, spontaneous erections, and all the other things that had a blush factor of 10 or more.

Along with a discussion about those issues, I wanted the therapist to help me instruct the boys on what was appropriate behavior—not simply sexually but socially—with members of the opposite sex. I knew that the boys had developed an interest in girls and women. I used to bring home outdated magazines from the office—*People* and *Cosmopolitan*, mostly—and Stephen and Phillip would read them. They both seemed to be drawn to the ones with the photos of female celebrities on the cover. That was fine and normal, but I also wanted them to learn that what they saw on the covers of the magazines and what was in store for them in reality were two different things.

Because of patient-client confidentiality issues—and even if there weren't those constraints placed on a therapist, I wouldn't have asked anyway—I don't know and can't tell you the details of the discussions the boys had with him. I respected their privacy enough and trusted in the therapist enough to simply take them to the appointments, sit patiently in the waiting room for the hour to lapse, and then drive the boys home. Later, when Doug learned that the boys had received some additional sex education through the therapist, he referred to him as "Doctor Las Vegas—what they discuss in his office stays in his office." And that's exactly as I intended it.

I knew my limitations, and I didn't want them to interfere with the twins getting the information they needed and deserved. I was willing to let go of my control over the situation and let someone with far more expertise than I possessed do the job for me.

Stephen and Phillip have both expressed a desire, as I've mentioned before, to date and to eventually marry. Stephen's first foray into high school romance serves as an object lesson in the ways of the autistic heart.

Stephen's self-confidence was boosted enormously by the press attention he was receiving. As one student told me when I went to pick the boys up from school—they were now considered BMOCs. I had no idea that kids in the nineties still used a phrase from my teenage years, an expression that even predates me, but if being a Big Man on Campus was what the twins were, then I was glad. I knew, of course, that this description was exaggerated. Agoura High was like most schools, where the football quarterback and the homecoming queen garnered the attention of the jocks and preps, were silently mocked by the skater dudes and the other social outcasts, and looked at with envious longing by the wannabes. There were other cliques, I'm sure, and Stephen's running achievements meant he was no longer among the anonymous, faceless crowd who secretly hoped for attention but found comfort in blending in. Though the Supreme Court had outlawed one kind of segregation in the schools, another remained deeply entrenched—the cool kids and the not-cool kids could occupy the same physical space, but in a physics-defying fact of high school life, the cool kids could render the others invisible and mute.

One young woman who seemed to operate beyond all the laws of the social physics of high school was Laura Jakosky. She was the lead runner on the girls' cross-country team, she excelled academically, she was a student leader, and she was one of the most popular and attractive girls at the school. A leggy blonde with long hair and eyes the color of the Pacific, she was a walking Beach Boys' song. One day, she did the unexpected. She broke ranks and asked Stephen his name. Who could blame him for falling instantly in love?

Each spring, the school held a Vice-Versa dance, their variation on the Sadie Hawkins Day dance, when the girls were expected to ask the boys out. Stephen convinced himself that Laura liked him and was going to ask him, so he purchased tickets to the dance and waited expectantly for her to call. We learned much of this after the fact. We knew that Stephen liked Laura. Doug and I both tried to talk to him about what was appropriate behavior and how he could go about asking her out on a date if that was what he wanted to do. Doug tried to impress upon Stephen the importance of not just being a gentleman but being confident and specific. He said that he should have a plan in mind for what he wanted to do on the date. He showed Stephen the movie section in the newspaper and told him that instead of just lamely asking a girl if she wanted to go out, he should say that he wanted to take her to the movies and that X was playing at this time at this theater and would she like to go.

We made it clear, or so we hoped, that we weren't talking about Laura specifically but with girls generally. We were trying to remain neutral on the Laura issue. We were in a tough spot. We knew Laura because of her association with the cross-country team, and we knew her by her very positive reputation. We knew that a girl like Laura could pick and choose from among the cream of the crop of young men at Agoura High School. How do you explain to your teenage son, one whose self-confidence was so newly formed as to be especially fragile, that he was aiming too high, that, as the expression goes, Laura was out of his league?

We could sense that Stephen was setting himself up for a painful fall, but who among us hasn't been in the same position? Though the inevitable would likely hurt, we felt that if we really wanted Stephen to socialize and integrate himself fully into life, some painful lessons were going to come his way. As hard as it was for me to let go, I knew in this case that my interfering would really disrupt Stephen's development. I had one ally in this regard.

Apparently, Stephen had made his feelings for Laura known. He didn't verbalize them, but when he was at track practice, at every opportunity he would maneuver around so that he could stand next to her. He lacked the courage and skills to say hello and engage her in conversation, so he was essentially lurking around. Of course, Laura knew about Stephen's condition and was patient with him, but she must have expressed her discomfort to her team-mates. Word got back to Coach Duley, but he refused to intervene on their behalf. He later told me that no matter who was involved, unless something illegal or potentially threatening was going on (which there wasn't), he would have expected the kids to sort things out themselves. He wasn't the type to cross the line and get involved in their personal lives unless there was a clear need to do so. We didn't know anything about this until after the fact.

Days before the dance, Stephen must have learned that Laura was not going with him but with someone else. He ran off instead of going to practice, a less-than-mature thing to do and a habit of his when he was disappointed. When I went to school to pick him up after practice, I immediately called the police when I learned he hadn't shown up. He had already been missing for three hours. The Lost Hills Sheriff sent forty deputies and park officers; they were joined by what must have been a hundred volunteers from the community—athletes, parents, store owners, and even one elderly woman whose self-sacrifice and compassion had me in tears.

The search went on, and desperate for clues, one of the deputies asked Phillip if he had any idea where Stephen might have gone. Not one to willingly disappoint anyone, Phillip said, "Yes." For two more hours a trio of deputies trailed after Phillip as he led them around and through the campus. He talked to them about his heroes, John Lennon and Eric Clapton. He asked the officers if they played a musical instrument. They tried to keep Phillip focused on finding Stephen, but Phillip had found three new friends. He would have kept them out there all night, but when the deputies worked their way back toward the front of the school, they spotted Stephen in a squad car. He was clutching a note in his hand. He'd written a love letter to Laura while hiding in the Andy Gump Porta-Potty less than a mile from the school.

I went to get him and did my best to find the words to console him, but he really didn't want to hear anything from me. I felt so bad for him. Coach Duley was sympathetic and called Stephen the next day to give him the "other fish in the sea" speech. I knew it was too soon to talk to Stephen about making more appropriate choices in terms of how he expressed his disappointment. Running away wouldn't solve anything, but I knew that he was angry, embarrassed, and possibly hoping that by running away he was showing Laura and everyone else the depths of his feelings for her. Though his choice didn't demonstrate the greatest degree of emotional maturity, he was still just a kid, as much a victim of his hormones and lack of impulse control as any teen. He was confusing getting someone to feel sorry for him with really having a deep affection for him, a trap that quite a few adults I know sometimes fall into.

Laura's family called us to explain her position. She wanted to be sure that Stephen understood, and that we understood, that she did like Stephen as a friend but that was all. I thanked them for phoning, wishing that Laura had made the call herself or, more especially, that she'd spoken to Stephen directly. We weren't in any way blaming her, but we were still left with the difficult task of explaining some of the social complexities and nuances of the situation to our brokenhearted autistic son. Stephen tended to exist in a more black-and-white, on-or-off world of absolutes. I think that was why running appealed to him so much. You knew who the winners and losers were because of the absolute certainty of the stopwatch. There were few gray areas in athletic competition. If you did lose, you knew by exactly how much, and you could measure the amount you needed to improve to become a winner. Games of the heart, Stephen was coming to realize, were played by an entirely different set of rules.

While Stephen's instincts and emotions led him to pursue Laura in the way he thought and felt was best, I was feeling my way along in the dark in dealing with the twins and their autistic adolescence. Letting go and learning to trust that my sons were resilient enough to deal with life's bumps and bruises was by far, and remains, the most difficult thing I've ever had to do. Maybe this has been God's way of testing me and making me a better person. I come from a long line of worriers, and maybe it was destiny to break that cycle somehow.

I know all parents worry about their kids. I know that my parents did and still do about me. I worry about all my kids equally. Ali is away at college, and I worry about her. She told me about an attempted rape in a campus parking garage, and I started to worry for her safety. Richard is in the Navy and away at sea on duty, and I worry about what might happen to his ship. I also worry about Doug. I worry about my dogs. I worry about my neighbors and the fires that swept through this part of Southern California. But with my autistic kids, the level or degree of worry I feel for and about them is somehow different from all the other worries I have and different from what I imagine other parents experience.

Maybe I'm wrong about that; maybe all this worrying and wondering and struggling to let go is normal. Maybe I'm no different and no more special than any other parent when it comes to the twin desires to hang on and to let go, to honor Phillip's cry of "Freedom" and to protect them from the harm that independence might sometime bring.

Chapter Six

Tilting at Windmills

MY parents worked extremely hard their whole lives to make my life and my siblings' lives better and easier than what they had experienced. Compared to the lives of a lot of people I've come to know, we didn't have a whole lot growing up, but I know that we had much more than my parents did. Every parent dreams and makes efforts to ensure that their kids have it better than they did. It's like we are all climbing a ladder to the next level with our kids on our backs, and when we grow old and too tired to carry on, we hope that we've taught our kids enough, instilled in them the proper values and the right work ethic, so they can continue the climb on their own.

I can still remember sitting in my mother's lap as a very young child as she read to me. She didn't have a lot of free time, but whatever time she could spare, she would make sure she spent with us. I can remember how she'd struggle to turn the pages in the book, her callus-toughened fingertips, made rough from hoeing and weeding and picking in our garden, numb to the sensation of the paper. But still she was there, her halting English spoken with a Mexican lilt from growing up in a Spanish-speaking house in Southern California. Education was going to be our way out, our way to a life free of the kind of back-breaking labor she and my father had endured.

I was no different. When my oldest son, Richard, was born, I was determined that he was going to have an easier time than I did. I thank God my parents instilled in me the values and work ethic that enabled me to get grants and scholarships for college. I suppose that was one of the reasons I was so upset with Big Steve, the boys' father. I didn't want to live in the lap of luxury, but the fact that he couldn't hold down a steady job meant that my kids would know the kind of insecurity that I had known. They might experience hunger and might not be able to enjoy the same kind of freedom from worry and want that I experienced. Worse, in order to obtain a better life, they might have to take out enormous loans and work part-time, straight through their college experience. In the meantime, they wouldn't be able to enjoy college life like their more financially stable peers.

Though I was certainly influenced by the thinking of the sixties, that didn't mean that I had entirely abandoned the American Dream for myself or for my kids. I still believed that it was possible for them to achieve whatever they wanted in life. I may not have had specific ideas of what my kids would do or be, but I did envision that the future was wide open to them, their possibilities limited only by the extent to which they could imagine and dream for themselves. I hated the idea that because of my financial situation both before and after Big Steve, I might somehow be putting blinders on them, not exposing them to the people and situations that would allow them to enlarge their horizons and expand their view of what was possible for them to achieve.

Unfortunately, my dreams for them did die in the immediate aftermath of the diagnosis. How could they not have? As I said, every parent wants their kids' lives to be easier and better than their own. The diagnosis laid waste to the idea that Stephen and Phillip could have an easier life than I did. In time, just as I'd arrived at a better understanding that their experiences would be different but not necessarily better or worse, I began to believe, and do so even more strongly today, that their lives are better. Their lives are not just better materially but richer experientially. I can say that with great assurance.

What I can't do is stack up our lives for comparison and say that theirs or mine is better emotionally or spiritually. I do know that their lives aren't in any way worse. They are different but equally rich and rewarding. I could say the same thing about anyone else's on the planet.

I realize now that many of the incidents I described to you in the previous chapters are things that I mourned in the first few moments postdiagnosis. My twin sons won't experience their first love and first heartache, won't enjoy the freedom of driving a car, hanging out with friends, enjoying the acclamation of their peers for some achievement on the playing field or in the classroom. All of that, obviously, was proven untrue. The twins have achieved those things, though maybe not exactly as I'd first envisioned them when they were born.

I never really doubted that Phillip and Stephen would achieve academic success. Their ability to read at such an early age, their intense interest in various subjects, the genetic legacy of their father and their paternal grandparents, all pointed toward them being brilliant. Frankly, I always considered them to be geniuses, and I attributed much of their early silence, and some of their enigmatic communication, to the fact that they were beyond me in intelligence.

I know that I was frustrated with their early performance in school, when in kindergarten and the first and second grades they received poor marks. Much of the reason for their poor performance had to do with social rather than intellectual influences. Their crying and acting out made it difficult for teachers to view them as anything but troubled and underachieving. Despite that, I clung to the idea that they were misunderstood. At one point in the fourth grade, I received Stephen's report card. He'd earned all A's for the marking period. I was gradually becoming accustomed to him earning that distinction, but amended to his grades was a note that said, "I wish I had a classroom full of Stephens."

I knew then that what I'd sensed in working with Dr. Koegel and employing his methods was truly working. Stephen had learned to control his crying and his outbursts. He was becoming a model student socially as well as intellectually. The work wasn't easy. I can remember spending countless hours instructing him in what on the surface seemed to be the simplest things but were for him quite difficult communication tasks.

I believed that Stephen needed to be independent and not rely on Phillip, Richard, Ali, or me to communicate his wishes for him. Getting him to ask for what he wanted off a menu took a great deal of perseverance. I can still picture everyone seated around a table, the waitress or waiter standing with pencil poised, eyes at first focused intently on Stephen and then scanning the rest of the room, all the other restaurant patrons, each of us, hoping that we'd intervene. Phillip was the one who was always most eager to blurt out something, to get the process moving again, but I'd squeeze either his hand or his forearm, signaling him not to speak. We weren't always successful in getting Stephen to comply with our wishes, and he strained the patience of and gave new meaning to the term "waitstaff."

When we were rewarded for his efforts, we'd cheer like he'd won a race. He'd respond by staring at his hands or his lap. He'd sip from his glass of water, not seeming to join in our mirth and satisfaction. I'd hope that someday he'd respond spontaneously and enthusiastically, be washed along and swim with the ebb and flow of normal human interaction, both with us and in the wider circle of people he encountered. But at least he had ordered from the menu, and achieving the next step would happen eventually.

I think that every parent wants his child to be not just polite and quiet, which Stephen certainly was, but gregarious and outgoing. I know that as a young person I'd struggled to emerge from my shell, and because of that, one of my dreams was that my kids wouldn't be as shy and withdrawn as I had been. With Stephen, that hope had to be greatly modified. I knew that he would never be the life of the party, but as his expressed desire to attend the Valentine's Day dance demonstrated, he'd at least want to attend.

In Phillip's case, as he aged, I never had to worry that he wouldn't communicate or interact. As strange as it may seem, his sticking up for me and even swearing at Doug was one of our prouder moments together.

I know that most boys go through life dreaming of being heroes. Whether it's climbing into a burning building, driving home the winning run in the championship baseball game, proving their courage behind the wheel of a race car, sacrificing themselves for the sake of their fellow soldiers, slaying the dragon, or whatever, the idea of overcoming obstacles and challenges defines much of their imaginative life. I've mentioned before that the twins loved the *Rocky* movies, and their fascination with them and other action-hero films and video games was another way that I got to know more about them and their struggles to form their adolescent and adult identities.

Rocky Balboa is the ultimate underdog, and that's one reason the boys could identify with him. No one expects this run-of-the-mill club fighter to really compete for the heavyweight championship of the world. I also think that the twins identified with Rocky because he wasn't the most socially polished or expressive guy in the world. In comparison to the polished Apollo Creed, Rocky wasn't so much a diamond in the rough as a lump of yet-to-be-compressed coal. They also liked the idea that Rocky gets the girl. Adrian isn't the cheerleader, beauty-queen type; in fact, she's in many ways even less communicative and outgoing and more unpolished than Rocky Balboa. She does possess an inner strength, however, and a kind of charm that takes a special insight and touch to uncover. As the series of movies progress, of course, Adrian blooms into a beauty, and I know that Phillip and Stephen saw something of themselves in her. All it would take was one person noticing them, one person willing to see beyond their disheveled state, and they, too, could blossom.

Rocky gets the girl, and his unconventional wooing and winning of her gave the boys hope that they, too, could be champions in the ring and in matters of the heart. Rocky was not a suave, sophisticated "player"; he was a lot like the twins. He was unschooled in the ways of flattery and not about to sweep anyone off her feet, but he wins the woman of his dreams. He proves that a guy doesn't have to have all the right clothes and all the right moves in order to find love and happiness.

Along with the romance element, *Rocky* is also obviously about facing physical challenges. The movie inspired Stephen to run and to work out. His devotion to his exercise was miraculous given that no one else in the family ever exhibited much interest or ability in athletics or fitness. (As much as anything else, our having no history of athletic achievement contributed to my thinking he was the water boy and not the star runner on the team.) The kind of discipline it took for him to rise every morning well before anyone else was remarkable considering that the rest of us struggled just to get out of bed. No one ever suggested to Stephen that he engage in this activity; he did it all on his own, without any prompting or, to be honest, any real encouragement from the rest of the family. We knew that he was doing it, but we were all so preoccupied with other matters, we seldom commented on it.

While I wouldn't suggest that parents take this kind of seemingly apathetic approach to their autistic kids' interests, I think that for someone as inner-directed and motivated as Stephen, this was an ideal environment for him. I think that because his running didn't attract much attention at home, he was more motivated to prove himself and to win the attention of others outside the family. I have no way of knowing how things might have been different if we'd been doting, intrusive parents who exploited his interest in the sport, tracked his every movement and bit of progress, and pushed and prodded him to get out the door each morning.

I think there is a lot to be said for Stephen having done all this independently. Once again, Phillip's shout of "Freedom!" echoes. It wasn't until Stephen's Miracle Run that it fully hit home that the boys could be independent. I've observed other kids and seen the "me do" phase they all go through. I don't recall Phillip and Stephen having that strong, stubborn, "I'll do it myself" mentality and exertion of independence that toddlers have. Part of the reason may have been that I was such a worrywart, and another part may have been that they didn't express this desire verbally. What I really think contributed to it is that autism made them more inner-directed and less likely to communicate their desires. The mistake that we can make as parents of autistic kids is to think that the lack of communication—for independence or anything else—represents a vacuum, a lack of desire, an absence.

As I said, I had to become a master interpreter of the relatively few things they said or did when they were very young, but as they got older, their desires and dreams were writ large and small in their actions and statements.

Toward the end of the seventh grade, a month or two after the Valentine's Day dance, Stephen came home from school and was visibly upset. Eventually, I found out why. He showed me a math test that he had taken. He got a B on it. To be honest, I was a little shocked myself. When Phillip and Stephen were first being given IQ tests, they'd do miserably because of their inability to answer questions orally for the verbal component. They scored off the charts in the math/computation parts of the test. I'd never seen Stephen come home with anything less than an A on any math test ever. I asked him what happened, but he wouldn't answer.

Later that evening, I got a call from Kathy Khmara, Stephen's teacher, one of the really good ones that he had. She told me that Stephen was so upset when he got his test back that he bolted out of the classroom and hid. It took the teachers and an aide about fifteen minutes to find him. He'd locked himself in a bathroom stall and put his feet up on the seat so that no one could see him if they just peered under the partition. Kathy managed to talk Stephen out of the stall and back to the classroom.

She knew how hard Stephen worked and the high expectations he set for himself, so she offered him the chance to retake the test. She sat Stephen down, put a new test in front of him, and watched wide-eyed as he took his pencil and with meticulous precision put a large X through each of the questions and then wrote an F on the top of the page. When she asked him why he did that, he took his pencil and added a letter N in front of the F.

Stephen didn't have to explain. Kathy knew what he was telling her. A retake would be NF—not fair—and Stephen wasn't about to accept charity. Whether it was going to a dance or taking a test, he approached school and all its associated activities from this perspective. He knew and understood all the rules and how they should be applied. All he wanted was to be given a chance to succeed or fail on his own terms. That's pretty much what I had been struggling to do for my kids all along—give them a chance. I was so proud of Stephen for doing that. I didn't like the idea of his running away—and I did stress to him that there were more appropriate ways to express his frustration. I told him I knew he'd do a better job of selecting one next time.

Later that evening, after dinner was done and the dishes all washed, I saw Stephen sitting at the table. He'd taken out the test on which he'd gotten the B and the blank test on which he'd crossed out all the problems. He sat with a tongue-pink eraser and removed all his cross-out marks on the second test. He dutifully copied all his correct answers from the first version onto the second. Then, his head resting on his hand, he wrestled again with the problems he'd gotten wrong, working through them slowly on a sheet of scrap paper. When he was satisfied that he'd gotten the right answers, he transcribed his work onto the test paper.

Well past his usual bedtime, he was still seated at the table looking back at his first test comparing answers, trying to figure out where he'd gone wrong the first time. I could relate to that. We'd all been facing tests and challenges, and many nights, far more than I cared to count, I'd sat in that same chair poring over the past wondering where I'd gone wrong, how I could rectify the mistakes I'd made.

What Stephen did next surprised and pleased me even more. When he was done comparing and correcting, he took both papers, folded them very carefully, stood up, and walked to the garbage can. He put the papers in the trash and walked away, not glancing back at all, satisfied that he knew what he'd done wrong, had fixed the errors, and was now moving on.

He'd succeeded on his own terms, and that was enough for him. That was a remarkable display of independence and self-assurance. I know that a lot of high-achieving, grade-oriented kids would have jumped at the chance for a do-over. His sense of fairness and the high standards he set for himself meant more than the grade.

Considering that Stephen was reluctant to speak generally and his running ability seemed to arise from nowhere in our collective family's abilities, it was surprising that he had no problem expressing his ambitions about running and the future he envisioned for himself. Whether it was telling a reporter for one of the many newspapers who interviewed him or standing in front of the congregation at the Born Again Baptist Church, he let everyone know that he planned to run in the Olympics someday.

I also remember something Stephen had once written in his school notebook. Among the inspirational slogans he'd collected, I found this:

The purpose of running a race is to test the limits of the human heart.

I asked Stephen who'd said that originally, and he told me, "Pre."

Unsure of whether I'd heard him right, I asked him again. I got the same reply. I asked who this Pre was but got no further with Stephen. He was working on an essay for his English class on *To Kill a Mockingbird* and didn't want to be disturbed.

I followed up on the lead that Stephen gave me and learned

that Pre was a kind of cult hero among the cross-country and track team members. His full name was Steve Prefontaine, and he ran track and field and cross-country for the University of Oregon from 1969 to 1973. At one point, he held the American record at every distance from 2,000 to 10,000 meters. Stephen later told me that he and so many other runners loved Pre because he was told early in his career that he should give up on his ambition to be the best—he simply lacked the physical characteristics necessary to be a champion runner. Pre refused to listen to the naysayers.

Spurred on by his critics, Pre developed an unusual race strategy. He pushed himself to his limits, taking the lead instead of laying back until the very end of the race and letting tactics decide the winner. He was a real free spirit, and his tragic death in a car accident at age twenty-four only reinforced his status as a legend. I'd eventually watch the movie based on his life and come to think of him as Stephen's nonautistic twin. They shared much more than a first name, and my Stephen modeled his running style on Pre's.

Stephen wasn't the most strategic of runners. He would start out of the gate very quickly and get out as far in front as he possibly could. He seldom held anything in reserve and would simply, as the saying of the time stated, "go for it." In many ways, Stephen was competing with himself, putting his heart and will as much as his opponents' abilities to the test. He may not have been the smartest, most analytical runner out there, but no one could ever doubt his desire and belief in himself.

I had always been a very cautious person, and Stephen's reckless style on the track and on the cross-country course was a revelation to me. I was never someone who could lay it all on the line; I was far too reluctant to put myself in such a high-risk/high-reward situation. Stephen never seemed to even consider the possibility that he would fail, that his "go for it with all burners at full fire" method could lead to spectacular flame-outs. I was proud of him for that, and if my dream of my kids having a better life than mine wasn't taking shape in the way I'd expected, the surprise was even more pleasing.

Both boys' willingness to put themselves out there, the audacity they exhibited in wanting to fully participate in life, was seeing my dream for them realized and beyond. Everything from joining clubs, wanting to drive, wanting to get jobs, wanting to live alone eventually, all added up to them breaking free of the limited expectations that had been placed on them by those who thought it best that they be isolated and institutionalized.

Much like Stephen's running, Phillip's music was an important part of his demanding that "out of sight and out of mind" was not going to be imposed on him. Even if it was frustrating to know that Phillip was trolling the Internet to find a lead singer for his band, Twist of Fate, and angering a Texas husband, I have to give him credit for trying to put together a band and not just being content playing in his room. I think that Phillip's big dreams and his enthusiasm were infectious. I couldn't figure out how Phillip was getting new picks, cords to plug his guitar into his amplifier, shoulder straps. One day when Phillip needed some sheet music, I accompanied him into the store. I asked the owner about Phillip's spending habits, and he confessed that he sometimes "forgot" to charge Phillip. He explained further, "You know how Phillip is; he gets to talking and I get all distracted."

Stephen's Olympic dreams had their parallel with Phillip's rock and roll fantasies. At one point, when we were trying to get Phillip into junior college, he told us, "I don't need college. I'm going to be a rock star."

We tried to explain to him that it was important to have a backup plan, that he would need to support himself.

"Bruce Springsteen makes a lot of money. He doesn't need college to support himself."

Every parent faces that dilemma—how do you not squash your kids' dreams while still getting them to be realistic? What do you do when the dreams you have for your kids are in conflict with the dreams they have for themselves? All I can say is that we were as supportive as we possibly could be, providing Phillip with guitar lessons, helping him get the next "best and last" guitar and amp he needed, and providing him and his band with rehearsal space.

I also admire Phillip's chutzpah, in particular when it comes to self-promotion. I was told by that same music-store owner that at one point one of the Backstreet Boys, A. J. McClean, was in the store at the same time Phillip was. My music-loving and music-wise son recognized the celebrity and approached him, saying, "I have a band, too. We're as good as you guys, but nobody knows that—yet." Later on, when Zac Efron was cast to play Stephen in the made-for-television film of our lives, Phillip was not shy about talking with Zac and telling him about his band and his aspirations. We knew Zac had some musical talent, but he wasn't yet one of the major stars of *High*

School Musical. Zac was so warm and humble, he chatted easily with Phillip about my son's dreams and his band's play list. I know that I could have never put myself out there like Stephen and Phillip did.

It might be easy to dismiss some of this talk of dreams and desires as simple boyhood posturing and fantasizing, except for the fact that I have concrete evidence of the seriousness with which Stephen approached his running generally and self-improvement particularly.

In the same notebook where I found the Steve Prefontaine quote, I also came across a list called "Priorities." The subheading beneath the title was, "Take <u>care</u> of business." Stephen's list consisted of the following:

#1 Family
#2 Educational Work
#3 Extra-curricular activity
#4 Fun
Important notice!!!—Make sure you are prepared, early on
     time, <u>NO</u> excuses!!!

He also created a timeline called "Stephen's Road to Greatness!" Along with that, he kept a detailed log of each of his training runs and workout sessions. What was interesting to me as I watched Stephen's progress was that his achievements in running paralleled his success in the classroom. Always a good student, he became far more organized, diligent, and focused. I know that being involved in a sport like running requires the kinds of skills that would easily transfer to other parts of life. Eventually other parents of special education students and even the special education teachers encouraged those kids to participate in track and cross-country. I was glad to see that. I knew the benefits of belonging were important, as were the lessons they learned about perseverance. In almost every speech, and in every interview, Stephen would always say, "I will never give up."

About five years ago, I was cleaning out Phillip's closet. In the very back corner of it I found a pile of bills and coins. I counted it out, and it came to $119.28. Along with the pile of money, there was a road map of California, with a route to Eureka marked in red. (None of us could ever figure out why Phillip was so fascinated with getting to Eureka, California, his whole life.) I found a small sheet of paper on which Phillip had written, "Dear Family: Thank you for raising me. It is time for me to leave home. Signed. Phillip Morgan." I added a twenty-dollar bill to the pile. I said a prayer in the hopes that one day Phillip will get to Eureka.

Only now as I write this do I realize the appropriateness of Eureka as the place of Phillip's dreams and my discovery. The thing about kids, whether they are autistic or not, and their dreams is that you never really know what they will be or where you will find them. And you never know just how far those dreams might take them.

Chapter Seven

Big Gifts Come in Small Packages

PHILLIP and Stephen continue to dream big and educate me daily on all they're capable of imagining and achieving. However, it's not just the major milestones that have revealed their potential to me. I've found that more often it's the little things they say and do that truly give me insight into their character and souls, allowing me to see the amazing men they are evolving into. Honestly, I can't afford not to allow myself to embrace these moments. Just as living with autism has taught me that one can't afford to focus only on limitations, shortcomings, or setbacks, one can't let life be all about major moments and milestones, as sometimes there are not enough of these. But there are so many smaller victories and special moments that are just as awe inspiring and remarkable as the bigger ones. I've learned to take victories whenever I can. And sometimes it can be tough to recognize them, especially when you're focused on avoiding major mistakes. (Remember when Doug and I were so uptight at the meeting with the movie studio? We nearly missed out on seeing Phillip engage the group and share his passion with them.) But when you pause to think about your kids, I think you'll agree that there's a lot to celebrate.

Each year at a site in Thousand Oaks, a festival called Conejo Valley Days is held. Along with the usual carnival midway tents and games, there are rides and other attractions. Special ed students from around the area got to attend, and they were given free rein to enjoy as much as the carnival had to offer—including food. Phillip came home from that festival full of belly and full of stories. I'd seldom seen the two of them so joyful after a day of school.

Recently, Phillip shared a journal entry with me about his trip to the amusement park that allowed me to understand why the boys loved the Conejo Valley Days.

When I was eight years old, we went to Magic Mountain Amusement Park to go on rides and to enjoy the rides. You see, I have a brother that makes noises too. When we made the noises at the park, people would look at me, and I would say, "What are you looking at!?" And my mother would say calm down and I would stay calm.

I realized that on that special education field trip to Conejo Valley Days, the twins didn't have to worry about being stared at or made fun of. They were surrounded by their subset of peers—special education students—and they didn't have to worry about being taunted or teased. Phillip especially was able to experience the kind of freedom he hoped for. I had been back and forth on how I felt about the twins moving into a mainstream class. I saw their potential taking them beyond their special ed class, but I also saw all that there was to gain in their current program.

What made it easy to deal with my complex emotions and thoughts about mainstream versus special education was that Stephen and Phillip emerged as role models for other kids with special needs. Even Stephen's teacher had told me she wanted a "class full of Stephens." What a compliment to my son! And that's when it hit me I could let myself continue to debate special ed versus mainstream, or I could spend a moment with what Ms. Koch said.

After the Miracle Run, I knew that something special was happening, the early stages of some kind of transformation in our family and in the community. The first clues came when we were at the Newbury Park race. Doug, Phillip, and I were standing on the far side of the chain-link fence that encircled the football field and track. We were near the finish line, and I was scanning the playing fields in the distance hoping to catch sight of the leaders. I felt a hand on my back and turned around.

Doug said, "This woman would like to speak with you." He nodded his head toward a petite blonde who stood next to him. She held her young daughter on her hip and shifted her weight to gain a better grip so she could extend her hand.

"Hi." Her voice was thin and reedy. The assembled crowd

was cheering loudly now, and I knew the leaders were getting close. I didn't know what to do or to say. I thought I knew what she was there for, but I wasn't certain. I could read something in the worry lines around her eyes and mouth, the weary agitation that expressed itself in how she bounced her daughter, rocked to and fro. She always had to be doing something, express kinetically the jumble of thoughts that ran through her mind. "My husband wanted to be here, but somebody had to stay home with our son." Her eyes went wide at his mention.

I nodded. I knew she wanted more from me, but I'd only just begun to store up enough energy for myself. I had so little in reserve.

The pack was making its way toward us, a mass of white, blue, and yellow interspersed with black and gold. Stephen was among a group of about seven runners at the front. I stuck my finger through the chain link, sighting down it until Stephen came into view. His posture perfectly erect, his head still, his arms like pistons, he kept pace with the two leaders from Newbury Park.

"That's my son," I said. "That's Stephen."

The woman stepped forward and she craned her neck to see around a fence post. She nodded. "I see."

And then a strange thing happened. She stopped moving. She stood stock-still for a minute while the leaders crossed the finish line. When she turned around, her face was composed, and she was smiling.

"Thanks." Her smile grew even wider. "Thanks."

She walked toward the parking lot, and over her shoulder her daughter waved. Then the mom turned around and waved as well. The eloquence of those gestures, hers and mine, didn't hit me until much later. I realized I'd given her what she'd come for—a glimpse of her son's future. She got what she wanted to see, a glimpse of a young man with a group of his peers, all looking perfectly normal. The future wasn't as bleak as it had perhaps once seemed. Stephen had erased the image of the gleaming tile floors, perky yellow walls, and equally perky staff members that all did their best to disguise the fact that the institution was little more than a holding pen.

More and more as the season progressed, parents and autistic kids began to show up at Stephen's races. I didn't realize just how powerful an experience it was until several weeks after my meeting with that first mother. We were at Waverly Park in Mountain View. Agoura was competing against Thousand Oaks and Royal high schools. As he usually did, Stephen broke from the starting gate and into the lead. We made our way from the start toward the finish area. I felt a bit like the Pied Piper of Autism, leading a group of about a half-dozen parents and kids. We all assembled near the finish line, and everyone was chatting amiably for about five minutes until the leaders came home.

Once again, Stephen was at the head of the pack, with another Agoura runner, Jonathan Goldman, right with him, stride for stride. We were all yelling ourselves hoarse, and with about ten yards to go, Stephen separated himself from Jonathan and leaned forward to break the tape just barely out in front. He'd won! I was so excited I was jumping up and down, and when I looked to my right to see the rest of the runners come in, I saw a woman sitting on the ground, sobbing.

At first I wondered if she was Mrs. Goldman and was taking his second place finish overly hard. Then I recognized her as one of the mothers of an autistic son. He was standing next to her, his hand on her shoulder. I began to choke up, and then the woman started to laugh, and her shoulders stopped heaving from her tears and shook with joy. "That was amazing! That was absolutely amazing. Amazing…amazing." Her words trailed off, but she didn't have to say much else.

Though the season was over, the attention Stephen received was only really beginning. The morning after the awards banquet, where Stephen was named most valuable runner, I received a call from a reporter for the *Los Angeles Daily News*. He introduced himself and asked me if I was willing to talk about Stephen, his running, his schoolwork, and so on. I wanted him to speak to Stephen directly, but he was at school. When I mentioned this, the reporter said he'd love to, but he was on deadline, and by the time Stephen got home, it would be too late. I also sensed that he was a little surprised that Stephen would be able to speak for himself. I passed that off and answered his questions. Later that afternoon, I went to get Stephen from school. For the first time that I could remember, Stephen and Phillip weren't standing or seated alone waiting for me. A group of kids were with them, talking and laughing. I couldn't hear what they were saying, but when Stephen and Phillip saw my car and walked toward it, the other kids all waved and said good-bye.

When Stephen got to the car, he immediately told me that he needed to be dropped off early the next morning. He was going to run with friends on the team. He asked if we could get extra PowerBars and Gatorade. I was glad to do it.

I wasn't very wise in the way of the media then, and I rushed home the very next day after dropping Stephen at school for his unofficial practice to grab our copy of the *Daily News*. I immediately went to the sports section, but there was no story on Stephen there. I then went through the rest of the paper from top to bottom and back to front, but nothing was there, either. I hadn't said anything to Stephen about the forthcoming article, just in case something like this happened. Each day, I dropped the twins off at school. Each day, I rushed home. Finally, after what seemed to me to be three very long days, I woke up to Stephen's excited shouts. He didn't have an early-morning practice that day, so he ran on his own. The paper had been delivered while he was out, and he grabbed it and brought it in. It wasn't as if he was looking for the article, since he knew nothing about it, but even if he had, he wouldn't have had to look very far for the story. There on the front page was a feature story about Stephen Morgan the runner.

"Look, Mom!" Stephen came into our bedroom pointing ecstatically at the headline. We both sat on the edge of the bed reading the article together. Phillip and Ali had heard the commotion, and they joined us in the room. I called Doug at work and shared the news that the story had finally run. He asked me to put Stephen on the phone, and I could hear him shouting and see Stephen's grin.

This was a big day in the Morgan-Thomas household, but everyone still had to get to school. I dropped them all off, went to the local convenience store, and bought every copy of the *Daily News* they had. I called my mom and dad and told them to go out and get the paper, too. Everyone was so excited. To celebrate, we went out for steaks at the Place. Once again, we were treated well, and the staff made sure to let Stephen know how happy they were to have a celebrity in their midst.

Much later, a friend of mine asked me how I felt about all the attention Stephen received because he was autistic. She wondered if he had been any other member of the team, regardless of how successful he was, would he have gotten that kind of publicity? She was genuinely happy for all of us, but wondered if Stephen's being marked as different was only doing to him what had been done before—setting him apart, excluding him. I told her that I had not honestly considered those issues at the time. I was so thrilled by his success and how Stephen's choice to join the team in the first place was such an act of inclusion that I couldn't imagine how all the press could have had any kind of negative effect on him. I also told her that as time went on and people read and saw and heard more about Stephen, I was acutely aware that the attention he was getting was about much more than just my autistic son. His story was bringing attention to autism in general and showing what autistics were capable of in such a positive light that I couldn't see anything wrong with it. I did agree with her in theory. In a perfect world, Stephen wouldn't be identified as the Autistic Runner. His recognition would be based on his accomplishments and not on his so-called disability. In the same way, it would be wonderful if everyone could be noticed and recognized for his or her accomplishments and not with additional identifiers such as race, ethnicity, or gender. I think that the world is getting closer to being that way when it comes to those traits, but we still have a ways to travel before someone with an obvious physical or mental disability isn't identified or labeled by that characteristic.

I saw no harm in the articles always featuring Stephen's autism for a couple of reasons. First, I couldn't see denying the truth. Stephen is autistic. Second, by presenting the fact of Stephen's autism up front and also chronicling his accomplishments, the reporters were doing a good job of achieving a highly desirable end. People were beginning to see Stephen as someone just like them or just like their own children. He was competitive, strong, smart, dedicated, and highly accomplished. "Autistic" became just one of a series of adjectives used to describe him instead of the only one. In that sense, I saw what was happening as part of a sociological change in and around Agoura High School.

Certainly the change came in small steps, like Stephen running with friends instead of alone, being invited to that postpractice McDonald's dinner, and other things of that sort. I might have wished that there was more of a tsunami effect, washing away any discrimination and having Stephen ride that storm surge to being chosen for the prom court or garnering enough votes to earn an elected class office. But when I looked back and remembered my sons being mistreated on the playground and having their coats tossed up onto the school's roof, being treated civilly was a huge step. I just had to keep these victories in perspective.

In addition, I also had to keep the twins' grooming and hygiene in perspective. The boys still needed to be constantly reminded of the need to bathe, use deodorant, brush their teeth, comb their hair, and put on clean clothes.

Most boys go through a phase when their personal appearance becomes more of a priority for them. I noticed this with Richard, our oldest son. Though he struggled with his weight, as a teen he became much more clothes conscious. Now that he's in the Navy, I notice that his level of neatness and fussiness over his appearance has increased even more.

As you saw from Stephen's "Priorities" list, he got the message from us about appearance. Stephen never liked to run with his glasses on, and we agreed to let him get contact lenses. This was a big step for him. While Stephen didn't exhibit full-blown signs of being obsessive-compulsive, he was meticulous and a perfectionist. When our optometrist explained the importance of keeping the contacts clean to avoid getting eye infections, Stephen took those directions to heart. I came across another one of his notebooks in which he'd scrupulously copied the instructions the doctor gave him:

—wash hands extra, extra, extra good!!!

—take out contacts, clean them gently for 20–30 seconds with lg. bottle solution!

—rinse contacts at least 5–10 seconds

—pour cleanser out of holder and replace it with fresh water solution!!!

—before insertment, wash hands extra, extra, extra good!!!

—trim nails weekly!

—when bringing contacts, bring solution w/ you!!!

—order new contacts every 3 months!

—contacts are a BIG responsibility, really realize it!!!

While it may seem somewhat trivial, Stephen undertook the task of writing these directions down on his own. All those years we spent reminding the twins again and again of what was appropriate and necessary were beginning to pay off.

Phillip's OCD and Tourette's made life even more difficult for him than the autism did. He needed a break and a morale boost, but little did he expect it on that night at the Born Again Baptist Church in 1998.

We were sitting and listening to the choir, knowing that when they finished rehearsing, Phillip would get his chance to play for them. I was so pleased they'd agreed to let him share the attention.

Then I looked over at Phillip. It may have just been his nerves or a reaction to his meds, but his head was shimmying and shaking worse than I'd ever seen. He got to his feet unsteadily. I knew he didn't want to be upstaged by Stephen, but his tics had seized complete control of him. He stammered out a few guttural sounds. Doug started to stand, but I put my arm on his and he sat back down. I knew Phillip would be humiliated if he wasn't able to get his time in the spotlight. I heard a few murmurs of encouragement and repetitions of "You take your time now" from the congregants.

Phillip stooped over, put his hands on his knees, and took a few deep breaths, but nothing could still his shaking limbs. He kept his feet firmly planted and stood, and I was reminded of those toys with the figure on a pedestal. You press the bottom of the pedestal, and the figure twists and moves spasmodically. That mind's-eye image was displaced when I heard the first rhythmic clap start. As the rest of us picked up the tempo, Phillips tics were transformed into a kind of dance.

Somehow that seemed to steady him, and he walked over toward his seat, under which he had stowed his guitar. He pulled it out of its case, and with the encouraging words of his audience, he started to play a few rhythm-and-blues chords. Reverend James stood up and went to a piano that was rolled off to the side. He began playing, and the members of his congregation stood up and started dancing. Phillip picked up on the line as best he could. The rest of our family stood up and joined in, adding our voices to the chorus, "Mama hallelujah, papa hallelujah, you can hallelujah, too."

Though Phillip wasn't playing "Twist and Shout" that night, I've come to think of his participation in that evening's festivities in that way. My perception about how we all might be received was certainly twisted into a more positive shape. The way the members of that congregation reached out and embraced us, and especially the twins, brought a song of joy to my heart. They weren't patronizing either of the twins, merely accepting them and their contributions to the evening, letting each of them participate in a way that was meaningful and, in my mind, magical.

Being vigilant about recognizing and celebrating the small victories is certainly important. I think my family managed to do that, and I believe that because we did, we also had some magical moments.

Though I refer to the Miracle Run as a miracle, I also know that another truth underlies what produced those moments. It is sometimes easy for me to forget that Stephen put in countless hours of running. He wasn't nicknamed the Bulldog for nothing! Each of us, in our way, put in a similar kind of effort. Maybe we didn't win medals and get our pictures printed in the newspaper, but we all contributed to the success that Stephen enjoyed.

While I'm not one who goes around looking for accolades and will never wrench my shoulder out of its socket by patting myself on the back, I did learn to enjoy some of the attention and some of the perks of Stephen's and our family's notoriety. Just as we had to learn to mark and honor the effort, we had to learn to enjoy the rewards, both large and small.

As a parent of an autistic child, I often wanted to fade into the woodwork, not stand out in any way. That can take a toll on you and diminish your ability to let go and enjoy, to occasionally step out of the part of your life that can so dominate your every moment.

Fortunately for us, we were able to enjoy some wonderful experiences, to fully embrace them, to literally and figuratively step out of our usual routine. One of those events that sprang from small victories and the larger Miracle Run was when, in October 2000, Phillip and Stephen appeared at a Cure Autism Now (CAN) benefit at the Beverly Hills Hotel. John Shestak, the Hollywood producer and founder of CAN, had invited us all to attend. He also arranged for Phillip and Stephen to speak. This was to be a really big deal of a fund-raiser, a black-tie event, so we were nervous and excited for weeks leading up to the event.

I even asked Mike Prevett, the agent working with Joel Gotler on developing the movie about our lives, to assist us in editing our remarks. Mike also did a great job helping us to keep calm. He reminded us that the people we'd be talking to had more money than we did but that didn't mean we had less humanity and less to offer. All they wanted was for us to be real, to, as we'd come to call it, keep it autistic. That we could do.

What was a little more difficult was for all of us to get dressed to the nines. As Doug put it, we were probably only at a six and a half collectively. We rented tuxedos for the twins, and in a way, this was their senior prom. They didn't have dates for the evening, but I think that it was important for them to get dressed up. A limousine picked us all up and drove us into Beverly Hills. The boys were enjoying themselves, but the clothes were making them a little self-conscious. When we got to Sunset Boulevard, and then the Hilton, that all changed. We were escorted along a path leading through the hotel's twelve acres of lush tropical gardens. Somehow those clothes and that setting all seemed appropriate then. A who's who of Hollywood fame had stayed at or been on the grounds of the hotel, and it was as if the air was infused with the collective class and sophistication of those legends. I don't know what it was, but it seemed as if we all walked a little taller, had words come more easily to our tongues, felt a certain something that we hadn't before.

As we walked through the hotel itself, we glided past the famous Crystal Ballroom and its art deco trappings. We marveled at the enormous chandelier that gave the room its name. Our event was being held in the Sunset Room, and appropriately enough, as we made our way into the space, the windows lining the room were set ablaze by one of those spectacular Southern California sunsets. We were introduced to a number of celebrities and other influential types, but were most impressed by Anthony Edwards. We all knew him from his work on the television show *ER*, but it took Phillip to mention two of his favorite movies, *Top Gun* and *Revenge of the Nerds*, to move the conversation from adulation to something a little more casual.

After dinner was served, the speeches began. Stephen and Phillip were well received, and though they would never be the most polished of speakers, their sincerity and their passion won people over. All in all, it was a transforming evening. A great deal of money was raised, Phillip and Stephen got a real taste of being in the limelight at a fancy Hollywood event, and they got a chance to speak on behalf of the millions of teens like them who were in need of a cure.

We could count the evening as another victory. Sure, we were still experiencing a few setbacks, and would continue to do so, but the course didn't seem as difficult as it had first appeared to be; the uphill sections were getting a bit easier to make our way up, our legs and hearts feeling stronger.

We were all riding high on the way home, our white whale of a Chevy Suburban traded in that evening for a white stretch Lincoln limo. As Hollywood and Beverly Hills receded in the rearview mirror, none of us knew or even wanted to consider just how symbolic that scene was.

Chapter Eight

Flying Solo

PARENTS of most children have to worry about the kinds of emotional and psychological abuse their kids will suffer as they grow up. A lot has been written about bullying and the many campaigns undertaken to eradicate it. I know that I was not alone in my worrying, and my boys were not alone in their suffering. I just don't understand the mentality of young people, or anyone for that matter, who want to heap abuse on someone who has already had plenty of difficulties presented to them by life. I understand on an intellectual level that that's the nature of things—that boys will be boys, that nature is red in tooth and claw, that nice guys finish last, that my sons should just rub some dirt on it and get back in the game. I understand that, but I don't like it. To this day, I struggle with shrugging that off and sometimes allow my frustration with injustice to get the best of me and sap my energy.

Given what we know about the oftentimes cruel environment in which our kids grow up, we're left to wonder just how we can finally let go enough to allow our kids the freedom they need to develop into adults. I know I've mentioned my experiences with the twins and this issue already, but because it is such an important one, I'm going to return to it.

I have a male friend who is the youngest of four boys, whom I'll call Bob. Bob's in his forties now, a well-adjusted father of two boys and a successful television writer with a beautiful wife. For the situation comedy he wrote for, Bob drew a lot from the experiences he had growing up. Laughingly, he says that he thinks that his brothers could have been trained by the KGB or the East German Stasi or some other CIA-like spy organization. He said that he was teased so mercilessly and picked on so much physically by his older brothers that when he got to school, no one was as good at the kind of mental and physical abuse his brothers handed out on a daily basis. (His brothers were as clever as they were cruel and never really harmed him physically—at least they never left marks that would show.)

As a result of his "training" at home, he was able to ignore most of the teasing he got for being tall and lanky and uncoordinated. He was able to laugh when anyone tried to trick him. He said that he'd learned the best way to defend himself was to ignore most of what was said and done, and only when someone crossed the line and tried to physically harm him would he retaliate. He also told me that he was grateful that his brothers were so mean to him, that they had toughened him up in ways that made the adjustment to school, and especially high school, so easy for him.

As his sons entered middle school, he was concerned that

they might have grown up in a household that was too protective. He and his wife preached the gospel of niceness and kindness, and the kids attended a private school that preached the same values. His wife was especially sensitive to teasing, since she knew the special kind of vindictiveness that girls can inflict on one another. Bob said he worried that they weren't really being prepared for what the real world is like.

I told Bob some of the stories about Stephen and Phillip and the teasing they'd endured—he especially liked the story about the kind janitors retrieving the twins' rooftop-tossed jackets—, and marveled that Stephen and Phillip hadn't turned bitter. I suppose if I had to objectively describe the twins to you as they are today, I'd say that they are nice, polite, and positive young men. If there's a miracle anywhere in their story, I believe these descriptions of them encapsulate that special quality of their lives. That's not to say that the twins are completely naive and Pollyanna-ish in their viewpoint. They do know that there are bad and unpleasant people in the world, but as far as I can tell, it hasn't tainted them. They are aware of the reality and have moved on.

Their tolerance and their willingness to block out the bad and focus on the good, or to at least develop a thick skin, was something that I had been working on for years. To see how easily they adopted that attitude and employed those strategies gave me hope. It is true that many autistics turn inward and inappropriately block out the rest of the world, but that doesn't mean that there isn't a lesson to be found in that behavior. Knowing when and how to carefully modulate that tendency toward introversion is just another of the social skills necessary to function—for them and for me.

Before I could completely let go of them, and before I could rest more easily at night knowing that they would be physically and emotionally safe, I knew that I was going to have to allow them to experience a few more of life's little bumps and bruises. They were very eager to get out in the world, and I knew that there was little I could do, or really wanted to do, to prevent them from seeing both the good and the bad.

I took my cue for how to approach this in adolescence and young adulthood from the experiences I had with them when they were children. They were both very afraid of thunderstorms and loud noises. So many times they would hear a distant rumble and become unsettled. At first, I tried to minimize the impact on their heightened senses by taking them into the bathroom or another secluded area of the house where they could feel safe and protected. In other words, I removed them from the experience.

As they grew older, I thought it was important for them to understand more about the phenomenon that had once terrorized them. Even before I could broach the subject of learning about "bad things," they came to me and told me that they wanted to understand the weather and storms. I bought them books about meteorology, astronomy, and other sciences. I took their wanting to understand what they'd once feared or what they viewed as unknowns and mysteries as a sign of their maturity. I also realized that book learning was an important and necessary part of their beginning to understand more about the world around them, but it wasn't the only way for them to learn.

If the twins were going to experience some of the painful realities of life, I would try as best I could to be sure that they received those lessons in measured doses, that their minds and souls had built up a tolerance for one level before being exposed to another. I also had to do the same thing for myself. I wasn't able to just let Stephen go to that Valentine's Day dance; I had to be nearby. As time passed, I was more able to just let them go places and experience things.

Letting Phillip work in the library was eased by our knowing and working with Barbara Mona. We trusted her and believed that he would be in safe hands. And he was. Later on, after high school, Phillip went to work at a Marshalls department store. He got the job through the auspices of the Department of Rehabilitation—an arm of the state mental health agencies. Phillip had a supervisor with that local agency, but he wasn't there day to day watching over Phillip. The job paid him minimum wage, and he worked in the backrooms mostly, unloading boxes, doing some folding, and he seemed content with that. There were never any incidents reported of him being teased or taken advantage of. We did have to provide him with transportation to and from work, and if we factored in the expense and time of that, his salary wasn't really covering our outlay of cash, but so be it—to a point.

Here's where the letting go and allowing Phillip to have his dreams become reality get a little confusing and complicated. Phillip never complained about the menial nature of the work or the minimum-wage pay. He was happy to be earning any money at all, which he spent as quickly as he earned (more on that later), and he enjoyed being able to tell people that he had a job. He was feeling pretty good about himself. That's a win. That's a big win, and I knew it.

Unfortunately, I also knew that Phillip was capable of far

more than working at Marshalls. I'm sure a lot of parents of nonautistic kids can identify with the feelings of a parent who believes that a son or daughter is underachieving. I could have accepted that if it were simply a matter of Phillip's choosing to limit himself. I could have easily stayed out of the matter entirely if I didn't see that greater harm was being done to him by the same agency that was responsible for him getting this job and getting "rehabilitated."

I understand that the world is a tough place and that there are individual bullies out there who will deny our kids some opportunities—to feel happy, safe, and so on—during some part of their day. Like my friend Bob, I believed that ignoring those people would eventually make them go away. I didn't like it if we were out somewhere and Phillip was gripped by a Tourette's syndrome tic and someone stared or laughed or looked in disgust at him.

For a long time as a parent of autistic kids, I believed that it was my responsibility to educate the world about disabilities. At the time they were growing up—the late eighties and early nineties—it really *felt* as if I had to be the one to educate people about autism and press for their rights and just treatment. I had no real option. I couldn't afford to hire a lawyer to do the work for me, so I had to become their advocate. By the time they were in high school and then of college age, I wanted to believe that the world was a more enlightened place.

Also, instead of confronting someone who looked askance at one of the twins, or counseling the parent of a child who gave Phillip or Stephen a hard time in public about how they should be instructing their kids, I adopted the "ignore them and they will go away" approach. It seemed to work. I couldn't save everyone from their wrong-mindedness, and if I focused on doing what I could through the foundation we established and didn't let my energy get sucked into trying to right every possible wrong, I could in the long run do a lot more good by staying positive and focusing on successes and not failures. I had to learn that sometimes letting go meant doing more good elsewhere. I also had to learn that letting go could sometimes mean giving up—in the sense of both losing something completely and settling for less than what you really wanted or deserved.

Because of those last lessons, I could not just sit idly by and watch Phillip trudge happily off to Marshalls, knowing that he was being denied the opportunity to go to college. Simply put: Individual acts of discrimination, while not being completely acceptable, were something I could let go of. Institutional acts of discrimination were definitely crossing the line, and I would not put up with them. We had worked too hard and for too long to let go of the idea that Stephen and Phillip would go to college.

I mentioned earlier that we had all taken a time-out after Phillip and Stephen finished up their last year of high school. It was a well-deserved break. We had all been working hard on a number of fronts. Inspired by Stephen's success on the track and the cross-country course, we'd gotten very involved in his races. We combined that interest and experience in running and a desire to be more out front about educating people about autism and fund-raising for the cause by hosting a Miracle Run race. The first was held in June 2000, and it was a big success.

Our collective hard work was also rewarded a few weeks before the race, when Stephen and Phillip graduated from Agoura High School. I was thrilled when Richard graduated, proud when he decided to enter the U.S. Navy, but there was something even more special about seeing Stephen and Phillip in their caps and gowns. I remembered when I first heard the dreaded word "autistic" and the dire prognosis that they'd be in an institution in a few years. I had mourned the fact that I wouldn't see them in their Little League Baseball uniforms, wouldn't see them marching in procession with their peers to receive their diplomas. For a long time, I felt the schools and the world at large weren't ready for autistics to take their rightful place in society. I knew that things were getting better but still weren't perfect. Seeing Stephen presented with an academic achievement award signed by President Clinton for having earned straight A's both took some of the sting out of and rubbed some salt in the fresh wound recently inflicted by the SAT test being denied to them and College Night being an education in how ill prepared colleges were for the presence of autistic students.

So we did take a bit of a hiatus. It wasn't, as you can now see, completely voluntary. Without the SAT test and without the kinds of special programs I thought needed to be available at colleges (what I'd learned on College Night), I thought the twins were effectively being denied entrance into college. We were going to have to figure out how to get around that obstacle. The time off would help us think, and as I said previously, it did release us from the notion that everything the twins did had to be on the same rigid timetable everyone else seemed to be adhering to.

But the time we took off wasn't spend idly wondering what the state was going to do for us next. I spent the time figuring out exactly what the state owed us.

Having the twins enrolled in public schools for twelve years had given me a certain level of comfort and familiarity. I could see on the horizon, however, that our comfort level would be tested. Public Law 94-142, which was enacted in 1975, had been amended periodically since then, but it still only provided legal protections for "school aged children" from the ages of five to twenty-one. We were clearly at the far end of that age spectrum in 2000, when Phillip was at work at Marshalls.

Provisions had been made in subsequent versions of the law that were more pertinent now. In 1990, PL 101-476 mandated that transition services be made available to assist students who were leaving the educational environment and entering the adult world. Phillip's job at the department store was a part of that legislation. That's where the Department of Rehabilitation came in. As much as they were providing Phillip with a transition to adulthood, I felt they were also setting up a roadblock, just as the Agoura High School District was by not allowing the boys to take the SAT test and just as the colleges and universities were by not having programs for autistic students.

I wasn't prepared to fight the fight right after high school, but I'd gotten my act together and wasn't about to let go of the idea that the twins deserved and were owed a chance to succeed or fail in college.

As much as I disliked the institutionalized forms of discrimination that the boys faced, I also understood that it was difficult to take on institutions. However, I did know this: Institutions are made up of individuals.

Phillip's supervisor at the Department of Rehabilitation, Mr. Sortino, was like a lot of other well-meaning people placed in his position. He had to toe the party line, and the party line was that, given Phillip's various conditions, he wasn't a good candidate to succeed in college. That's why he'd recommended Phillip for the job at Marshalls.

Of course, I disagreed with his assessment of Phillip. Yes, Phillip had tics, and he sometimes struggled to control his impulses, but he was a smart guy. Surely anyone who dealt with him could recognize that.

As the 2001 school year approached, I finally confronted Mr. Sortino. I wanted Phillip's case to be reviewed. I wanted him to be switched out of the job-training program and into the college education program. This was a case of Phillip not really understanding the long-term impact of a decision that was being made for him. I had to let go of the idea of letting go and allowing things to happen on their own without my intervening. This was a case of greater harm being done by my standing by than my acting to intervene on my son's behalf.

I tried my best to stay calm during my phone conversation with Mr. Sortino, and I did until he responded to my statement that Phillip wanted to go to college to major in drafting by saying, "Mrs. Morgan-Thomas, my job is to rehabilitate Phillip, and his going to college would be a waste of the taxpayers' money. You do pay taxes, don't you? You wouldn't want your tax money wasted, would you?"

Sortino was the one man who stood in the way of the state approving funding for Phillip's tuition and fees. His comments about whether or not we paid taxes was a subtle dig. He knew all of our financial realities. I let the dig pass, but what I didn't let pass were his seemingly contradictory remarks. I was not about to let go when I knew I had the advantage and he'd made a stupid comment.

I asked him if it was his job to rehabilitate Phillip or to protect the financial interests of the taxpayer. As I figured he would, he told me he was trying to do both.

I had no choice; I had to let him know that I'd done my homework. "Mr. Sortino, you are familiar with the Americans with Disabilities Act, aren't you? You are familiar with Public Law 94-142? You are aware that this is federal legislation and that you are not guaranteeing my son the right to an education?"

I imagined Mr. Sortino's face losing its smug expression and his eyes sweeping the ground as though he were looking for the smarmy smile that had fallen off his face.

"Mr. Sortino, if you're denying Phillip his rights, then we as taxpayers are wasting money on you."

I heard the sound of a hissing flat tire on the other end of the phone. "Of course we wouldn't deny your son his rights. That's not what we're here to do. Unfortunately, since Phillip is now over the age of eighteen, any request in regard to a change in status has to come from him."

I was steamed. Just another hoop to jump through. If I had a dollar for every page of paperwork I'd had to file over the years, I could have bought my own college.

"Hold on. I'll get Phillip."

I didn't bother to cover the mouthpiece as I shouted, "Phillip, come here!" When Phillip ambled into the kitchen, the omnipresent earphones mugging his ears, he looked at me and smiled.

"Tell this man you want a review meeting. Say, 'I want a review meeting.'"

Phillip hit the stop button on his disc player and shrugged off his earphones. "I want a review meeting." He handed the phone back to me and smiled.

A few hours later Mr. Sortino called back. Phillip would have his meeting in two days.

We didn't have a lot of time to prepare Phillip for the meeting. We'd seen how he acted in some of our movie pitch meetings and were a little concerned that if he didn't stay focused on the task at hand, convincing everyone that he wanted to go to college, all could be lost. The meeting was to be held in Thousand Oaks, at the headquarters of the Department of Rehabilitation. Along with Mr. Sortino, Phillip's case manager, Ms. Terazin; the state transition counselor, Sandy Moshin; and the regional manager, Rhonda Wolfgang, would also be in attendance. I told Doug that since I had spoken out and not gone along with the system and just let them decide that Phillip should stay in a job-training program, they were probably going to have a social worker there to scare me into behaving myself. I had made such a big stink about this issue, I was sure they would retaliate in some way.

As the president of the Miracle Run Foundation, I had fielded many calls and letters from other parents who were fed up with the system and the runaround they were constantly forced to endure from all layers of the bureaucracy that managed the social welfare agencies. These groups were supposed to help us, but too often they ended up being a hindrance. I was tempted to just give in, take on other work to earn extra money, and pay the tuition myself, but something told me that would be the wrong thing to do. I'd been advising other parents to be aware of their rights, to fight for what was legally theirs, and to know the system and work within it rather than throw their hands up in frustration. We couldn't let them win. All the regulations and steps and filings seemed designed simply to wear us down to the point at which we surrendered. I couldn't do that now, not after seeing the example that Stephen had set; not after having heard all his words about not giving up.

The morning of the meeting, I awoke early and pressed Doug's only suit. I needed him to be there with me, and I needed him to look as authoritative as possible. If there's one thing Doug is not, it's authoritative. Not that people don't believe what he says or listen to him, but he is just a tie-dyed-in-the-wool, laid-back hippie type who is completely distrustful of any form of authority. I had to impress on him the fact that just because he was wearing a suit we'd bought from Marshalls using Phillip's employee discount didn't mean that we'd sold out completely to the man. He had to drop that attitude and his regular-guy blue-collar persona for just one day and be a model of middle-class respectability and comportment. I knew that wasn't going to be easy, particularly since I hadn't taken the time to hem his pants. I couldn't let him walk around with them dragging, so I pinned them up, telling him to be careful and to be ready to jump in with whatever support he could.

We'd briefed Phillip several times on what to say at the meeting. We also bribed him. If he said, "I want to attend college as a drafting major," we'd buy him a new game for his Nintendo console.

God love him, Phillip is a really honest young man. When we told him that he needed to make that statement, he said,

"But I want to be a musician in a band. I'm working on a screen-play. I don't need college."

I didn't have time to refute his irrefutable logic. "Okay, but do you have money for video games now?"

"No."

"Then you are going to have to kiss these people's butts. That's how it is sometimes when you're an adult. So, just for an hour or so, I want you to be a drafting major."

"I want to be a musician."

I put my hands on the top of Phillip's head and inclined it so that our foreheads touched. "Remember these words, Phil-lip: Kiss butt."

"Okay."

I handed Phillip a short stack of papers I'd printed out. Copies of the ADA, Public Law 94-142. I also had a similar stack for Doug and me. Hopefully our props would convince them that we were fully prepared and fully informed and not just fully full of it.

We were optimistic on the drive to Thousand Oaks. Phillip gave us the rundown on his possible video game selection. Doug looked great in his suit, and I was as put together as I ever could be. I'd walked out of the bathroom after having put my hair up in a nice chignon. A bottle of Phillip's Xanax had tumbled out of the medicine cabinet when I went to return my brush. Sorely tempted but knowing better than to face the state in an altered state, I had walked away, hoping I wouldn't regret my decision.

Doug was particularly upbeat. Ever since we'd gotten Bev-erlee on board to help sell our life story, he'd acted as if we were a team of destiny. I love his optimism—it serves to offset some of my natural skepticism—and I found myself caught up in his positive vibe.

"Let's have dinner after this," Doug said to me. "To celebrate our upcoming victory."

"Sure, let's. Why not? Phillip's going to college."

"I'll be glad to be done with this. This rehab stuff is a bunch of crap." Phillip sounded convincingly angry. I just didn't want him to use that kind of language.

"Remember what we told you, Phillip?" I asked.

He nodded. "I remember, Mom."

We walked toward the building's entrance. Phillip was standing tall, walking without his sometimes autistic gait. Wearing a nice pair of slacks and a button-down-collar shirt, he looked handsome. For the moment, his tics had subsided.

"This is too easy," I said, and took Doug's hand.

Maybe it was because we were accustomed to our meetings with various Hollywood types—we'd just had one with Valerie Bertinelli and her production company—but the Rehab Center's office seemed even shabbier than before. The conference table we sat at was chipped and stained, and around it sat the principal players all clad in some variation of the social services uniform—a drab-colored polyester suit. My heart went out to these people in spite of all the obstacles they threw in our way. I knew that for the most part their motives were pure, but their strict adherence to guidelines and procedures and protocols had worn on our very last nerves. Though we were familiar with one another through our dealings with the various branches of their agencies, we exchanged introductions. We were sitting at a round table, but I found it odd that the two "teams"—us versus them—were positioned on opposite sides of an imaginary line bisecting that circle.

"So, Phillip," Ms. Terazin said, "you want to attend college. You know it's not in your plan." Ms. Terazin tapped a blood-red-tipped finger on a document. I recognized it as his Individualized Education Program. He'd filled it out along with his teachers at Agoura High during his senior year. I was about to state that the document was nearly two years old and that much had changed during that time. I refrained from responding, remembering that Phillip was the one who had to say that he wanted to go to college.

Phillip was nodding his head, looking pensive and not at all like he was seized by a Tourette's tic. He licked his lips and was about to speak.

"What the *fuck!*" I recognized the voice as Doug's but could have sworn it had come out of Phillip's mouth. Except, of course, Phillip seldom swore and never used the F word.

Doug squirmed in his seat as though he were channeling Phillip's condition. He held up a pin for everyone in the room to see. "This thing stabbed me." Doug and I were the only ones who knew the identity of the real culprit—his makeshift seamstress (aka his wife).

I felt all the blood drain out of my face and pool in my big toe. I saw Phillip beginning to shake. I thought of that Xanax and wished I had taken it, or at least snuck it into Doug's juice that morning.

I tried to say something but couldn't find my voice. I felt paralyzed. I moved my eyes to check in on everyone else's reaction. For the most part, they sat there with their professionally composed expressions on. These people had seen a lot in their careers, but this had to be a first for them. Mr. Sortino took over, acting as if nothing had happened.

"Since Phillip is over eighteen now, he has to make this declaration of intent himself."

Sitting there asking myself why he had to phrase it that way and wondering if Phillip would understand that "declaration of intent" was his cue, I suddenly tapped into my inner screenwriter. In my mind's eye, I saw this scene as it would appear in the film. The camera would pan from one face to another, showing their reactions to Doug's outburst. Everyone would be clearly agitated, talking over one another, and then from another angle, a second camera would focus on Phillip. He would compose himself, and a look of fierce determination would settle over his features. The camera would slowly zoom in until we saw a tight close-up of his face. He would rise, and the camera would rise with him. We'd see reaction shots of each of the meeting's participants growing still and then nodding thoughtfully as Phillip's eloquent words about his dreams and desires, his vision for his future, his belief that all autistic people could one day take their rightful place in society, had their effect on the room. Everyone would rise to their feet and applaud him. Doug and I would rush up to him and proudly throw our arms around him.

Back in Realityville, Phillip did stand. "I have something to say—" All eyes were riveted on him. He took a deep breath, and as he exhaled, it was as if an electrical charge coursed through his body. His arms flew up and a Little Richard–like squeal came out of his mouth. In an instant he'd gone from placid and composed to doing the Mashed Potato.

My mind had left my body in California and gone to Catatonia. For all I knew, drool was pouring out of my mouth. I imagined I was making as much of a spectacle of myself as Phillip was.

We all have fantasies.

My first one of that day, Phillip's rousing speech, had been shattered.

I looked over at Doug, my knight in shining wool blend, and knew that he would come to our rescue. He'd done it before, and though a White Suburban is a poor substitute for a White Charger, his heart was always in the right place. He put the palms of his hands on the table and pushed himself upright. His face contorted and he collapsed into his seat. "Shit! How many of these fuckers are in my pants?"

Everyone just stared at Doug.

My husband raised his hands in surrender. "I'm sorry." He rubbed his chin and tried to calm himself. "Look, the thing is, let's look at Phillip. How can anyone deny him access to college? He's intelligent. He behaves appropriately in public. More than anything, though, he wants to succeed."

All eyes turned to Phillip, evaluating him.

At this point, Phillip had finished the Mashed Potato and was into the Twist, making Chubby Checker look like a fallen pawn.

"EEEK! EEEK!" Phillip screamed.

Doug didn't miss a beat. "His language skills, after completing years of therapy, are outstanding."

"VAGINA! VAGINA!" Phillip shouted.

"See, he *does* know how to act in college," Doug responded.

At that point, Phillip's body stilled midtwist. He stuck his right middle finger out and bunny-hopped around the table singing "Christmas Time Is Here" in a falsetto Alvin and the Chipmunks' voice.

"He's a musical savant. Have you heard him play?" Doug asked.

Sandy Moshin pointed at Phillip and said, "*He's* going to college?"

"Then we're all in agreement, that's great." Doug gathered his papers and stood as if to leave.

"Hold on, Mr. Thomas." Rhonda Wolfgang's basso profundo squashed Phillip's singing. "There's a simple matter of regulations that hasn't been attended to."

Phillip stopped moving and singing. He took his place back at the table and stood behind his chair with his fingertips resting on its back. "I would very much like to go to college to study drafting."

"We are all in agreement, aren't we?" Doug asked.

All our adversaries around the table nodded or shrugged their shoulders in resignation. They knew they had no choice. They'd invoked the rule of the law, and Phillip had abided by it. But he wasn't through yet.

"One more thing," he said. I sat there hoping my cinematic moment would make a late entrance.

"Of course, Phillip," Rhonda Wolfgang said. "It's your meeting." She looked as if she were about to vomit.

"Butt kissers." Phillip smiled. He handed his copy of the Adults with Disabilities Act to Rhonda. "This is a bunch of crap." Phillip's echolalia was kicking in and he was now channeling Doug. He began repeating everything Doug had said, beginning with, "Shit, how many of these things do I have in my pants?"

Doug took Phillip by the arm and escorted him toward the door. "What the *fuck* is this?" Phillip said, in parting.

I pushed my chair away from the table, all of my faculties once again intact. "Thank you for your time." I hustled out of the room before anyone could respond.

I met up with Doug and Phillip in the truck.

Doug fired up the engine, and once it had settled down from its rapid idle, he looked at me and said, "Even though my wife is trying to kill me and I'm bleeding, I still think that went well."

"Do you think they liked us?" Phillip asked.

At the time it was difficult to find a lot of humor in the incident, but the story of Phillip's triumphant "I have something to say" meeting has metamorphosed into one of our favorites.

The Rehabilitation Center classified Tourette's syndrome as among the most serious of disabilities. They felt it represented a "serious drawback" to Phillip's potential and also would effect the ability of other students to learn. That was no laughing matter. Years later, Ali, who is in college now and studying to be a special education teacher, wrote a paper about Tourette's syndrome and higher education. She posed a very good question. Were the policies designed to punish the Tourette's or the person with Tourette's? Obviously, we saw it as the latter and wouldn't let that distinction go unchecked.

Phillip and Stephen would go to college in August 2001. The law stated that as adults older than eighteen, all they had to do was say the words. Phillip just added a few more for emphasis.

Those additional words might have been directed at me— not in the sense of Phillip swearing at me in anger, but in expressing a lesson I'd been learning all along. As much as we worked to prepare Phillip for the meeting, as many times as we warned him that he had to behave and speak politely, as much as we rehearsed, planned, and envisioned outcomes, the reality was that Phillip was Phillip, Doug was Doug, Stephen was Stephen, and I was Corrine, and we were all unpredictable and prone to surprise one another. Phillip and Stephen were not puppets. As much as behavioral modification therapies were based on positive rewards, that didn't mean that they were guaranteed to produce the kinds of behavioral results I wanted.

I was not a puppet master pulling strings. Like any parent, I had to evaluate certain situations and make judgment calls. I did have to step in from time to time, but as the boys got older, those situations were becoming fewer and farther between.

I know that I'm hard on myself, and for a long time I questioned some of the decisions I've made. One of my biggest mistakes had been in believing for so long that I was the one who was responsible for teaching the boys. Phillip's actions made me realize that they had a lot they could teach me.

It was also slowly dawning on me that if we were running a race, then throughout their childhood and into their adolescence I had been carrying the boys on my back for so long I was getting exhausted. It would take the Miracle Run to really let me see that I wasn't running alone, that this was in many senses a relay race. In my desperate attempts to ensure that the race was run fairly, I may have held the twins back, slowed them down too much. We all still had a lot to learn and teach one another. The next step was to widen our scope, expand our sphere of influence, and let more people know what they and we are capable of.

Taking on the challenge of getting them into college was another much-needed reward; other challenges lay ahead, and we'd need the energy to get there. Thankfully, the twins are taking on much more of the work for themselves.

I can remember taking Phillip to the movies. As a child, he was content to sit with us, and it was easier to monitor his behavior. Now, as an adult, he doesn't want to sit with Mom and Dad. At times, his Tourette's syndrome erupts, and he may make noises or vocalize things. He knows that if it gets too loud or too distracting, he should leave. The stares of disgust he sometimes receives irritate me no end, but I don't intervene on his behalf. Phillip will frequently tell people on his own that he is autistic and has Tourette's and OCD. I'm not convinced everyone he says that to understands or even cares. Phillip's efforts may not seem like much, but they are motivated by his desire to inform and educate more than they are to provide an excuse for his behavior. One of the things I admire most about Stephen and Phillip is that they take responsibility for the things they do that draw attention to themselves or that negatively impact other people—especially Phillip, who will go out of his way when he first meets people to tell them about his various conditions. He's not seeking sympathy or attention but understanding. I have to admire anyone who has the courage to say to the world, "This is who I am," warts and all. I hid for so long that I'm still not entirely comfortable with the idea of being that open. But I'm trying to keep it autistic.

Phillip and Stephen still live with us, though they have both moved out of the house. Doug, ever the handyman, built a twelve-by-twenty-foot outbuilding on our property, where Phillip now spends most of his time. Doug ran electricity and an Internet connection (a must-have, it seems, these days) to it as well as a cable for his small television. And Stephen now lives in a motor home parked in our driveway. It was originally owned by my ex-husband, Big Steve, and his wife. They'd bought it years ago, but since they were no longer using it, they'd put it up for sale. The twins loved to travel and talked all the time about the camping trips they took with their grandparents. The motor home was large enough to accommodate us all, and since we still had some funds left over from the movie proceeds, we decided to splurge. When we aren't traveling in it, Stephen uses it as his residence. He has everything he needs in that self-contained space, and that seems appropriate for him and his temperament.

Phillip's place doesn't have running water, so we see him frequently, and he often eats his meals with us. We're fortunate we live in the climate we do. The exterior walls of the outbuilding are plywood, and the interior walls are unfinished. It never gets so cold at night that we feel the need to put up drywall and insulate it.

For symbolic reasons, I kind of like the idea that it isn't insulated. We haven't banished Phillip from the house, nor have we provided a protective cocoon to keep everything potentially harmful away from him. He is living both at home and not at home. I do have to admit that sometimes when he is playing his guitar loudly or when one of his Tourette's syndrome vocal tics has him shouting, I do long for a sound barrier to keep the peace and quiet I treasure so much these days from being disturbed. I also know that when the day comes and Phillip and Stephen aren't living in close proximity to us, I will miss what have come to be the familiar sounds of our days.

It also seems appropriate that Stephen and Phillip live in more or less temporary quarters. The motor home can be on the road in a moment's notice, and Phillip's "pad" was designed and built to be dismantled quickly when he no longer needed it. For now, the twins are parked here, living on some part of the property where they spent the most important years of their lives, the place where they took so many monumental strides toward growing up. I've come to think of this place as the pad as well— a launching pad and a staging area, a place where one day they will take off from to explore other places on their own.

Like most parents, I feel a mixture of apprehension and anticipation about the day when Phillip and Stephen are officially and permanently on their own. Mentally and emotionally, I think I'm most of the way there in terms of letting go. I still enjoy the security of knowing that they are so close by, but I also have some worries about their capability of being fully independent. One of the most troubling issues we have to deal with is money. Phillip is quite able to carry on a phone conversation with anyone. Because most of his Tourette's syndrome symptoms are his physical tics, and he avoids speaking on the phone when they are manifesting verbally, you would think as the person on the other end of the line with him that you were dealing with just another customer. As a result, he has signed up for numerous credit cards and ordered all kinds of electronic devices, CDs, video games, and such that he doesn't have the money to pay for.

For a while, it seemed as if there were a never-ending parade of UPS, FedEx, DHL, and USPS couriers traipsing up the steps to our place, all laden with packages for Phillip. He was also smart enough and eager enough to receive all of this bounty that he would wait at the top of our street for the postman or deliveryman to arrive every day. Eventually, no matter how hard he tried to hide from us what he'd ordered, or what credit card he'd received, the bills would eventually come to us. Doug and I are very good about not invading the boys' privacy, so we would never open their mail, but we would notice and ask about the packages that were coming with such regularity. We decided that we wouldn't intervene unless the companies contacted us and our own credit rating and standing were threatened.

We've tried not to put the responsibility for these actions on anyone's shoulders but Phillip's. I don't know if it was the economic deprivation that he experienced as a kid that has him acting out in this way, but it is a reality that we have to deal with. If nothing else, we hope that Phillip's desire for material things will motivate him to finish college and land a job that will enable him to live the lifestyle to which he has grown accustomed—if not fully capable of affording.

I suppose that in some way my attitude toward this financial stuff is indicative of how I've grown. I used to worry so much about money, would fret and lie sleepless for days wondering how I was going to find enough money in the budget to pay one bill and hold off another creditor until the next payday. I hated that feeling and was so ashamed that I couldn't meet my financial responsibilities.

Now, I realize that Phillip is at an age when he has to assume those responsibilities himself. We have to provide him with guidance and educate him about potential scams, identity theft, the importance of maintaining a good credit score, and all the rest of those issues. In a lot of cases, we have bailed him out financially, but we have also, as my father used to say, "bawled him out" for his irresponsibility and given him ultimatums. I don't worry about this as much as I used to, and I've adopted a "we'll take care of it when we have to" stance. I'm not going to let Phillip's fiscal misadventures ruin my day, and I'll step in only when they threaten to ruin a part of his or our life. I guess it's all a matter of attitude and a question of degree.

Some people might read this and think that we are on the verge of financial ruin, that Phillip's behavior is typical of a society that worships things and lives on overextended credit. I look at this as one particular quirk in Phillip's personality, one that is bothersome but manageable. Like most other parts of his and our lives, we'll get to a solution that works for all of us eventually. In the meantime, there are puppies to be fed and my garden to tend to. All in good time; all in good time.

Chapter Nine

Give and Take

I grew up in a house in which the statement "To those whom much is given, much is expected" was a part of our daily lives. Even though we didn't have a whole lot of money or material possessions, whenever someone needed anything, my mother and father would give what they could. If that meant helping someone out by providing free labor, cooking a meal to help out a family when the mother was ill, or contributing our weekly tithe at church, we were giving in whatever form we could whenever we could.

I'm sad to admit that the above statement about expectations took on a different meaning when the twins were diagnosed. I felt as if I had been given a whole lot of worry, work, and woe, as if I was being expected to do so much more than other par-

ents, and that the burden of autism placed on the boys and by
extension on me was something to be endured. The expectations for the kind of lives they were going to live were dim at
best and completely dark at worst. At those early stages of coming to terms with the diagnosis, I could not imagine a time
when I could have done anything but concentrate on the lives
of my own children, that the only contribution I was capable
of making (and at times I doubted I could successfully manage
even this) was to be sure that they were raised with the proper
values, had enough food not to starve, and had a safe haven to
come home to when others treated them poorly.

That didn't mean that I wasn't compassionate. I could feel a
great deal of compassion for anyone who was downtrodden. My
heart went out to victims of natural disasters across the globe, I
empathized with the parents of other special needs kids in my
community, and I admired and was eternally grateful to the people in my life who had assisted me in so many different ways. I just
really didn't have enough energy to do anything other than feel.

As a result of Stephen's Miracle Run, my attitude toward
other people in need and my willingness and ability to reach
out to them came closer to merging. In the months after seeing
Stephen run, change came incrementally.

So there I was, in 2001, with the boys approaching eighteen. They were both in high school and had done well enough
to be given the option of enrolling in mainstream classes. One
was working after school, and the other was involved in extra-
curricular activities. We were driving them back and forth to
this practice and that job, working and still trying to get our

foundation off the ground, and having an agent shop our life story around Hollywood.

I don't know how many candles my mother lit at church to get us to this point, but I had visions of forest fires in my mind. And to think that I'd once been told that the boys would have to be institutionalized. I didn't like to think about how different things would have been for them if I'd made that choice.

The Stephen that we saw on the cross-country course, on the track, and in the classroom was a very different person from the one who was observed in the last year of junior high by Cathy Khmara. She sat in on his language arts class. She witnessed Stephen crying and telling another student to shut up when he couldn't find his homework in his binder. Her evaluation stated that Stephen "keeps very much to himself" and "didn't seem to know that he could get a tissue for his dripping nose." As a final summation of that observation, Robert Cunha, the school's psychologist, noted, "He showed stronger reasoning with the task of discerning the relationship in designs than he did with understanding everyday life experiences. It seems that he deals with abstraction rather than reality."

Maybe some parents would be dismayed by having their son characterized as having difficulties with reality, but I firmly believe that it was Stephen's ability to retreat from his harsh reality and go someplace else in his mind that really enabled him to become a good runner and an outstanding student. In talking with Doug and with several other adult males over the years, I've come to understand far better the importance of a young man's imagination and thinking of himself as a hero. The movies the boys watched and the underdog mentality that they developed really helped make them a success. Being on the cross-country team gave Stephen an outlet for those impulses to triumph over the odds and over adversity. It also gave him a place where his oddity was rewarded. The cover of the 1999 Charger Cross-Country Yearbook announced this; it read: "Why Be Normal? BE POSITIVE."

This was among the many slogans that I eventually saw Stephen write down on various sheets of paper. I know that some of them came directly from the coaches, who gleaned them from movies like *Star Wars* ("Do, or do not, there is no try"), literature ("Courage is not the absence of fear, but it is the mastery of fear"—Mark Twain), and popular culture ("No pain, no gain. No guts, no glory. Winners don't quit and quitters don't win!"). I was particularly struck by two others: "It's not always possible to change the world, but it is possible to change yourself" and "Train yourself to let go of everything you fear to lose."

These last two seemed particularly appropriate for my changing circumstances. As I said, more and more people with autistic kids were coming to the races. The newspaper story earned us a lot of attention, and I saw an opportunity to be of greater service to those parents. You know I was initially reluctant, and my first experience speaking at a support group for autistic parents in Ventura County didn't exactly set the world on fire and make me a passionate advocate for the cause or a highly sought after public speaker, but it was a start. As Stephen had written: "Why Be Normal? BE POSITIVE."

In a sense, I also learned from Stephen's example of withdrawal. It was for him—and had been for me—a necessary survival function. We were not interested in just surviving any longer; we wanted to thrive. I couldn't continue to isolate myself; I had to get out in the world and do. Although I wasn't ready to fully take on autism, I found another cause that showed me how willing other people would be to reach out to those in need.

In October 1999, torrential rains had caused enormous flood damage in Mexico. They were the worst floods in forty years, and more than two hundred people had been killed in ten states in southeastern Mexico. Having Mexican ancestry certainly made me more attentive to this situation, but it wasn't just that accidental heritage that made me realize I had to do something. Before the Miracle Run, any pictures or stories of others' suffering were too much for me. I would think, "I'm just one person. What can I do? Look at the burdens I've got to carry."

Instead, I spoke with the people at the Coldwell Banker realty office I worked in and told them that I wanted to spearhead an effort to collect donations for the Red Cross relief efforts in Mexico. Everyone responded wonderfully. I felt good.

No, I hadn't gone down to Mexico myself to help repair a mudslide-damaged home, but I had at least done *something*. Ever since Stephen's Miracle Run, I'd had it in the back of my mind to create some kind of charitable organization or to at least participate in one. I started to do more research.

Jonathan Shestak and his wife, Portia Iversen, were another gift in my life. They had contacted me because they were producers and were interested in developing our life story for a film. At the time, Jonathan's most successful production was the thriller *Air Force One*. We recently rented the comedy *Dan in Real Life* and saw that he'd produced that as well. Portia had worked in various capacities in the industry, including art directing and writing. More important, they had a son who was diagnosed with autism. In response to that, they formed an organization called Cure Autism Now (CAN).

They were both highly successful and highly motivated individuals, and the name of their organization says a lot about them and their mission. They were raising millions of dollars in the hopes of finding a cure, and they moved in circles populated by people I could never imagine getting to know. I was excited about the opportunity to meet them. I didn't know how they managed to do their day jobs in the entertainment industry and found and run such an impressive organization.

Seeing what Jonathan and Portia could do to contribute amid their busy, successful lives didn't give me the motivation I needed to get started in this direction; it was meeting them and understanding what they were doing that helped sharpen the focus of the organization I was in the process of starting. The motivation and desire came from within, but was also influenced by Stephen and what he had accomplished. In the months following his Miracle Run and into his junior year, I was transitioning from someone who focused primarily on preventing bad things from happening to someone who wanted to do some good in the world. There's not just a semantic difference here. My attitude really started to shift. Hearing from all those other parents made me realize that we weren't the only ones who were struggling. I had always known that in abstract terms, but once I began to get involved in the lives of others and saw and read about the specifics of their lives and obstacles, I stopped focusing so much of my attention inward.

Jonathan and Portia were invaluable in educating me. I also spoke with the man who helped run pro football star Doug Flutie's organization. Doug and his wife, Laurie, had founded the organization just a year before my call. Their son, Doug Jr., had been diagnosed at the age of three with autism, and the Doug Flutie Jr. Foundation for Autism was named after him. Its mission was to provide support for parents of autistic children. I'd also previously met and lunched with Dr. Bernard Rimland of the Autistic Research Institute (ARI) and knew the kind of scientific work that his organization was doing. The more I looked, the more I saw that there were hundreds of organizations already out there serving others in all kinds of capacities.

One group that caught my eye was the AFA in New Delhi, India. Action for Autism was founded in 1991, and as the organization's website states today, "We provide support and services to persons with autism and those who work with them in South Asia. Founded in 1991, we work from legal, medical, and educational perspectives to 'put autism on the Indian map.'"

At the time I came across them, they had put out a request for Legos, Duplo blocks, jigsaw puzzles, toys, children's books, erasers, and, for their office, an electric teakettle. I can't say that my heart broke, but it certainly expanded. I'd been so focused on our needs, and yet my kids had most of those things AFA was asking for—and much more. I couldn't imagine a group of people trying to raise awareness about autism in a country like India, which in 1999 had not yet started its economic boom.

At that point, I was still both marveling and chagrined at my failure to really focus on autism as a worldwide phenomenon. I knew that personal evidence to the contrary, America was the richest country in the world. As bad as things might have been for us, I couldn't imagine what someone in an impoverished part of India would do with an autistic child. We had public schools, support groups, and these people needed a teakettle! What about the estimated one million kids in India with the condition?

I tapped on the collective shoulder of my real estate colleagues again, and we collected boxes and boxes of toys, puzzles, and games. I contacted UNICEF for assistance, and they told me that it would be a logistical nightmare for them to try to ship and distribute our contributions to a group in India. In the past, I might have given up, said we tried, and then donated the gifts to Toys for Tots or some other worthwhile local organization.

With Stephen's never-give-up slogans echoing in my mind, I couldn't just give up on my desire to get those kids in India what they needed. Though there was a tangle of customs forms to fill out and a considerable expense in shipping the boxes to India, we did it. I didn't realize before this experience that "relief agency" had more than one meaning. I can't express how good it felt, the enormous relief and feeling of satisfaction in overcoming obstacles to get these things done.

I also realized that the work that the people at CAN, ARI, and the Doug Flutie Jr. Foundation for Autism were doing was extremely important and extremely valuable. I could only hope to do a fraction of the fund-raising that they were doing, but that didn't mean that I would be doing only a fraction of the good they were. I wasn't capable of structuring a foundation that could impact scientific research. To be honest, I didn't want to. As important as a cure was, I wanted to do something for the parents of autistic kids right then, that day, in a way that would improve the quality of their lives immediately. I was already doing some of that, but I wanted and needed to do more.

The people I spoke to with experience in this area told me that creating a 501(c)3, a nonprofit organization, was the way to go. Because I wanted contributions to be tax deductible, I would have to register with the IRS and California's Franchise Tax Board. If UNICEF thought I was presenting them with a logistical and paperwork headache, then what I faced in creating the Miracle Run Foundation was a nightmarish avalanche of forms and figures and statements to be found, filled in, and filed. It was going to be a daunting task, but I was now asking myself, "How can I possibly not do this?" Before, I was always asking myself, "How can I possibly do this?"

Learning to ask for help was tough for me. I'd been raised in a family in which suffering in silence and waiting for your reward in the afterlife were dominant ideas. Seeing my twin autistic sons taking chances and seeing how people responded to them inspired me. Joyce Pearson was another of those people who taught me about giving. I'd heard about her during my inquiries into various other foundations. She was a lawyer who'd assisted others in the arduous process.

I walked into her office and told her my story. She looked at me and nodded silently as I spoke. When I was through, she sighed heavily and looked down at her hands.

"You don't have any money, do you?"

"Some."

"Well, we'll work that out later. For now, let's get started on this. I imagine you don't want to waste any more time, do you?"

With Joyce's aid, the paperwork was filed. We didn't talk at all about her fees and how she would recoup the money lost for taking on a charity case.

I guess I didn't really take the time to think about it much, but as Stephen's story spread and more and more people contacted us, people remarked on the courage it took for all of us to take on so many challenges. While I was flattered to be thought of in those terms, I saw nothing heroic about it; I was simply doing the right thing for my family. Now it was time to do the right thing generally.

To me, courage was exemplified by other people doing work with autistic children in other countries. I was fortunate to have a good education; full employment; and the resources of federal, state, and local governments that made provisions for disabled individuals. Yes, I had to learn a lot about how to work within and to sometimes contravene the system, but at least there was a system in place. That isn't the case in lots of places in the world. As I was doing more research on establishing the foundation, I came across the listing of an agency in Chile. There was no real description of the program, just an email address. I emailed the agency, explaining briefly that I was starting a foundation and was wondering if there was any way I might help. After a week or so of no response, I dug up a mailing address for them and wrote a hard-copy letter and mailed it off. I was as brief as I had been in the email. I wasn't comfortable with opening up with too many details of my life to someone I didn't know at all.

Just after New Year's in 2000, I received a letter postmarked from Chile. In a neatly precise script, Dr. Eulalia Monge de Barros wrote to me from Limache about her work with autistic children. Limache is a city of some 50,000 residents in central Chile, just east of Valparaiso, and a hundred miles from Santiago. It is surrounded by small villages, impoverished by our standards, and it was in one of those small villages, Olmué, that she had established *La Casa Esperanza*. The House of Hope was an old home that some kind neighbors, Catholic Charities, and various volunteers had rented and renovated. It housed a group of about twenty autistic youngsters. The Ministry of Education had declared them uneducable, and without Eulalia and others, they would have already been placed in an institution or left at home. The state provided no services for them, offered no form of aid—financial or otherwise. The same was true for the House of Hope.

Eulalia wrote to me, expressing all of this as well as her surprise that anyone outside the immediate region had ever heard of the organization or her efforts. She went on to say that a few of the children were higher functioning, capable of reading and writing. The younger children and those without speech were shown the few picture books they had. Most would never acquire the ability to speak. Though Eulalia didn't write this,

I knew from her tone and the description she provided that unless something changed, these children would eventually end up in an institution. They'd exist in a very bleak world.

For days after reading her letter, I cried whenever I pictured those kids and the conditions they must have lived under. I hadn't cried much with Phillip and Stephen. I knew that I had to be strong and felt that crying was an emotional extravagance I couldn't afford. If I permitted one crack in the façade, the entire structure might come tumbling down on top of me. Prior to the Miracle Run, in my mind sorrow equaled despair. Since the Miracle Run, I understood that sorrow in and of itself was a good thing. It meant that you felt something, that you hadn't numbed yourself (as I felt I had to do to survive) to the point that little registered in your heart or mind.

The other day, I was working in the garden doing some planting. I seldom wear gloves when I do this. Maybe its my Mexican roots that have me so tied to the earth, but I like the feel of the dirt against my skin. I had my watering can with me, and when I was done planting the bulbs, I mixed up a batch of earth and water into a thick slurry I worked by hand. Doug was outside doing something else in the yard, and he called me over to look at some repair he was making to a trellis. We stood and talked for a few minutes, and when we went our separate ways, I noticed that my hands were caked in rapidly drying mud. My skin felt entombed, warm but unnaturally dry and lifeless. I went to the garden hose and began to rinse my hands off. The mud softened and dripped off me, leaving a residue of dirt like a chalky shadow. That feeling reminded me of what I'd experienced in the first years following the Miracle Run. It was as if that wizened crusty old self had to be washed away, and my tears were doing that bit by bit.

I gave myself permission to cry but not to despair. As heart-rending as Eulalia's letter was, it would have been useless had it only elicited tears and not action. Once again, I called on the folks at the real estate office and in the community at large to join me. They responded magnificently. We collected children's books, toys, clothes, blankets, and assorted other goods that filled boxes and boxes. Some people wanted to donate money, but the foundation's paperwork was still in progress. I told people we couldn't give them receipts for their taxes, but they didn't care. They handed us cash, told us to do with it what was necessary to defray shipping costs or however we saw fit. I wasn't sure what to do with the cash and how to get it safely into the hands of the right people in Chile.

I took to stuffing bills in the pockets of the shirts and pants we'd collected, figuring that whoever was in need of clothes would also be in need of money. I didn't give much thought to the fact that we were sending American dollars, where they might exchange the money, what the rate was, what kinds of fees they'd incur. What was important was imme-diate action. So off the boxes went, and later, in came the let-ters of thanks. Those expressions of gratitude were wonderful, but I often thought they were misplaced. Instead of thank-ing me or the people of Agoura Hills, they should have been thanking the young man who ran his race and taught us all a lesson about courage and winning. Later, packages went out to Argentina, the West Indies, Australia—anywhere we saw a need.

By February, we received notification that the Miracle Run Foundation was formally and officially a not-for-profit organization that could receive tax-deductible donations. We were in business. Given the inspiration for the organization, we decided it was only natural that we host a race as our first official fundraiser. We had no experience as event organizers, couldn't afford to pay for the services of professionals in the field, and decided to start figuring out what it took to host a race.

We had selected a date in June for the inaugural Miracle Run Foundation five-kilometer cross-country race. Stephen had participated as a volunteer for a number of road races, and we'd attended and volunteered at a number of Stephen's high school races, so we weren't completely unfamiliar with what needed to be done.

Doug loves to tell the story of getting up early one Saturday to take Stephen to a race. The local Chamber of Commerce was hosting a road race, and Coach Duley had offered the help of the Agoura High Cross-Country Team. The team was not allowed to run but would act as volunteers along the racecourse, to hand out water and assist in any other way they could. When Stephen told me about this, I wondered who Coach Duley had volunteered to keep an eye on my son.

"I have to be there at six in the morning," Stephen ordered Doug in his usual flat tone. The next morning at exactly five thirty, Stephen knocked on our bedroom door. This was our sign, to get him breakfast and take him to his destination. Doug and I were both really tired, so I volunteered him to do the driving. Doug had had a hard week at work, and this was really early on a Saturday morning, so he was in a fog as he made his way on autopilot to Kanan Road. Once there, he realized he didn't know where the race was being held. No problem, he thought, all he had to do was ask Stephen.

"Okay, Steve, where are we going?"

Stephen sat stone silent.

Now you have to remember that autistic people are sometimes dead silent, and you have to ask the same question a few times before getting a response. Doug thought that maybe Stephen's brain hadn't processed the words, or maybe he, too, was suffering from early-morning fog, or maybe he simply hadn't heard him over the road noise.

So this time, Doug spoke louder and enunciated each word, "Stephen, where is the race?"

Stephen continued to stare straight ahead, still not speaking, still not acknowledging Doug's presence.

Doug was getting worried. He knew that Stephen had promised to be somewhere, and he wanted to follow through on that commitment. He asked again louder and impatiently, *"STEVE, WHERE AM I TAKING YOU?!!!"*

"That's a problem," Stephen answered, in a cool, collected voice.

Doug lapsed into silence as he drove Stephen to Burger King for his sausage-egg-without-cheese breakfast. He was by no means a psychologist and hadn't read any books on autism; he wasn't even Stephen's biological father. But he did have something in common with Stephen that we all have in common: We can run from our obstacles, or run to them, but that does not mean we give up.

Doug finally saw a sign for the Pumpkin Run in Westlake Village and learned the starting line was about five miles from home.

"That's a problem" has become a refrain in our household, one we turn to when our frustration levels are high and we need to let off some steam through humor. So when we first decided we were going to plunge into hosting a fund-raising race, we were fully prepared to have to utter "That's a problem" quite frequently.

That said, we had no idea until we really started how much needed to be done or how expensive it would be to hire someone who could organize the race for us. There are businesses out there who organize these kinds of events regularly, so we contacted a few of them, and the lowest quoted price we got for orchestrating a fund-raising event like ours was $10,000. There was no way we could come up with that kind of money; we didn't have enough to even put down a deposit on that amount. We also couldn't guarantee we'd raise that much, and we certainly didn't want to take $10,000 out of the charitable proceeds to pay for what needed to be done.

Doug and I joked about hosting a fund-raiser to raise funds for the fund-raiser, but we'd need to host a fund-raiser to raise funds for the... You get the idea. Since the Miracle Run Foundation was primarily concerned with doing grassroots work to raise awareness and to alleviate the stresses on families with autistic members, it made sense to take on the task ourselves. I have a to-do list from the preliminary planning stages of that first race that encompasses everything from legal issues (park permits, permission to post signage, insurance) to race logistics (course measurement, printing and distributing two thousand entry forms) to racer and spectator comfort and enjoyment (procuring three hundred bananas, twenty dozen bagels, fifty cases of beverages) and so on.

We sought out sponsors and were enormously grateful that the people at Saucony, Inc. (Stephen's favorite maker of running shoes) donated T-shirts and shoes, the Dole Food Company provided us with bananas and fruit drinks, *Runner's World* magazine promoted the race and provided us with race numbers for the participants, KLSX did radio spots to help get the word out, and our local papers also chipped in with ads. The Rainbow Connection—a local organization based in Oxnard, which did outreach in the tri-county area for adults and children with developmental disabilities—provided a lot of assistance in spreading the word about the race. We started with very modest expectations, hoping that we might attract about two hundred runners, but as February 2000 turned into April and then May and the race was only a month away, we realized that for a bunch of volunteers and first-timers, we were doing okay for ourselves.

We always had our sights set high—for example, I wrote to *People* magazine hoping they would do a profile, and through our new Hollywood connections we were in touch with a number of celebrities—but were prepared to settle for less if necessary.

Coach Duley was also extremely helpful. Through his Future Track Running Center, he had a pipeline into the running community. His sponsorship of the race and his help and guidance in organizing it were invaluable. In addition to his duties as a high school coach, he also worked with elite, world-class athletes like Brian Damesworth, a national champion in track and field. Brian agreed to participate, and though his name didn't mean that much to me, having a national champion in the field gave the race credibility and drew in additional runners.

Though we wanted to have a strong field and a really competitive race, the main purpose of the event was to raise money and awareness. The runners were primarily helping us out with the first of those goals. Their $40 entrance fee entitled them to run the race, get a T-shirt, win a trophy if they placed high enough in their age group, and enjoy the entertainment and camaraderie that comes with racing. We also asked everyone to join us for a postrace presentation at which some of the most prominent doctors in the field of autism—doctors who knew Phillip and Stephen from early on—would speak. I was thrilled that the Koegels from UCSB and Dr. Freeman from UCLA agreed to attend the event and speak.

More and more groups agreed to sponsor us or serve as volunteers. The outpouring of cooperation was enormously rewarding. The Agoura Hills Boy Scouts came and helped set up the water stations in the staging area and along the course, the Optimist Club assisted with the Kiddie Walk, our local Ben and Jerry's franchisers provided refreshments after the race, as did Kim's Mandarin Express. Just what really fit runners wanted—ice cream and Chinese food. No one commented or complained; they understood that everyone was putting their hearts in the right place and doing whatever they could to make the event a success. Doug posted a notice on the set of the production he was working on for volunteers to assist with the race setup, and a few more than I can name showed up and pitched in.

While the focus was on running, and that meant Stephen, we didn't want Phillip to be excluded. His newly formed band, Twist of Fate, was scheduled to play a couple of ten-minute sets as part of the postrace entertainment.

I can't adequately express how grateful I was to everyone nor can I express how gratifying it was to see a field of about a thousand runners streaming across the fields where Stephen had done so much of his solitary running workouts. He'd started to run because he wanted to be a part of some group larger than himself. I think he succeeded.

The day of the race was exhausting. We began setting up at 6:00 a.m., but were up hours earlier going over many of the details. The last postrace presentation ended at 2:30 p.m. We were done cleaning up at almost 5:00, more than fourteen hours since we'd started working. We had done so much, and then the event was over. Surprisingly, I didn't have that Christmas Day letdown feeling—the "all that time preparing and now it's over" kind of feeling that puts a damper on much-anticipated events. Frankly, some of the reason for not feeling that way was simple exhaustion. Most of it, though, was due to how energized I felt, how fulfilling it was to see so many people from so many disparate parts of our world and beyond uniting behind a cause we believed in so strongly. The money we raised was wonderful as well. We hadn't earmarked any of it for any specific projects, preferring instead to be flexible and use it on an as-needed basis. I liked having that kind of flexibility, and it paid off for us and for the recipients of the funds generated.

The year following the boys' graduation saw us hold our second Miracle Run five-kilometer race. The preparation was a little less intense since we'd been through the process once. Doug and I continued to work hard at our day jobs. While we were busy with all those things, we were also making preparations to get the boys enrolled in the local junior college—Moor Park. Phillip's declaration that he wanted to attend college had meant that we were on our way up the ladder of higher education.

California has a wonderful system of junior colleges. Many students attend them right out of high school and then go on to attend a four-year university. The facilities are wonderful; they offer opportunities for students to compete in many sports and be involved in other activities. Even better, they offer a low-cost alternative. Today, tuition at Moor Park, where first Stephen and then Phillip enrolled, is $20 per unit. A full-time student is one who is taking a minimum of twelve units, so tuition is only $240 per semester. That doesn't sound like much money, and it isn't when compared to the tuition at most state schools or private universities and colleges, but even though tuition was less than $200 for Stephen, we were still hard-pressed to come up with the money.

When you factored in fees, transportation costs, and the like, the bill was even greater. Fortunately, because we qualified for assistance through the North Los Angeles County Regional Center, which served the needs of disabled individuals, we were entitled to financial support.

In August 2001, Stephen and Phillip both attended Moor Park Junior College. To be more precise, all four of us attended school at the same time. As the story of Phillip's meeting demonstrated, his Tourette's symptoms were not under control. As much as we tried and despite the many doctors we

saw, combinations of medicines he took, and dietary modifi-
cations he made, his outbursts were simply too unpredictable
for him to function in a regular college classroom. We knew
that going into the situation, but we still felt that he deserved a
chance. Moor Park did offer some programs and services for students with special needs. The twins enrolled in classes designed
to ease the transition from the special education courses they
had been taking at Agoura High to the mainstream curriculum.
Counselors were available to help them with course selection
and other things, but there would be no aides in the classrooms.
Their instructors would be informed of their disabilities, but
they had no special training in how to best teach special needs
students. We were treading on new ground.

To make Phillip's transition to college course work easier,
and to help him and the other students and the faculty adapt
to his presence, Doug and I attended his classes along with
him. The reception that Phillip received was mixed, but not in
the way you might expect. Even though the students at Moor
Park were only one or two years removed from high school,
they were in so many ways light-years beyond the immaturity
that marked their younger years. Doug and I spent a lot of time
on that campus, and I can't really think of a single incident or
look the boys got from a fellow student that made obvious that
person's surprise, anger, or disgust at being around an autistic
individual. Stephen was able to blend in a little more seamlessly
than Phillip, but neither of them was subjected to the kind of
teasing and mockery that I had so feared during their days in
high school. That was an enormous relief.

They each took four classes that first semester. Stephen

received three credit hours toward a physical education require-
ment by being on the cross-country team, so he really only had
three academic classes. One of those was College Strategies. In
it, he learned about the school and its policies, degree require-
ments, and strategies that students could employ to succeed. It
wasn't a particularly challenging class, but it did help Stephen
focus on what his academic program would be if he wanted to
work toward an associate's degree. He completed a Student
Educational Plan, in which he outlined in advance what his
next three terms at the school would look like. As part of his
work in his College Strategies course, he had to write a paper
comparing the associate's and the bachelor's degrees. I came
across it and was struck by a line he might have gotten from a
brochure or some other research material he found, that "the
degrees are not designed to teach a student a trade or a career,
but make a person well-rounded and educated in all aspects of
life and in the world."

That pretty much summed up my view of education. I had
pressed Phillip to declare that he wanted to study drafting
because I knew he had an aptitude for it. Not for a minute did
I think of pushing him down that career path. I had an ulterior
motive for encouraging both of the twins to pursue the same
field. They would adjust better to college life if they were in
the same classes, and it would be easier for me to attend classes
they took together. I still had Ali at home, a job to go to, and
duties around the house to fulfill. I remember someone suggesting that as long as I was going to be on campus, I should
take a class for my own enjoyment! All I needed was more
work, and even if it had been a class in receiving therapeutic

massage, I would still have looked at it as just one more thing on an already too crowded to-do list.

I think that Phillip was too caught up in the excitement and worry of being in a new environment to have strong feelings about having his mother tag along to his classes. Sometimes I sat in the classroom; other times I waited outside. If I heard that Phillip's Tourette's episode was being a distraction, I'd go in and calm him down or else take him out of the room. A few times when they had classes together, I'd go to the library or to the cafeteria and wait for them. Stephen had a good sense of when things were potentially going wrong and could step in on my behalf.

A few of Phillip's instructors were less tolerant than others, but for the most part, they cooperated with our efforts. I've found that most people, after they have Phillip's condition explained to them, are understanding. As we learned from Coach Duley and his initial impressions of Stephen, an autistic student isn't likely to draw any attention to himself or stand out in any way. Stephen's reluctance to speak up in class or to make direct eye contact is probably only slightly more extreme than what instructors encounter all the time with shy students.

I've probably uttered the words "Poor Phillip" thousands of times more because of his Tourette's syndrome or OCD than because of his autism. It's not that I pity him—far from it. It's just that his Tourette's and OCD really do get in the way of his functioning normally in social situations. As I've noted many times, he is by far the more vocal of the twins and has a gregarious nature, but people see the facial and body tics, hear the vocalizations, and make all kinds of assumptions about intelligence that just aren't correct. That's a lot for anyone to have to overcome.

One of the episodes that was most frustrating for him to deal with occurred, unfortunately, in a piano class. I don't know what Phillip would do or what kind of person he would be if it weren't for music. I've come to think of music as Phillip's mood and state-of-mind barometer. If he is playing his guitar, singing, or listening to music, I know all is right in his world. When he's not, I know that he's in the grasp of Tourette's or OCD.

When he enrolled in a piano class at Moor Park in the spring of 2002, I knew going in that this class would be different from some of the others he'd taken. A combination of both music theory and practice, the success of the course depended on establishing a certain mood, a level of comfort and familiarity that was different from a history or a math class. I met the instructor and came away from the meeting feeling her sensitivity, her more artistic temperament. She seemed somehow more fragile than some of the other faculty members I'd met. I have to admit those weren't bad qualities, since they translated into her being a passionate and mesmerizing teacher. She was, however, easily distracted and flustered.

When she was lecturing, Phillip's every twitter and exclamation seemed to throw her off. It was as if she were a classical pianist in the middle of playing a piece, and Phillip intruded upon her reverie with clanging honky-tonk or jazz improvisations. They weren't that loud or attention grabbing, but they were enough to disturb the harmony and euphony of her compositions. Personally, I sometimes felt as if she could have used

Phillip's vocal tics as a so-called teachable moment to make her points, but she never did that. Instead, she'd turn her back to the class, inscribe some musical notation on the chalkboard, and suggest through tight teeth that maybe Phillip needed a break.

As was true in most of his courses, Phillip's classmates were more sympathetic and accepting than disrupted. A number of times, one classmate or another would comment on how great it was to see Phillip in school. Their empathy arose from an understanding, I believe, that what he was doing was anything but easy. Most of them were not top-of-the-heap kids; otherwise, they would have gone on to some major university. They understood what it was to struggle with things, and something of an anti-elitist agenda seemed to pervade the place. It truly was, in the best sense of the word, a community college.

As much as the course content and the curriculum mattered to me and to the twins, that sense of a bond and belonging still mattered a great deal. I don't know if they would have gotten that same inclusive experience elsewhere or through distance learning programs or other alternatives. For Stephen, his integration into college life was smoother. He had cross-country and a built-in group of, if not friends, then at least teammates. Many of the young men on his team he had competed either with or against in high school. His training discipline carried over into his studies, and by the fall of 2002, his course schedule read much like any other student's: Drafting MO2; English 104; Modern American Literature; Astronomy 1; and Cross-Country.

Phillip was also enrolled in that same section of Drafting MO2. Their instructor, Mr. Tom Craft, was wonderful. He stands among the all-stars of our story. Stephen and Phillip had always loved to draw, and drafting, though not as expressive or creative as a sketching or painting class, seemed ideally suited to their interests and temperaments. The class sessions were a mix of brief lecture demonstration and then independent practice. There was not a lot of reading, and very little if any interaction among the students. That seemed to play to Stephen's strengths, and he was thriving in the class. Mr. Craft would circulate around the room while the students worked on their projects and offer his gentle criticisms and frequent praise. He was always very careful to modulate his tone when talking to Stephen, and he would bend over and keep himself in Stephen's peripheral vision when he spoke directly to him.

I guess that some people are natural teachers and communicators, and Mr. Craft was one of the finest I'd seen. I didn't want to speculate too much, but I suspected that he had someone with special needs somewhere else in his life. He just had that reassuring confident tone and manner of someone who'd had a great deal of experience. He never condescended, and he did something else that I admired. If Phillip piped up, which he did far less frequently in that class than in others, Mr. Craft would sometimes just ignore it. Other times, he would pick up a T-square, a lettering template, or an architect's triangle and tap out a bass line to accompany him. The other students would pick their heads up from their work and smile; occasionally, a few others would join in to create a tympani section. By the end of the first month of the semester, even Phillip's tics had become fully integrated into the landscape and soundscape of that room. Doug and I both found ourselves wanting to sit in on the class just to feel those soothing vibes.

One day, that vibe came to a nerve-jangling halt.

After dinner one evening in October 2002, I found Stephen sitting at his desk staring straight ahead. He had his drafting tools and paper laid out in front of him. He was wearing a pair of yellow latex dishwashing gloves. His elbows were resting on the table, and his hands were standing perfectly vertical, fingers slightly splayed. He looked like a surgeon who had just gotten through scrubbing up for an operation. I asked him what he was doing, but he continued to stare straight ahead. I asked him again if everything was okay, but he refused to answer. In situations like this, I had learned that it was always better to walk away and give Stephen the space he needed. He's always been the less communicative of the twins, and particularly when his emotions are running high, his slower speech functioning frustrates him even more. Whereas Phillip will have outbursts, Stephen turns inward. I had to learn to understand and respect those differences.

The next day, Stephen had his drafting class. After Mr. Craft did his introduction and demonstration, the students in the class took out their materials and began their drawing. Stephen did not. He sat at his drafting table with his elbows resting on it as he had at his desk at home the night before. I tried to talk to him; Mr. Craft came over to see if he could help, but he couldn't get a thing out of him, either. This went on for a few class sessions. Stephen improved to the point that he would get his materials out and put his mechanical pencil in his hand, but he would put the tip to the paper and then just lock up. I could see the tendons and veins in his hands and arms standing out like features on a relief map, but there was no relief from the tension that consumed him. Mr. Craft seemed as worried as I was, and the rest of the students, who usually engaged in a low-volume, collegial banter, also fell silent. Everyone knew that something wasn't right.

That same day, Stephen had a cross-country meet. I went to watch him. He lined up at the starting line with everyone else and looked fine. The gun went off and the rest of the runners took off at a fast clip. Stephen plodded along, trailing the field. He had been a middle-of-the-pack runner in college, but now he was left in the dust. Something was definitely not right.

Based on how Stephen's muscles seemed to become so rigid, I was immediately concerned that something neurological was going on—that he was manifesting symptoms of some physical problem. I did some checking around, and based on a recommendation, I made an appointment with Dr. Dave, a neurologist in West Hills about a half-hour drive from our home.

I'm usually hyperaware of the importance of being on time. I don't like to be late, and I don't like to be made to wait. For that reason, though we had a nine o'clock appointment, we left the house at eight. That gave us an hour, double the amount of time needed to get there, in case Southern California traffic acted up in some way. It did. We got to Dr. Dave's office at nine fifteen. The receptionist asked us to take a seat in the waiting room. A half hour passed. I don't like to be made to wait, as I said, but I understand that sometimes things happen. At about ten o'clock, the door to the waiting room opened and in walked Dr. Dave. "Is this the Morgan boy? You were fifteen minutes late. I have a very busy practice. I can't see you now. Maybe I can fit him in later."

I was stupefied and insulted. This was my first contact with the guy. He could not have been ruder. I tried to explain but he cut me off. "Later. Maybe." I was sitting there worried sick about my son, I had an armful of his medical records from all the other doctors and specialists he'd been to, and I needed some reassurance that my son hadn't blown an aneurysm or something. So I did what I'd instructed Phillip to do at his meeting. I kissed butt. May we please go get something to eat? We'll be right back. Here's my mobile phone number in case Dr. Dave has a moment to see us.

As it turned out, I needn't have bothered with leaving my phone number. We ate, came back, and sat for another five hours. Finally, we got in to see Dr. Dave. I had all of Stephen's medical records, and mixed in among them were a few photographs. One of them was of Stephen at the Beverly Hills Hotel with Anthony Edwards. Dr. Dave spotted it, and suddenly he became more interested in Stephen's case.

I told him that this photograph best represented who my son used to be up until two weeks before. The smiling, speech-giving young man with the bright future. I saw that Dr. Dave was fixated on the photo, and it wasn't my son who had caught his attention. At that point, Dr. Dave began behaving more like Dr. Jekyll. He told me not to worry. He would make sure he found out what was wrong with my son. Then he asked me about CAN and the event Stephen spoke at.

Stephen was subjected to some tests, and Dr. Dave reported back to us that he could find nothing physiologically wrong with Stephen. That was a relief, but still left us with the question of why he was behaving the way that he was. Another round of doctor visits, and this time the conclusion was that Stephen was likely experiencing the onset of OCD. The cause? Stress. The solution? A prescription for Paxil. I didn't bother to fill it. Phillip had been through the vicious cycle of pharmaceuticals. Stephen didn't need that. Paxil wouldn't reduce his stress level. We needed to step back and evaluate what was going on.

One of the difficulties in dealing with an autistic like Stephen is that he seldom complains. His tendency to turn quiet and internalize whatever emotions he's feeling can easily turn into depression, anxiety, or any of a number of other disorders. I was aware of that, but getting Stephen to really open up and express what was going on in his mind and heart was not easy. He was, and is, such a perfectionist and sets such high standards for himself that he seldom complains. To do so would be a sign of weakness. In my mind, the amazing thing was that he had not succumbed to the stress before. Our household was a stress factory.

Consider this: Stephen was autistic; his parents had split up when he was a young boy; he was teased and tormented as a youngster; he lived in a household where financial security was seldom present; he had a brother for whom he felt responsible and who endured even more traumatic episodes; he turned his life in a positive direction through running, but his dreams of Olympic glory seemed to be fading in the face of stiffer competition. Despite his achievements, he still wasn't fully integrated into the social sphere—he'd had a few friends at Agoura High, but he didn't keep in frequent contact with them; he wanted to date but had no prospects we knew of. That's a pretty substantial laundry list, and those are only the concerns that I was aware of. I really didn't know what else was going on in his mind.

Stephen always kept himself so busy and so occupied with studying and running that he seldom seemed to take time out for fun. Does that sound at all familiar to you? He was like an adult in his mid-thirties experiencing a bit of burnout. And I don't think the rest of the family or our circumstances were helping matters much. We were still struggling financially. Doug had gone in for arthroscopic surgery on a chronically bad knee and was not working. Fortunately our insurance was good, but Stephen didn't know that. All of our original excitement and hope about the film had gradually leached out of us after multiple delays and long stretches of no news.

I mention all these factors because I'm still seeking an adequate explanation for what Stephen did about two weeks after we first met with Dr. Dave.

We woke to the sound of a vehicle alarm going off. Actually, Ali heard it and alerted us by screaming. She'd looked out the window and saw the interior of Doug's truck in flames. By the time she let us know what was happening and Doug hobbled down the hillside to the driveway, it was too late to do anything to save the truck. I called 911. We all stood in mournful silence watching Doug's pride and joy go up in flames. He needed a truck for his job and had purchased a heavy-duty Dodge Ram pickup. Doug usually doesn't get attached to things, but he took a lot of pride in owning that vehicle. As we all stood on the patio above the driveway watching it go up in flames, I had a lump in my throat.

I looked around, and Phillip and Ali were both crying. Stephen wasn't around. That's when I knew. A car's interior doesn't just catch fire; someone has to light it. I tried to convince myself that some neighborhood kids, or kids from anywhere else, really, had vandalized it. Then I remembered. Earlier that evening, Doug had told Stephen, in a tone uncharacteristically sharp for him, to get his homework done. I knew Doug was in pain and upset about the surgery and the prospects of a painful and protracted rehab, and he let some of that out on Stephen. I'd seen a look in Stephen's eyes that I seldom saw before. He was really angry. I think that what hurt him was having to be reminded to do something that he so often did without being told. The perfectionist in him was wounded, and I feared that all the cumulative stress had finally burst the dam.

I could hear the sirens in the distance echoing through the hills. A few moments later, Stephen joined our circle and watched as the Mars lights of the emergency vehicles flickered like fireflies in the distance. The smell of burning plastic was horrendous, but that wasn't what was making my eyes tear. Stephen stood and stared horrified at the spectacle. The heat from the fire shattered the windshield in a fiery kaleidoscope. I walked up to Stephen and looked him directly in the eye. Normally, he would shy away, but he held my gaze.

"You did this?" I pointed down the hill to where firemen were now hosing down the truck.

Stephen flinched when the vehicles' emergency lights strobed his eyes, then he nodded.

This was *definitely* going to be a problem.

Later on, I would learn that Stephen's drastic acting out was a blessing in disguise.

I began this book by stating that sometimes the things that we are forced to do turn out to be the most beneficial for us. I couldn't have seen the truth of that statement as I stood facing an Agoura Hills police officer and the captain of the fire department. We all knew that trucks don't just spontaneously combust, and with Stephen's confession making it clear how the fire started weighing heavily on my mind, I started in on the story by saying, "My son is autistic."

In my heart and in my mind, I knew that didn't excuse Stephen from responsibility for his actions, but I wanted to be sure that everyone understood that mitigating circumstances existed. I had to be careful in how I presented the facts because I knew that some people believed that autistic individuals are conscienceless, amoral individuals who are the victims of their impulses. I knew of rare exceptions of severely low-functioning autistics of whom this could be true, but in my experience generally, and with Stephen and Phillip specifically, they have a moral compass as strong and as true as anyone's. The twins are both deeply spiritual, and along with understanding what is right and wrong in the eyes of the law, they have a highly developed sense of what is right and wrong in the eyes of God. Stephen knew that destroying Doug's property was illegal and sinful.

I was grateful that the police officer and the fire official both knew of Stephen and his story. They were entirely sympathetic to our plight, but they also had jobs to do. Because Stephen was autistic, they weren't going to arrest him, but they needed our assurance that we were going to do something to make it clear to Stephen that there were serious consequences to his actions. This was not something we could lightly blow off with a "please don't do that again" warning. He needed to have it reinforced deeply in his mind that what he did endangered our lives and the lives of those who had come to put out the fire.

Also, the subsequent explosion when the gas tank caught fire had roused the neighborhood, and we had to be held accountable for that disruption and the disquiet Stephen's actions caused. The police officer reminded us that our neighbors wanted, like anyone else, to live someplace safe. Stephen's arson (that word had never sounded so sinister to me) would undermine that sense of safety. The fire captain reminded me of what I needed little reminder of. We lived in a hilly, canyon-filled area, where wildfires were common and exacted a heavy toll. He said we should consider ourselves very fortunate that the fire hadn't spread to our house and to our neighbors' property.

We all agreed that because of the lateness of the hour, we wouldn't make a determination at that point about Stephen's punishment. I knew they had to make an official report to several agencies, including the Department of Rehabilitation. They might be able to recommend an appropriate course of action.

Having been through so many ups and downs through the years, I thought I'd be able to put this incident in perspective more easily. I couldn't. Doug blamed himself for having hurt Stephen's feelings, and I was deeply troubled by what Stephen's actions implied. Every parent I know has experienced one or more of those "Where did I go wrong?" moments, but this moment spread into hours and days. The word "stress" kept creeping into my thoughts, and I wondered if we had pushed Stephen too hard for too long. I knew that by nature Stephen was a driven individual, but for not the first time I wondered just how much he was suffering in silence.

After a few days of brainstorming options and considering alternatives, we did the thing that I had worked so hard for so much of my life to prevent: We placed Stephen in an institution for the mentally ill. His sentence was only three days, but my Judas-like feelings lasted long after he returned home. In some ways, Stephen's being detained seemed pointless. He had immediately expressed his remorse to Doug and me. One thing he said to me when we brought him home did make me feel that the experience was beneficial. I asked him if he could explain to me what he was feeling and why he was angry enough to have set fire to his stepfather's truck.

Stephen turned his head to the side. His tongue ran along his lips and his Adam's apple bobbed several times before he said haltingly, "Don't worry. That's dead in me."

I cried. I cried because I was grateful that he understood the consequences of his actions. I cried because my son was trying to reassure me. I cried because I despised the idea that any emotion, however negative, was dead in my son. I wanted him to experience the full spectrum of emotions, but as we always had to do with the twins, we had to again explain to Stephen the difference between appropriate and inappropriate. I cried because I felt that somehow I had failed. I hadn't done a good enough job early on to get Stephen to understand that he could express himself and his emotions freely. It didn't have to come to this, but it had and we all needed to move on.

One benefit of the incident and having it reported to the various state agencies was that Stephen and Phillip were assigned monitors who would come to the house and spend time with them. Because Stephen had posed a potential threat to his safety and the safety of others, the state wanted to be certain that inappropriate behavior wouldn't be repeated. While it may sound as if these monitors functioned as parole officers, the truth is that they were more like the aides who'd been in their special education classes. By that, I mean that while we were still their primary teachers and caregivers, we would now have some assistance in our home from these individuals. At first I was a bit skeptical about the idea of having someone come into our home—again the impulse to do everything ourselves and be the be-all and end-all of our sons' transition to adulthood was difficult to put aside without feeling as if we were abandoning the twins. That may sound like an exaggeration, but even though we had the schools and other agencies involved in the twins' lives, it still felt as though every burden was on our shoulders.

Allowing the monitors to assist us in the everyday tasks of helping Phillip and Stephen learn to manage their lives independently was just another lesson in my learning to let go. As much as I felt that Stephen's acting out was a product of him hitting the wall (a term runners use to describe a total lack of energy that sometimes occurs during a long race), we had in fact all hit that wall—perhaps so many times that we didn't realize we were banging our heads against it until we stopped doing it.

The monitors help fill a void that, as the twins' parents, we can't fill. They socialize with them by going out to eat, attending movies, and becoming surrogate friends. In some ways, their role reminds me of the Big Brother or Big Sister programs. The main difference is that they have some therapeutic training and do work with Phillip and Stephen on specific social and vocational skills. While they are not with the twins every day or even an entire day, the fact that they are available to work with Stephen and Phillip even part time has done a lot to lift the weight off our shoulders.

In the immediate aftermath of the fire, the presence of the monitors also served as a reminder to Stephen and Phillip that some changes were going to be made in their lives. Stephen finished out the fall semester of 2002 at Moor Park, but he has not reenrolled. It became clear to us that he needed a break.

I've already mentioned my feeling that arbitrary timetables do more harm than good when too strictly adhered to. Stephen does want to go back to school at some point, but he has voluntarily told us that the pressures to succeed and excel did get to him. We never found out the source of his mysterious freezing at the drafting table, but have assumed that it was a result of a combination of things—stress, overwork, his intense competitiveness, and hormonal changes that altered his brain chemistry. I've long since concluded that for as many advances as researchers have made into the study of the brain, so much still remains shrouded in speculation and mystery. I've stopped chasing cures and causes and have instead tried to assist the twins in making the necessary adjustments to their lifestyle that will keep them happy and healthy.

With Phillip, we chased the dream of the gluten-free diet for a while but saw little change. Today, Phillip eats what he likes and is more content as a result. The less anxiety and agitation he has, the less he has to worry about whether or not something he enjoys eating is in some way harmful, the more in control of his Tourette's syndrome symptoms he seems to be. Autistic individuals are so acutely sensitive to stimuli that we've now sought the path of least resistance. That doesn't mean that we have given up—far from it. We simply manage our expectations more efficiently.

Ironically, if Stephen hadn't made such a dramatic plea for help, I don't know if we would have gotten to this point in our lives. I think that one of the frustrations we all experienced in having the boys attend Moor Park was the sense of déjà vu, more of the same tedium of being in school. We all need a break every now and then, and the autism fatigue syndrome we experienced should likely be cataloged along with it.

I know this comes as no great revelation, but to be an effective caregiver, you have to take care of yourself first. While things had certainly gotten better in our lives as the boys were finishing up high school, we were operating on adrenaline. All our systems were stressed to such a point that it's a wonder we didn't spontaneously combust. Giving yourself permission to say you're tired, you need help, you need a break, and all those other statements of "failure" is not an indulgence—it's a necessity.

These days I hear more and more people using the expression "It is what it is." As much as I dislike clichés, I think that saying is a shorthand way of stating what I'm attempting to describe. I don't think we adequately celebrated our successes with the Miracle Run Foundation, with the twins' graduation from high school, with Stephen's running success. Stephen's Miracle Run energized us and gave us the power we needed to accomplish more. What we didn't recognize is that some of the laws of physics and the conservation of matter and energy applied to our hearts and our souls. We could only do so much. Resting was not a sign of losing or quitting; taking care of ourselves was not selfish. Having someone else around to help care for Stephen and Phillip was the best way that I could see for Doug and me to take care of ourselves.

In some ways, I think the "hurry up and wait" experience of having a movie made about our lives was a very positive and beneficial one. From first contact by agents interested in representing us to the first airing on Lifetime took more than five years. By the end—the last six months when the filming began and the finished product was shown—we'd learned a lot more about letting go of expectations about how things ought to proceed. I don't think any of us has a long list of daily to-do's. We don't mark our calendars or keep track of the days when someone promised us a phone call, a draft of a script, or anything like that. We let life dictate the pace these days; we don't try to exert any control over time. With Stephen and Phillip here but not here in the house, with Ali well on her way to earning her degree in special education, and with Richard married and still in the Navy, we're enjoying the sense of ease that comes with knowing that you are fit and that the race is nearing the end.

We couldn't rest completely. I had had to push hard and cite the Americans with Disabilities Act to keep the state funds flowing to us for the boys' monitors. Having them there forty hours a week had been transformative. I'd taken up gardening again, with a passion that I'd not had the time to experience for years. I come from a farming family with deep roots in the soil, and it felt so good to be able to indulge a pastime all about nurturing and growing.

Shortly before filming began, my father revealed that he had cancer. He was admitted into Sharp's Memorial Hospital in San Diego. I packed a bag and drove down there to join my nine siblings. They all told me that they'd come prepared with clothes for the funeral they were sure was imminent. Dad hadn't been eating for two weeks and was struggling just to take a breath. I was sitting by his bedside, holding his hand, when he told me he was going to die.

"You can't die. Who'll take care of Mom?"

"Your sister Peggy will do it."

My dad was eighty-four, riddled with cancer, and wanting to let go; I wasn't prepared to let go of him. My father was given a device he was supposed to blow through to improve his lung function. Each time a doctor came in and instructed him to use the device, my father put it to his lips and then let it fall. He had given up.

Doug was with me, and he shook his head. He said he'd be right back and returned with a pint of my dad's favorite Ben and Jerry's ice cream—Chunky Monkey. He ate. I insisted he use his breather. He did. The crisis passed. His cancer went into remission. I needed some more clothes, and so did Doug, so we drove up to Malibu Lake to pick up a few more things. When we got home, we found out that our beloved dog, Patches, had died. I was fifty years old and crying like a baby over the loss. I'm a big believer in the power of dogs to teach us and to heal us. In my mind, Patches had sent his life force to my father to save him. I was so upset and so wanting the companionship and comfort of a dog that I ran to the pet store and bought the only dog they had, a little lap dog, a Shih Tzu we named Song.

I had seen a PBS special about a woman with cancer who claimed that her three dogs had helped her heal. I couldn't get the picture out of my mind of that seriously ill woman sitting propped up in her bed surrounded by her three dogs. She was beaming. Her smile stayed imprinted in my mind. I decided I had to have three dogs. Doug was all for it. He knew the calming effect that Patches had had on me, and he saw how instantly Song and I had bonded and how beneficial she was for me. So Hannalei and Snowflake came to live with us—a black-and-white Shih Tzu and an all-white one. The house was filled with the sounds of puppies yipping and barking. The kids adored the dogs as well, and I truly believed they helped Phillip through some rough spots. Their unconditional love and playful nature soothed us all. They also kept me active. A friend once commented that she was surprised I hadn't ballooned up to three hundred pounds given all the anxieties in my life. I owe that to the dogs. They insist that I play with them, take them for walks—during which I frequently carry them in turns—and are such a pleasant presence that I wish that I'd taken the step to have more dogs sooner.

To celebrate my father's cancer going into remission, we added Carebear, Snowbear, and later Jasmine to the pack. As soon as we had our first litter of pups, we started to get visitors from the neighborhood. Kids especially love to see and hold and play with the pups. They help to socialize the dogs and get them used to human contact, and in a way they do the same for us. We'd lived in a closed circle for so long, and with the dogs and the constant flow of visitors, that circle was growing ever wider. Stephen and Phillip are often around when guests drop by to see the dogs, and the focus is on the pups and not on them. That's a nice change of pace. No one mentions autism or any other issue. They just enjoy being with the dogs and us.

We find good homes for the puppies and never charge any-one for them. We feel so good about spreading the joy of a dog's companionship that it wouldn't feel right to take money for it. I used to think that I was doing whatever dogs we had a good turn by providing them with shelter and love and a good life; I now realize that it's the other way around. I've always loved St. Francis of Assisi and his namesake prayer, and really do believe that it is in giving that we receive. As I write this, it's nearly four years after my father told me he was going to die. The fact that he's still with us is a testament to that belief.

Other visitors dropped by and enlarged our circle. The cast of the movie stopped in during filming. I can't say enough about how wonderful they all were, but I have to make special men-tion of Zac Efron and Aidan Quinn. They both seemed to bond instantly with all of us, but especially with Stephen and Phil-lip. Neither of them had a pretentious bone in their body. If you didn't know that they were actors/celebrities, you wouldn't have been able to tell by how they interacted with all of us. I don't know if Ali or I was more smitten with the two male leads.

They were both such incredibly warm and genuine people. As much as I was eager for the movie to air, I was sad when shooting wrapped up. I wanted these people to be a significant part of our lives for many years.

We all enjoyed the experience of the movie being in production. We weren't present for much of the taping, and it all felt somewhat surreal to know that incidents from our lives were going to be shown to people around the country and other parts of the world. It was difficult to get our minds around that concept no matter how much we discussed it and speculated about what it was going to feel like. I understood the reasoning behind the decision, but I still felt bad about Richard and Ali not being included in the television version of our family. I knew that they had endured as much if not more than the twins had. They were the unsung and now unseen heroes of the story. Ali had been forced to grow up so fast and to deal with so many issues and complications, but she handled them all well.

When the date of the first showing on television approached, we weren't sure how we wanted to handle it. Throwing a big party was out of the question. I kept remembering Stephen's reaction when we watched him on the newscast. His running from the room gave me some idea of how I might react when I saw incidents from our lives, quite a few of them painful ones, replayed before our eyes. I decided that I didn't want to do anything special that night; instead, we'd all gather in Doug's and my bedroom and watch it as a family. The trepidation I felt had nothing to do with the quality of the movie or my trust in the people involved in the making of it. Having to relive and reexperience many of those moments was going to be difficult. I would have felt like a fraud if I had thrown a party and been forced to react inauthentically. I also wanted to protect Stephen and Phillip and their sensibilities. I didn't know if it was going to be too difficult for them.

I didn't eat much the night of the first showing. I was far too nervous and anxious. We all gathered on the bed and on a few chairs and watched it. I kept my eye on Stephen, but he seemed fine this time. Phillip told me that the movie made him realize how much he'd had to overcome. Doug said that being with me and helping with the kids was the really only lasting and important thing he'd ever done with his life. He said that he was so used to working in a world of make-believe that he welcomed coming home every day to something real, no matter how difficult that reality was.

In some ways, I need not have worried about the emotional reaction we'd all have. I'm not saying that the film wasn't good or that parts of it didn't ring true and evoke some emotion. What I am saying is that television distances us. The script took some liberties with the reality of our experience, but I knew going in that it would. It was surreal to see someone else going through the events that I'd experienced. The performances were wonderful, but they were exactly that—performances. The movie was so good that I found myself getting caught up in it. Even though I knew what was coming next, I still felt the dramatic tension. I was simultaneously empathetic to what those characters on screen were experiencing, and remembering and reliving the events as they happened to us. Is that not the definition of surreal?

I suppose that I'm not a very good critic. How could I be?

I had put up a wall, not wanting the intensity of the experience to overwhelm me. I was and am incredibly grateful to be a part of something that showed autism in a positive light. I was and am incredibly grateful that we got to know such a wonderful group of people. I was and am incredibly grateful that the movie so moved people that they wanted to be in contact with us to offer support, to ask for advice, and to be consoled. Laying your family's life bare is not easy. We made the choice to do so not only because of the financial rewards but also because we thought we could be of service to others.

The number of phone messages, emails, and letters we received staggered us. Even today, five years after it first aired, each time Lifetime shows *The Miracle Run*, people still reach out to us. I'm always particularly moved by autistic adults who share their stories with us. Those stories are too personal and too private for me to share. Suffice it to say that almost universally, people found the story moving and inspirational. Simply seeing a young man set a goal for himself and then achieving it may seem to most of us unworthy of such attention. The crippling stigma of autism has always been the belief that people with the condition can only achieve so much. Stephen demonstrated that isn't the case, and we have struggled mightily as a family to chip away at that perception. It took some time for us to get to the point where we could really believe it ourselves. We had mouthed the words, but it took Stephen's running the reality to make us true believers.

AFTERWORD

I still find it difficult to believe it's been five years since the movie first aired. In some ways our lives are fundamentally different now from what they were then. I'm leery of leaving you with the impression that it took a movie to make the difference in our lives. It doesn't take something as rare and unpredictable as having your life story told to millions of people around the world to demonstrate the power that you have to alter your own perceptions. The film was just a part of the greater process we were all experiencing. I can't deny that we benefited in tangible ways. For the first time in my children's lives, they didn't have to worry about where their next meal was coming from. I know that those awful days profoundly affected my kids.

I remember that at one of the many meetings we had with producers, someone said to Stephen that he was going to be rich and famous as a result of the movie. Stephen said, "I don't want to be famous, just rich." Some parents might have cringed at what seemed like a selfish remark, but rich is a relative concept. I do know that Stephen and Phillip and all my kids are more materially focused than perhaps I'd like them to be. I try not to be judgmental about that, knowing where it stems from. We live in a very materialistic society, but the reality is that on many occasions, one or another of my children would say to me, "Mom, can we please have some food in the house?"

For a lot of years, my first thought after waking up every morning was how I was going to provide my kids with what they needed and wanted. I don't know how many other people wake up with that same worry, but I suspect it's quite a few, and that reality both sickens and motivates me.

One of the things we did in the wake of the film was to add another element to our Miracle Run Foundation, which we called the Change Autism campaign. Continuing our grassroots focus, we tried to alleviate the financial hardships that many parents of autistic children endure. I knew what it was like to go hungry; I knew how it felt to struggle with the horrific reality of not being able to adequately provide for your children. I wanted to do whatever I could to make sure that other families didn't have to experience what we did. No one should have to face the decision between providing much-needed medicine for their afflicted child and food for the rest of the family. To that end, we began distributing clothing, food, and other essentials to families with and without autistic children. We went door to door to collect donations of food, clothing, and cash. We also distributed bags that individuals can use to collect loose change at home, at the office, or wherever, which can eventually be used to purchase much-needed items for families.

I approached a friend once and asked her for a donation. She said it must have been really embarrassing to do that. I told her I had no idea what she was talking about; it would have been embarrassing for me not to have been doing that.

Along with serving those immediate physical needs of families, the Miracle Run Foundation is dedicated to educating people about autism. What we have been attempting to do our whole lives is to get our kids, all of them, out in public so that they can enjoy as full and unrestricted a life as possible. I know that the teasing, stares, and looks of disgust that autistic people endure do far more damage than the condition itself. I also know that you can't force people to accept the admittedly odd behaviors that autistic people sometimes engage in. Just as we've always stressed to Phillip and Stephen what is appropriate and acceptable, we've been working to let other people know what are appropriate and acceptable responses to our children in public and private encounters. Expanding the parameters of acceptable has also been one of our goals.

Since the movie was first shown, Phillip and Stephen have turned twenty-six. For now, they are taking classes online. They both pursue their current interests—geology and astronomy and a host of other subjects. While they don't get the social benefits of attending classes in person, they are making progress toward a degree. In short, they are still in the race. Their expected running times have been adjusted, but my belief that they will cross the finish line has not changed. I also know that life is a series of races, not just a single one.

I'm not sure what it is about vehicles and motion, but when we take one of our infrequent road trips in the motor home, Phillip and Stephen seem most content. If they could, they'd be on the road all the time. We've taken trips to visit Richard where he was stationed in Texas, to tour the Redwoods in northern California, and to see Ali at the University of California at Channel Islands. The routine we follow has become a kind of ritual. I tell the twins the date of departure and that they need to be packed. The morning we leave, I go to the motor home and see that Phillip and Stephen are already waiting for Doug and me. They've packed their iPods, their guitars (Stephen now plays as well), their video games, and everything else they deem valuable. I ask them where their clothes are, but already knowing the answer, I then assist them with the no-fun task of packing shoes, socks, T-shirts, underwear, and the rest.

Doug does all the driving. Stephen is the navigator. He has one savant-like ability of being able to determine the day of the week for any date you give him, but he's even better with directions. He loves to sit and pore over maps and atlases, calculating distances and driving times, verbally ticking off major way points and intersections along the way. I know that he would love to drive, but we're still not convinced his focus and concentration are sufficient to allow him that privilege. Phillip is much more of a fussy traveler. He loves it but finds it hard to just sit still and watch the miles roll by. As much as he loves the travel, he enjoys the stops even more. Road trips and junk food go hand in hand in most households, and ours is no exception. Let me tell you, it takes a long time to fill the gas tank of a thirty-two-foot motor home, but we still have to sit and wait for Phillip to emerge from whatever quickie mart is part of the gas station. I used to worry about turning Phillip or Stephen loose in any kind of store or other public place, but I know that Phillip will most likely have found someone with whom to share his gift of gab. Stephen will quickly have decided what he wants to eat or drink and return to his command post.

I like to sit in the passenger seat with the window rolled down, the wind whipping my hair, and whatever concerns we had growing small in the mirror until I stop looking for them at all. I know they're there. I've made a conscious decision not to focus on them when we take these trips. All is not completely well. Phillip's Tourette's syndrome kicked into an aggressive phase that had him melting down with increasing regularity both at home and on the road. For a while I'd grown so frustrated, so angry that the damn Tourette's syndrome had such a stranglehold on Phillip, that I was fighting back. It took a while but I eventually realized that some of Phillip's meltdowns were the result of how I was responding to him when he did act out. Pouring gasoline on the fire wasn't the answer. As you can tell, I'm still learning to let go. It's a long process.

I find it fascinating that motion seems to calm both Phillip and Stephen. It has since they were very young, and it seems to me to be more than just their desire to travel and to see new places that soothes them. I've read of other kinds of movement that provides relief for autistic kids. I saw the website of Israel and Danielle Paskowitz. They have a son, Isaiah, who was diagnosed with autism at age three. Like Phillip and Stephen and most autistic kids, sensory overload seemed to afflict him. The parents noticed that when they were at the beach, Isaiah seemed much calmer.

Israel had been a competitive surfer, so he started taking his son out on his board. The changes were remarkable. The couple founded an organization called Surfers Healing, and they host day camps where parents bring their autistic kids to the ocean so that they can experience the benefits that Isaiah did. I hope that researchers investigate this phenomenon. There might be something to the sights and sounds associated with being in a car or on a surfboard that offer some clue to mitigating the suffering of autistic kids. For the most part, I don't keep up with all the current research and theories. We focus on the immediate with the twins, but I'm still keenly aware of the rising incidence of autism and hope that some breakthrough will occur.

The family experienced another breakthrough recently. We were profiled on CBS's *Early Show*. A crew came out to the house and interviewed us all. I marveled as I watched Phillip and Stephen interacting with the young woman, Flavia Colgan, who asked them both questions. In many ways, if you didn't know that they were autistic, you might think that they were a bit shy and nervous on camera. They handled themselves with a great deal of poise. At one point, Ms. Colgan asked Stephen what he saw for himself in the future. He looked over at his twin and asked, "Phillip, do you think we could get an apartment together?"

This was a bit of a bombshell. Though in the back of my mind I knew that someday the twins would want to, and needed to, live independently, we hadn't really ever talked about it as a reality. Emotionally, the twins are ready to leave, and that is our focus right now. They're still at home, but every day Doug and I sit down with them to discuss some aspect of independent living—handling finances, grocery shopping, public transportation, and so on. While they will face many challenges, I will, too. Letting go and not having them here at home is going to be very hard for Doug and me. Accepting the diagnosis was difficult, and letting go of the protective impulses and instincts has been something I've had to teach myself day by day.

One sign that I'm changing is that in the last few months I've started to watch a sitcom on HBO called *Curb Your Enthusiasm*. The brains behind the show and its star is someone who lives fairly close to us, Larry David. The show is very funny, but darkly so and often risqué. When I was a kid, my mother and father were so devoutly Catholic that we never heard any one swear or make any reference to sexual matters, and we certainly never saw images of naked people. I guess you could say that *Curb Your Enthusiasm* is about as politically incorrect and borderline insensitive as a show can get. The first time I stumbled across it, I think I blushed as much as I laughed. But I did laugh—a lot. Watching it became a kind of guilty pleasure that Doug and I hid from the rest of the family. It wasn't that hard to hide it since Phillip and Stephen now have their own places.

A few weeks ago, Phillip and Stephen both decided that they were going to hang out with Doug and me after dinner. It was a Sunday, and I kept one eye on the clock and another on whatever was on the TV screen. As darkness crept across the windows and the time for *Curb Your Enthusiasm* approached,

I dropped a couple of hints about the lateness of the hour. I still had in mind Stephen running to turn off the television set whenever he saw people about to kiss—something he did because my mother did the same thing. I also thought of Phillip and his discussions with the Jehovah's Witnesses who come around. He has lots of questions for them about the nature of sin and evil and forgiveness and Heaven. The twins weren't taking my hint, and it was good to have us all sitting around together as a family again. They have their own interests and schedules, and with Richard and Ali away, the house sometimes feels empty—save for the dogs.

Phillip could serve as a personal *TV Guide*, and at nine o'clock he asked for the remote and turned the TV on. *Extreme Makeover: Home Edition* was just starting, but he switched channels. I stood up to get a beverage for Doug and me, and I was surprised when I heard the static sound of HBO's theme and then the jauntily familiar first notes of the theme song from *Curb Your Enthusiasm*. I'd just about resigned myself to not seeing that week's episode, but I handed Doug his glass of water and retook my seat. I was surprised that Phillip had selected that show, and I asked him why he had, but he shushed me and said he didn't want to miss anything. I looked at Doug, and his attention was focused on the screen, as was Stephen's. The episode began, and I found myself fighting a smile. Larry had learned from a female friend that his best male friend/manager had a small penis. Now, I don't think in my entire life I was ever in the presence of my parents when that word was spoken, read, or likely even thought about. Stephen and Phillip didn't react to the use of the word, but they both, along with Doug and me, burst out laughing when we heard that episode's catch-phrase: "These women with big vaginas are getting away with murder."

We all looked at one another, and I don't know if we were all laughing at the concept and accompanying hand gesture that kept getting repeated like an OCDer's fixation or if we were all laughing about the mention of a word that Phillip frequently used in the midst of a Tourette's outburst. All I know is that what we were watching was funny to me, and I remembered how mightily Stephen and Phillip once struggled to get any jokes at all. I was also laughing because here we all were, sitting in our family room and laughing at a show that always revolves around the violation of some subtle social insinuation or misrepresentation or another, and the twins seemed to get it. They weren't just laughing because Doug and I were; they were laughing because they understood the nuance and the absurdity of the social interactions that were going on. I was laughing because it all felt so normal and natural for us to be together, four adults sharing a laugh about a sophisticated (though some might say juvenile) bit of humor. I laughed because we were being true to ourselves.

When the show ended, Phillip told me that *Curb Your Enthusiasm* was one of his favorite shows. Stephen nodded in agreement. Doug and I confessed that we'd been hooked on it for a few months, and Stephen said, "It's funny and believable."

We don't always watch the show together, but it's nice to know that Phillip in his pad and Stephen in the motor home and Doug and I in our house are all enjoying the same show on television. I'd been hoping that somehow and someday we'd be a "normal" family, but it took the Big Vagina episode to make clear to me that we'd never measure up to anyone else's definition of "normal." And that was perfectly fine with me.

When I thought more about it, I realized that a lot of other things we do and say and believe probably don't fit within the framework of the typical American family—if such a thing even exists. Doug befriended a squirrel a while ago, and she now lives in our bedroom. Doug will take her along for rides when he does errands, putting her in the chest pocket of his shirt. People have grown so accustomed to seeing Doug with her when he's in the grocery store that he gets more questions when the squirrel isn't with him than when she is.

I also noticed that far fewer people comment or look askance at Stephen or Phillip in public places. The only Rainman-esque thing that Stephen and Phillip like to do is gamble. Not to the extent as portrayed in the Dustin Hoffman–Tom Cruise movie, but they do enjoy going to casinos when we take a road trip. Phillip likes the Wheel of Fortune slot machine. Stephen isn't as particular about what machine he plays. Phillip has been through so much, and we're all pleased that he seems to have the magic touch when it comes to gambling. He wins a lot, and when he's sitting at those machines, his Tourette's syndrome tics just seem to disappear. He'll let out a loud whoop every now and then, but only when he's won. People gather around him and they seem to share in his joy. The world truly does work in mysterious ways.

They're both good and smart players. I used to work in a casino, and I know how the odds favor the house, but the twins do pretty well for themselves. Phillip is about as gregarious as you might expect, while Stephen tends to keep to himself—only to the extent that people think he's very shy or a very serious player who doesn't like to be distracted. Stephen's perfectionism comes into play. He has a self-imposed $20 limit and gets frustrated easily when he doesn't win. They fit in well enough that frequently the staff will ask them if they'd like a drink. Phillip, of course, explains to everyone at the table that he has OCD, Tourette's, and autism and that he doesn't drink at all. Stephen politely declines or asks for whatever version of a Shirley Temple they serve. He also has a self-imposed eating limit—three hamburgers—and when he's either lost his $20 or had his fill of food, he's eager to leave. I think Phillip could spend much of his life in a casino and be perfectly content.

These outings are a far cry from when they were toddlers and their screaming and acting out were a cause of such angst for me. I know that their affect is slightly off and that most people probably think that they are a bit nerdy and a little socially awkward. Doug and I can laugh about that and say that they get that from us.

For so long, I hoped for and worked feverishly toward the goal of getting the twins accepted and treated as equals by other people. It was as if I wanted them to be transparent, to blend in so well that no one would ever take notice of them. I realize that I may have been in error in wishing for that, both because I now can't imagine anything worse than being so normal as to be invisible and because that would have been asking them to deny their true nature. I've come to think of their autism as another feature of theirs, just like Phillip's dark curly hair and Stephen's lanky limbs. I would love it if there were a cure for autism, but I've also become realistic enough to know that waiting for that cure instead of adapting to our reality would be a mistake.

People frequently ask me about Stephen and his running. He doesn't do it competitively anymore. He does not get up every morning to train as he used to. His Olympic dreams were a lot like those of many young people—dreams. He's awakened from them and realized that he has other aspirations and other ways he'd like to spend his time. He wants to finish college, get a job, get married, and start a family. I've also come to realize that sometimes when we are running toward something, we are in fact running away from something else. None of us feels such a strong need to escape as we once did. I think we all learned what we needed to from the experience.

At the end of one of our Miracle Runs, I spoke to a participant who seemed remarkably fresh after completing what I considered to be a grueling five-kilometer race. He told me that he was in the middle of training for an upcoming marathon. I said that I didn't understand how anyone could run twenty-six miles. His reply was very interesting, and I think it relates to our story.

The idea of a race that was just over twenty-six miles didn't fit into his head. He couldn't think about all those miles. So instead, he redefined a marathon as a series of four six-mile races, with an easy two miles to the finish. That made a lot of sense to me.

I wrote earlier that running is a good metaphor for my family's story. Our efforts are perhaps better compared to a marathon. And yet like that insightful runner, we have learned not to think about the entire distance all at once, but to break it up into shorter, more manageable runs. Looking back, we've been able to finish a whole slew of difficult races, one at a time, and there are more to go. But we won't think about the finish line—only the next easy stretch ahead.

The fight against autism and other disabilities can seem as long and as daunting as a marathon. But as you put one foot in front of the other, don't think about the distance. Don't count the mile markers. You have to find other things to think about, diversions that give your mind a break. The next thing you know, you're at the water station, enjoying some well-earned and much-needed refreshment. There's no dishonor in slowing to a walk. You're not really competing against anyone else—just moving forward. Your time is your own, and you're the best judge of the appropriate pace.

Right after I had that discussion with the marathoner, I came across an article about the so-called penguins in a marathon: the back-of-the-pack people who are waddling along as the jackrabbits dash off. What I read became a kind of mantra for us: The miracle isn't that you had the courage to finish the race, but that you had the courage to even start.

We're still out there, somewhere in the pack, plodding along as best we can, enjoying the journey, finding more and more friends like us, stopping occasionally for snacks and some rest but certain we'll get there all in due time.

All in due time.

A NOTE ON THE MIRACLE
RUN FOUNDATION

SINCE establishing the Miracle Run Foundation in 2001, we have assisted hundreds of families in ways large and small. As we intended from the beginning, the foundation is a grass-roots-level organization designed to assist families in need. As I've said throughout this book, we were constantly faced with choices, but no parent should ever have to choose between paying for their autistic children's medication and putting food on the table. That guiding principle remains fundamental to the work we do.

In addition to offering financial support, we remain a clearinghouse of information on the latest advances in autism education and treatment; however, our focus remains on providing emotional support for parents. I continue to receive hundreds of emails and phone calls a week. Often, what I offer is a shoulder to cry on, an ear to listen to a parent's sadness and frustration (and sometimes joy), and the benefit of my experience. This book is an extension of the work of the Miracle Run Foundation. I shared our story in the hope that we can educate, enlighten, and inspire hope for parents of autistic and other special needs children.

We are about to launch a new venture for the foundation.

My father and mother, Ralph and Lupe Mount, bought a twenty-acre ranch in Warner Springs, California, when my father retired from the aerospace industry. He wanted out of the city. I don't know how they found this ranch, because it is in the middle of nowhere. It is miles from the nearest grocery store, and that store is no bigger than a convenience market. Twenty-something years later, my parents moved to Chatsworth, California, so they could be closer to their doctors. Refusing to sell the ranch, they offered it to me. My parents are saints.

Part of a more frugal and forward-thinking generation, fortunately for us, they carried no mortgage on the place. We took them up on the offer because we saw a new opportunity to help other families with autistic children. We are working toward converting the ranch to a place where autistic families can bring their children and not have to deal with the conflicts and interruptions of a fast-paced society. We needed a time-out ourselves, and now we hope to provide one for autistic children and their parents, a place where they can spend a few hours or a few days.

And so Miracle Run Ranch was born. Today, we are busy turning twenty acres into a garden, playground, and grazing area for animals that we hope will become a kind of petting zoo. In a way, we are back where we started, operating on a shoestring budget as we attempt a complete renovation of the facilities. Of course, we will not charge any kind of admission to the ranch, and the overnight accommodations will be free as well.

This time, as before in all our efforts with the foundation, we are not alone in this. We are grateful to have received left-over building materials and other donations. Though Doug is retired, he's putting his carpentry skills to use for a larger cause. We continue to solicit donations through CraigsList and our newspapers. The response has been heartwarming, and while there's much to be done, I have faith that we will all be pro-vided for. To obtain additional information about the founda-tion, or to check on our progress at the Miracle Run Ranch, go to www.themiraclerun.com.

Our first family will be at Miracle Run Ranch by 2009.